SCALING UP

SCALING UP
THE UP
CONVERGENCE
OF SOCIAL
ECONOMY
AND
SUSTAINABILITY

EDITED BY MIKE GISMONDI, SEAN CONNELLY,
MARY BECKIE, SEAN MARKEY,
MARK ROSELAND

AU PRESS

Published by AU Press, Athabasca University
1200, 10011 – 109 Street, Edmonton, AB T5J 3S8

ISBN 978-1-77199-021-9 (print)   978-1-77199-022-6 (PDF)   978-1-77199-023-3 (epub)
doi: 10.15215/aupress/9781771990219 .01

Cover and interior design by Sergiy Kozakov
Printed and bound in Canada by Marquis Book Printers

Library and Archives Canada Cataloguing in Publication

 Scaling up : the convergence of social economy and sustainability / editors, Mike Gismondi, Sean Connelly, Mary Beckie, Sean Markey, Mark Roseland.

Includes bibliographical references.
Issued in print and electronic formats.

 1. Cooperative societies—British Columbia—Case studies. 2. Cooperative societies—Alberta—Case studies. 3. Sustainable development—British Columbia—Case studies. 4. Sustainable development—Alberta—Case studies. I. Gismondi, Michael Anthony, author, editor II. Connelly, Sean, 1975-, author, editor III. Beckie, Mary, 1954-, author, editor IV. Markey, Sean Patrick, 1970-, author, editor V. Roseland, Mark author, editor

HD3450.A3B74 2015   334.09711   C2015-906796-0
                  C2015-906797-9

We acknowledge the financial support of the Government of Canada.

 Canadian Patrimoine
Heritage canadien

Assistance provided by the Government of Alberta, Alberta Media Fund.

Government

Chapter 10, "Strong Institutions, Weak Strategies: Credit Unions and the Rural Social Economy," is a revised version of

 Kristensen, Freya, Sean Markey, and Stewart Perry. 2011. "'Our Liquidity Is Trust, Not Cash': Credit Unions and the Rural Social Economy," *Journal of Rural and Community Development* 5 (3): 143–61.

For those seeking transitions to socio-ecological sustainability, thanks for your inventiveness. This book is for the rest of you.

Contents

Tables and Figures

Acknowledgements

Our work emerges from seven years of research as part of the British Columbia–Alberta Social Economy Research Alliance, or BALTA (socialeconomy-bcalberta.ca). The editors would like to thank all our friends associated with BALTA and with its Scaling Innovation for Sustainability project (balta-sis.ca).

We gratefully acknowledge research funding support from the Social Sciences and Humanities Research Council of Canada and from our home universities: Athabasca University, the University of Alberta, the University of Otago/Te Whare Wānanga o Otāgo, and Simon Fraser University.

Thanks also to each of our co-authors and to the many graduate student researchers, social economy practitioners, and community friends who helped compile research notes and case study information, many of whom are named alongside the case studies in the text.

Cheers to Don McNair for his careful reading and suggestions. And a special thanks to Mike Lewis and Stuart Wulff, BALTA's heart and soul, for their leadership, inspiration, and steady hands.

Introduction
Social Economics and Sustainability

Mike Gismondi, Sean Connelly, Mary Beckie,
Sean Markey, and Mark Roseland

When we began this project, our perspective on the social economy and sustainability was based on our work as theorists and practitioners active in the environmental movement. Over the years, however, that viewpoint has changed through our participation in an alliance of academics and community practitioners whose mandate was to research the role of the social economy in western Canada. This experience brought us into contact with many leaders from Canada's co-operative and enterprising non-profit and community development sectors. While we had been building the environmental movement, they had been building—some of them for over forty years—the social economy movement and its networks.

We discovered that social economics is connected to all aspects of sustainability: ecological conservation, social justice, gender equity, cultural health and continuity, human well-being, and ethical responsibility for future generations. More importantly, we found in the practice of social economics new strategic directions for both the politics of sustainability and the organizational and institutional setup of sustainability alternatives. We saw how local, democratic organizations can advance ecological and social sustainability. By the very initiatives that they define and carry out, often to meet basic needs in a community or region, these small organizations practice sustainability. They "social economize" sustainability, you might say.

While we see a convergence occurring between social economics and sustainability, we do not want to overstate the wonders of the social economy. Let's be frank: the theory and praxis of sustainability are a mess. At the same time, our transition to sustainability is no longer a choice but an imperative. Today's coincidence of climate change, degradation of planetary ecosystems, and global financial uncertainty poses a threat to all communities. For some, the threat is more immediate than for others. The relocalization of economies may be a way both to protect environments and to empower the most vulnerable of populations. The crucial question is whether the transition to a relocalized economy can be accomplished in a manner that is low carbon, ecologically sustainable, and socially fair.

In *Scaling Up*, we explore the possibility of a just transition to sustainability: one that is sustainable in social, economic, and environmental terms. We assess a number of initiatives in social economics and sustainability in western Canada. In light of that experience, we argue that the social economy sector is a small but effective piece of the transition challenge. Indeed, social economy leaders are old hands at running robust, resilient institutions and networks that can advance the sustainability agenda. In the chapters to follow, contributors examine issues ranging from attainable, affordable housing and local capital financing to local food and community-based energy. They show how these development issues link to issues of state power and structural change, which are concerns common to communities all over the world. They explore obstacles and challenges to achieving structural change, as well as strategies for deepening and broadening the impact of innovation and for interconnecting, horizontally and democratically, across the wider "green" social economy.

The innovations discussed in this book have been proven to work at the local level, but the question remains of how to deepen and broaden their extent—how to scale them up and out so as to create structural and societal change. *Scaling up* means escalating the impact of a particular innovation within the sector in which it operates, from community to city, from region to nation. *Scaling out* means taking innovations that have proven effective in one place, extending their impact through diffusion and adaptation into new geographical locations and new sectors. But scaling an innovation successfully often requires changing the very social and technological systems that make our current way of life unsustainable. The spread of these innovations implies profound changes in social systems of provision, in democratic practices and beliefs, and in state policies and economic power. In order for sustainability innovations to grow, the right conditions must be introduced. Strategic interventions and support mechanisms are required. Change will be resisted. The politics and practice of transition will be difficult, to say the least.

Notwithstanding the obvious challenges to altering the dominant capitalist system, the examples that we profile here demonstrate the emergence of innovative, democratic ways to create change. In chapter 1, Sean Connelly, Mike Gismondi, Sean Markey, and Mark Roseland introduce the concepts of social economy and sustainable community development and the connections between them. They set out the distinction between strong and weak sustainability initiatives, emphasize the need to take ecology seriously, and explore the social economizing of sustainability. Chapter 2, by Mike Gismondi, Lynda Ross, and Juanita Marois, offers a socio-historical account of the social economy in Alberta and British Columbia and, using survey data, paints a picture of the current green social economy sector in both provinces. In chapter 3, Mary Beckie and Sean Connelly present examples of various ways in which people are relocalizing and resocializing food. They demonstrate that consumer demand for local food is growing, in part motivated by concerns about health, food safety, and environmental stewardship but also based in the desire of consumers to reconnect with farmers and the land. In chapter 4, John Restakis introduces social care as part of the sustainability equation. Challenging the status quo, he claims that the provision and consumption of human services is not the same as the production and consumption of material goods. His story of social co-ops in Italy emphasizes the importance of focusing on relational goods. Julie MacArthur discusses energy and sustainability in chapter 5. Faced with the dual challenge of climate change and uncertain future energy supplies and costs, how will we find the clean energy needed to run local economies? Her work addresses the power of capitalism and the challenge of developing renewables democratically to engage local people in ownership and profits. She offers strategies for launching an energy innovation and for scaling out a successful project from its originating community to a wider area. In chapter 6, Kelly Vodden, Lillian Hunt, and Randy Bell demonstrate how ecology, tourism and economic activity, and culture intertwine in First Nations' efforts to strengthen community resilience. They stress the importance of culture and sense of place for generating the capacity of First Nations to take an active role in the protection and promotion of their cultural heritage. The tourism and economic development proposals discussed in this chapter involve local environmental management as well as alliances with other communities, private businesses, the state, environmental groups, and non-profit organizations in the region.

In chapter 7, George Penfold, Lauren Rethoret, and Terri MacDonald explain how affordable, attainable housing is critical to sustainability. In their review of housing research in British Columbia, they found that challenges differ in rural and urban settings. Replicating successful community projects from one place in other communities or across a wider region has not been shown to be successful, particularly in rural Canada. In chapter 8, Marena Brinkhurst and Mark Roseland show how collective land ownership and community control over land can be linked to sustainability. They explore a variety of land tenure models that can increase community control over the use of land for local housing, agriculture, and even wind farms or other energy projects. A partnership of a non-profit group, a land trust, and a municipality is a highly effective way to reduce land costs for a housing project, a cultural arts building, a farmers' market, a social care co-op, a community kitchen, or a building for local food storage and distribution. Any discussion of multistakeholder coalitions, whose construction is far from easy, turns our attention to engaging the power of government, at all levels, to meld sustainability and social economy, a theme that arises across other chapters as well. Yes, inertia and ingrained habits must be overcome. Trust is also a challenge, as are the oppositional interests and influence of private capital and the managers of incumbent systems who are keen to maintain the status quo. But the role of the state remains important.

In chapter 9, Noel Keough, Mike Gismondi, and Erin Swift-Leppäkumpu claim that heritage conservation can contribute to sustainability in built environments. They show that the repurposing of unused, derelict, or failing older buildings can rejuvenate neighbourhoods. The preservation of heritage buildings conserves embedded energy, reduces demolition waste, cancels out the energy costs of new construction, and preserves architectural elements that define the character of city neighbourhoods and their buildings. Moreoever, the memory of a building's previous uses and its social meanings are recovered as well. The authors demonstrate that involvement of municipal planners and support from higher levels of government is key to such preservation initiatives. In chapter 10, Sean Markey, Freya Kristensen, and Stewart Perry discuss the financing of the social economy. They analyze the uneven effectiveness of most rural credit unions in supporting community development and explore Vancity Credit Union as an example of a large credit union (Canada's largest, in fact) that, through engagement in a wide range of initiatives, promotes both social innovation and sustainability.

Throughout the book, we provide examples of green social economy organizations. Each outlines the sustainability issue and social economy mission and its transformative potential.

The many small social economy sustainability initiatives found across western Canada can be thought of as seeds of innovation, a recurring metaphor in this volume. Each initiative strategizes differently to provide an alternative narrative to that of the dominant economy. Collectively, these stories demonstrate that democratic institutions, social markets, a socio-ecological ethos, and coalition building provide a nurturing environment for incremental and transformative change. It's all part of a growing global movement for sustainability and social justice. While some seeds may fall on stone, many others hold the promise of spring.

Towards Convergence

An Exploratory Framework

Sean Connelly, Mike Gismondi, Sean Markey,
and Mark Roseland

The roots of the modern environmental movement in the Western world can be traced to the publication of Rachel Carson's book *Silent Spring* in 1962. The book was a very public wake-up call of our human impact on the environment. Supported by meticulous research, Carson clearly outlined the devastating environmental costs of America's postwar economic progress. A decade later, in *The Limits to Growth*, Donella Meadows and colleagues measured the thresholds of the earth's ecosystem and horizons of resource exhaustion. *Our Common Future* (1987), the report of the United Nations' Brundtland Commission, warned of increasing environmental degradation, as well as the challenges of under-development and the growing gap between the world's rich and poor. The report asked current generations to reduce consumption and conserve ecosystems for future generations—to practice what the report termed *sustainable development*. As government and business embraced the term in the 1990s, however, many in the environmental movement began to reject it. They feared that its original meaning had been co-opted by corporate messages equating sustainable development with more rapid economic growth allegedly intended to alleviate poverty, increase productivity and consumption standards, and diversify economies (Block 1912 Collective 2007; Rees 1990). As Tim O'Riordan put it (2007, 325), "Sustainable development has become a universal phrase. It means everything, and is in danger of meaning nothing."

In this discussion of the transition to sustainability, we return to centre stage the complex of ecological limits, social inequalities, and moral obligations encompassed by the term *sustainable development* when it was first introduced by the Brundtland Commission. Neither economies nor ecosystems have stood

7

still since Brundtland. If anything, the politics of sustainability has entered a new stage. Today, some 60 percent of the planet's ecosystems are at risk (Millennium Ecosystem Assessment 2005). Greenhouse gas (GHG) emissions are rising year after year. The demand for oil has far surpassed the supply of conventionally produced oil, so governments and corporations are turning to unconventional sources that are much more costly to extract, both financially and environmentally (Davidson and Gismondi 2011). With the rapid decline in the price of oil in 2014 and 2015, the future of investments in these unconventional supplies is being questioned. Investments in unconventional oil run the risk of being stranded assets, with commentators such as the Governor of the Bank of England, President of the World Bank and the U.S. President referring to the vast majority of these and older reserves like coal being un-burnable (Rusbridger, 2015). The certainty of a steady future supply of energy is in doubt (Aleklett et al. 2010; IEA 2008, 2010). Furthermore, leading scientists now argue that we have breached critical planetary boundaries. Global patterns of climate change, resource exhaustion, species extinctions, and environmental pollution confirm that we have surpassed ecological and thermodynamic limits. Only a massive reduction in carbon usage and emissions over the next fifty years can correct our error (Barnosky et al. 2012).

In addition to these disturbing trends, social inequality remains high, both globally and locally. In the past, unsustainable practices and ways of being were justified through their development benefits. In simple terms, burning fossil fuels in the present could be traded-off for rising incomes, with the expectation that rising incomes would result in more sustainable practices in the future. Evidence of increasing inequality and worsening environmental conditions suggests such an argument is not tenable. Today, the effects of unsustainability are often unanticipated and unpredictable, and continuing along the path we are on will endanger the livelihoods of millions well into the future (Rockstrom et al. 2009). Poor and marginal populations are the most vulnerable (AtKisson 2011; Srinivasan et al. 2008; Urry 2011). As changes in the ecosystem accelerate, we must accelerate our response. Radical change is needed.

How can we respond quickly and effectively to this sustainability challenge? Information is not enough, that much we know. We cannot just put information in front of decision-makers and wait for them to make the right decisions. Nor can we expect information—even the best information—to change public behaviour or to cause firms and states to steer economies wisely and equitably towards sustainability. Nothing short of a seismic shift in consumption, technologies, values, and political organization will suffice (Shove 2010; Shove and Spurling, 2013).

In this book, the contributors argue that the social economy is strategic to this great change. Research has shown that the social economy has the potential to be catalytic—as having the potential to lead a transition to a more humanized economy, one that is attentive to local and global sustainability (Bouchard 2013; Buchs et al., 2011; Connelly 2010; Gertler 2006; Gibson-Graham, Cameron, and Healy, 2013; Gismondi & Cannon, 2012; Restakis 2010, 2011; Wittman, Beckie, and Hergesheimer 2012). Our perspective is also based on some foundational principles of social economics: the interdependence of parts within the whole, a dependence on robust democratic institutions, and innovation that is locally defined and controlled to meet sustainably a community's or a region's basic needs for energy, food, shelter, and work.

The transition to a more sustainable economy has barely begun. The power and politics involved in maintaining the status quo are daunting. Yet change *is* underway. The intentional adoption and merging of the alternative structures, principles, and practices of sustainability and social economics may facilitate a just transition to sustainability.

WHAT IS THE SOCIAL ECONOMY?

Most readers are probably familiar with the social economy. If you volunteer in your community, you are part of it. So, too, if you are a member of a credit union or a non-profit society. You encounter the social economy if you participate in a community centre or support a women's shelter, live in a housing co-operative, or shop at a social enterprise.

But let's be more specific. The social economy can be understood as a "third system" of the economy, in addition to the public and private systems. In this third system, citizens take action to satisfy their own and others' needs by working together in some way (Pearce 2003). The social economy includes non-profit organizations whose actions enhance communities socially, economically, and environmentally, often with a focus on disadvantaged community members (Neamtan 2009). The social economy, according to some writers, encompasses the work of any democratically controlled organization whose mission is both social and economic in nature (Amin, Cameron, and Hudson 2002; Lionais and Johnstone 2009; McMurtry 2009a; Neamtan 2009). Some define social economy organizations as those groups whose members and supporters are fired by the principle of reciprocity. Such groups pursue economic, social, and environmental goals through the social control of capital, including the use of market mechanisms, to pursue explicit social and environmental objectives (Lewis 2006; Restakis 2006; see also Fairbairn 2009; Neamtan and Anderson 2010; and Pearce 2003).

How big is the social economy? Researchers estimate that it generates $79.1 billion (7.8%) of Canada's annual gross domestic product and employs over two million people (Amyot, Downing, and Tremblay 2010, 14–15). And it is growing rapidly. (See chapter 2 for figures on British Columbia and Alberta.) The size, scope, and impact of the social economy, however, differ from region to region. In Québec, the social economy is large and well known and is recognized as a distinct form of economic activity with its own social and cultural values. The Chantier de l'économie sociale acts as the social economy's umbrella organization in that province, unifying an array of non-profit groups, mutual associations, co-operatives, and community economic development initiatives. The organization has thus been able to secure legitimacy and support from the Province, universities, and public policy research centres (Bouchard 2013).

Elsewhere in Canada, the social economy is not as well recognized by either the public or government, despite a long history of community action in response to social and economic restructuring. All the same, its work and impact are significant. Numerous non-profit societies, co-operatives, mutual associations, and foundations pursue economic activities on behalf of vulnerable individuals and groups: farmers, rural resource communities, the urban poor, and other disadvantaged populations.

BRINGING THE SOCIAL ECONOMY AND SUSTAINABILITY TOGETHER

Two recent English Canadian books explore Canada's social economy in depth, analyzing how it is organized and what it does (McMurtry 2009b; Quarter, Mook, Armstrong 2009). Surprisingly, ecological sustainability is rather marginal to both of these studies: in the words of John Pearce (2003, 43), "It should be axiomatic that an enterprise which has a social purpose will have a clear positive environmental policy, for to be environmentally irresponsible is to be socially irresponsible." Graham Smith (2005, 125) speaks of "the mutual, common or general interest that is fundamental to the ethos of the social economy": surely, environmental sustainability is in the common interest of us all.

The engagement of social economy actors with environmental sustainability has been uneven, but it is growing (Smith 2005). We propose that a serious effort to bring about a convergence of the social economy with critical sustainability theory and practice can create a whole that is greater than the sum of its parts.

This book is about social economy organizations that grapple with sustainability in its fullest sense: their structures, like their enterprises, target a triple bottom line of mutual economic, environmental, and social sustainability. Although the examples explored in this volume are all located in western Canada, we recognize that they are part of something bigger. As Nancy Neamtan, the past president of the Chantier de l'économie sociale, reminds us, "the social economy has grown into a global movement. It does not only respond to the repercussions of repetitive crises. It proposes an alternative: a pluralist and inclusive economy within a framework of sustainable development" (Neamtan 2009, 1).

It is essential, however, that environmental sustainability be integrated into the politics and practice of the social economy. The reverse is also true. Some environmental researchers and activists ask which social and economic practices and values align well with sustainability. They recognize a need to "social economize" sustainability in order to increase the impact of sound practices (Connelly, Markey, and Roseland 2011). The effort to connect the two fields, in terms of both research and practice, has just begun. Little attention has been paid, for example, to what such a convergence could do for social sustainability. In this book, we attempt to begin filling that gap. We investigate how innovations from both movements might be united, thereby accelerating the transition to sustainability.

Community Bike Shops I
Celia Lee, Kailey Cannon, and Juanita Marois

From St. John's to Victoria, community bike shops have been cropping up throughout Canadian urban centres. Although the structure and goals of these shops vary, most are driven by concern for mobility that reduces impacts on the environment, as well as for social justice and equality. Their goals range from reducing the number of bikes taken to the landfill by repairing old bikes and reusing parts, to offering free bike mechanic workshops that empower people to do their own repairs, to redefining how we move through the city.

Community bike shops are generally non-profit co-operatives and mostly—if not entirely—volunteer run. St. John's Ordinary Spokes, Edmonton's Bikeworks, and Winnipeg's The Bike Dump, for example, are managed completely by volunteers, while Calgary's Good Life Community Bike Shop recently created some part-time paid positions in addition to relying on a large volunteer base. Most bike shops make their services or membership available in exchange for volunteer hours; indeed, Victoria's Recyclistas and Vancouver's Pedal Power: Our Community Bikes have work-trade programs in place for people without money or who want to learn how to fix bikes for free. Most community bike shops strive to be non-hierarchal in terms of workplace structure, access to services, and decision making. Many shops have policies that explicitly assert zero-tolerance for discrimination, and most shops attempt to make their services accessible to all by keeping prices low, offering free services, and/or accepting non-monetary forms of payment.

Edmonton Bike Works. 2015. http://edmontonbikes.ca/services/bikeworks/
Good Life Bikes. 2015. Calgary. www.goodlifebikes.ca
Pedal Power. 2015. "Our Community Bikes." http://pedalpower.org
Recyclistas. 2015. Victoria. http://www.recyclistas.ca/
The Bike Dump. 2015.Winnipeg. www.bike-dump.ca

We explore this potential as it relates to a number of the basic needs associated with life and livelihood. The case examples herein cover such topics as local food, transportation, housing, social inclusion, job creation, heritage conservation, tourism, land, finance, and advocacy. Each chapter begins with "green social economy" innovations in western Canada, followed by a discussion of patterns emerging in other parts of Canada or internationally. For decades, practitioners in the areas of environmental sustainability and social economics have known and respected each other. Occasionally, they have even worked on projects together. But something new is afoot. Something is driving innovative connections of thought and practice. This book aims to expand and strengthen those connections.

THEORIZING PRACTICE: THE WEAK-STRONG CONTINUUM

The concept of "sustainable development," while broadly recognized, is interpreted in different and often competing ways (Mebratu 1998). Early discussions of sustainable development concentrated on conservation of non-human nature and management of the environment. Today, sustainable development encompasses issues of employment, equality, and the economy (Edwards 2005). The concept itself has been subject to much criticism because its ambiguity leaves it open to widely different interpretations (Dale 2001; Keiner 2004; Robinson 2004; Sneddon, Howarth, and Norgaard 2006). Indeed, many argue that the concept is used to perpetuate overconsumption and the destruction of ecosystems driven by the process of capital accumulation (Johnston, Gismondi, and Goodman 2006). In addition, much discussion of sustainable development occurs at a level of abstraction that means little to the general public (Bridger and Luloff 1999).

Weak-Strong Sustainable Community Development

Critics make a significant distinction between sustainable development and sustainable community development, or SCD. Responding to the severe limitations of mainstream models of economic growth and of sustainability and ecological modernization, SCD applies sustainable development at the local level, with an emphasis on providing essentials like food, shelter, and clean air and water (McMurtry 2002). In the SCD model, democratic processes enable citizens and their governments to channel diverse values, visions, and activities into a program of change (Roseland 2012). SCD has had its successes. It has combined environmental and economic concerns at the local level by, for example, integrating green jobs with low-growth economics and eco-efficiency. Yet this approach has failed to come to grips with such social justice issues as equal access to an acceptable quality of life for all members of society (Agyeman and Evans 2004; Jones 2008). For its part, the social economy has long supported marginalized individuals and communities through job training, social enterprise, affordable housing, and the like. Yet only recently have social economy actors begun to think more critically about what it means to integrate environmental issues into its mandate.

As with sustainable development in general (Rees 1991, 1995; Williams and Millington 2004), it is helpful to consider SCD in terms of a "weak" to "strong" continuum, depending on how problems and solutions are perceived (see table 1.1). Weak SCD recognizes that economic growth has to address environmental issues in some way but does not challenge the concept of economic growth. This approach assumes that environmental (and social) problems are offset by advances elsewhere: in other words, such advantages as greater cost efficiency, manufactured capital, or scientific insights counterbalance a depletion of natural capital. For example, hydroelectricity generation and job creation compensate for the loss of a wetland when a dam is built. These gains are presumed to outweigh losses to the ecosystem and its social and cultural role in people's lives.

Table 1.1 Characteristics of weak and strong sustainable community development

	Weak SCD	Strong SCD
World view	Anthropocentric	Biocentric/biotic rights
	Rational individuals	Collective action
Role of economy	Economic growth	Qualitative development
	Centralized	Community based
Source of problem and solution	Supply problem	Demand problem
	Technocratic	Social relationships
	Use of Environmental Impact Assessments, cost-benefit analysis	Small scale decentralization
		Self-sufficiency
	Efficiency	

In contrast, strong SCD recognizes the finite nature of the earth and the need to reduce demands on all its life systems and realizes that the depletion of natural capital may have irreversible or, at best, uncertain consequences. Strong SCD assumes that the idea that manufactured capital can "substitute" for natural capital is dubious, at best: job creation may not compensate for the loss of that wetland, for example. This uncertainty compels strong SCD proponents to consider alternative sources of energy.

Strong SCD strives to enhance well-being by balancing the development of capital in all its forms: social, human, cultural, physical, economic, and natural (Roseland 2012). According to this approach, gross quantitative measures of growth, wealth, and consumption do not measure success, and solutions are rooted in social rather than technological change. Collective action, social innovation, and finite growth are key to strong SCD initiatives (Rees 1995).

For many practitioners, strong SCD proponents also aim for social justice, considering essential the redressing of inequalities in quality of life based on race, gender, and poverty (Agyeman and Evans 2004; Pearsall and Pierce 2010). This emphasis on social equality and solidarity determines the trade-offs that strong SCD practitioners are willing to make between social and environmental benefits.

Admittedly, much SCD falls at the weaker end of the spectrum in that practitioners emphasize efficiency in the use of resources as a means of conserving the environment; respect existing power structures; and aim for incremental changes to social, economic, and environmental relations. According to this approach, markets can be trusted to prompt people to behave more responsibly towards the environment. A good example is the recycling movement that began in the 1980s with the blue box program. Promoted under the motto of "Reduce, Reuse, Recycle," this program was more about the technological fix of sorting recyclables than about issues related to overconsumption, with all of its social and political consequences (Connelly, Markey, and Roseland 2012).

Note that this analysis does not use the word *weak* in a derogatory manner. Many organizations engaged in SCD or the social economy do important work using practices that fall at the weak end of the spectrum. For example, technological advances and efficiencies in the use of resources may be important in our response to climate change and energy use. They could reduce greenhouse gas emissions in the short term. Unfortunately, big efficiency savings only occur once and subsequent savings diminish over time. To date, it is strong SCD that has allowed practitioners to most effectively bring together the ideas and alternative practices of environmental sustainability and social economics.

Weak-Strong Social Economy

Like SCD activities, social economy initiatives can be understood as arrayed along one or another type of spectrum: from weak to strong, from high road to low road (see Lewis and Swinney 2008), or from pragmatic to utopian (Fontan and Shragge 2000). Critics of weak social economy initiatives see such endeavours as working on the margins of the larger capitalist system: they help the poor while embracing the mainstream (Amin, Cameron, and Hudson 2002). They do not promote or facilitate societal transformation, and they pay scant attention to issues related to capitalist accumulation and environmental degradation. Most food banks are considered examples of weak social economy endeavours. Following a charity model, they play an essential role in providing food for the hungry, but they are often critiqued for depoliticizing hunger and poverty. While the public may get the impression that corporations (or individuals) "address poverty" by donating remnant stock to food banks, critics charge that the opposite is true. These donations solve problems of agribusiness waste, and donors are rewarded with tax credits (Poppendieck 1999). Meanwhile, the social causes of hunger remain untouched (McDonald 2005).

Rather than simply patch up problems, strong social economy initiatives contribute to transformative change. They undertake community-based actions that incorporate the principles of equity, redistribution, resilience, solidarity, and mutuality. They meet social needs instead of maximizing profit (Pearce 2003). Consider the alternative food movement, for example. Community supported agriculture, good food boxes, farmers markets, community gardens and local food hubs often use education, self-empowerment, and a systems approach to address the root cause of hunger and food insecurity. This approach addresses inequities and environmental degradation at each stage of the food chain, from field to fork to waste. If food initiatives do not highlight the relations between people and nature, the deep structural changes that are necessary for the emergence of sustainable communities, including changes in the ownership of agricultural lands, will not be realized (Allen 1993). In community-supported agriculture, for example, residents invest in farmers or in farmers' market associations. Such schemes bring together diverse producers and consumers to share the risks and benefits of a resilient local food system.

If contribution to transformative change is one measure of a strong social economy initiative, local financing is another. Strong approaches generate a large proportion of their own capital, thus reducing their reliance on banks, government subsidies or on charitable donations. That is why so many non-profit societies, co-operatives, and mutual associations are turning to social enterprise. These ventures sell or provide goods and services that meet social and economic needs, returning the profits to the organization. Table 1.2 contrasts weak and strong approaches to social economics.

Table 1.2 Characteristics of weak and strong social economy

	Weak social economy	Strong social economy
World view	Marginalized orientation	Mainstream orientation
	Neoliberal service provision*	Roll-back neoliberalism
Role of economy	Corporate social responsibility	Core business practice
	Charity, redistribution	Asset generating, equality
	Gap filling	Social and economic transformation
Source of problem and solution	Behavioural	Structural
	Capacity	Competition

*This refers to the provision of government services. The neoliberal model emphasizes managerial efficiency instead of equity in the provision of services (Polèse 1999). This managerial focus is said to offer greater bottom-up participation and control. In fact, the real motivation is to reduce government funding. Weak social economy initiatives fill the gap left by this retrenchment. Strong social economy initiatives organize in opposition to it.

For social economy organizations at the weak end of the continuum, day-to-day commitments tend to absorb all of their time and effort, leaving no resources to take part in the politics of broader structural change. Their provision of food and shelter to marginalized communities is admirable, as is their contribution to incremental change. In the long run, however, strong social economy approaches do more to strengthen sustainability and resilience and to counter socio-economic inequality and environmental degradation. We encourage approaches that confront root causes and ideologies and that strive for alternatives and transformational or structural change. In our view, then, and that of other researchers, sustainable development recognizes not one imperative but three: it requires that we reconcile social, ecological, and economic values and goals (Dale 2001; Robinson and Tinker 1997).

Community Bike Shops II
Celia Lee, Kailey Cannon, and Juanita Marois

Increasingly, community bike shops are encouraging use of their services by historically marginalized groups by offering monthly women-only and queer-only workshops (e.g., Our Community Bikes, Bikeworks, and Good Life). One well-known program is Wenches with Wrenches, which is run by the non-profit Community Bicycle Network in downtown Toronto to offer bike repair skills to women (Community Bicycle Network 2015). In line with their commitment to egalitarian principles, many community bike shops practice consensual decision-making to ensure that all members have a voice (e.g., Good Life, Ordinary Spokes, Our Community Bikes). Other shops, such as Bikeworks in Edmonton, have annually elected volunteer boards whose meetings are open to all members.

The popularity and geographic spread of community bike shops speak to a desire among urban residents to reduce automobile use—be it for environmental, health, or financial reasons. Community bike shops are highly networked and have created a lobby that focuses not only on individual cyclists but also on the road and transit bylaw structures fashioned by the long-dominant car lobby. The bike transportation lobby is often intentionally more grassroots and inclusive. Many bike shops practice radical inclusion and respond to a number of current social policy preoccupations such as creating community, reaching out to youth, quieting downtowns, increasing access to mobility, and challenging the association between masculinity and biking.

Community Bicycle Network. 2015. "Wenches with Wrenches." http://www.communitybicyclenetwork.org/wenches-with-wrenches/.
Good Life Bikes. 2015. Calgary. www.goodlifebikes.ca.
Ordinary Spokes. 2015. https://sites.google.com/site/ordinaryspokes/.
Pedal Power. 2015. "Our Community Bikes." http://pedalpower.org

TOWARDS CONVERGENCE: STRONG SOCIAL ECONOMY AND STRONG SCD

It is at the local level where SE and SCD convergence is most apparent. It is the context specific interventions in particular places that provide opportunities to connect problems and solutions across communities. SCD and SE address realities at the local level, where people generally experience economic and social marginalization and environmental degradation most acutely (Bridger and Luloff 1999, 380). In the last two decades, climate change and energy issues have taken an especially large toll on Canada's poor, including the working poor. Energy costs have spiked and energy supplies have grown uncertain. The portion of household income spent on cooling and heating, light, water, and waste removal has risen, resulting in "fuel poverty"—the inability to stay adequately warm or cool at a reasonable cost—for large numbers of citizens. At the same time, transportation costs have escalated, with a concomitant growth in the portion of the household budget spent on personal transport and on groceries and household goods.

Faced with the mounting impacts of these trends, individuals, communities, and municipalities are collaborating with social economy organizations. Social economy models of organization offer strong platforms for generating knowledge and innovation relevant to sustainability. Indeed, the theory and practice of both SCD and social economy offer us an entirely new ethos: they provide us with novel and valuable ways of thinking and organizing. Table 1.3 compares strong approaches to SCD with strong approaches to social economy.

Table 1.3 Characteristics of strong social economy, strong sustainable community development

Sustainable community development	Strong/Strong criteria	Social economy
Strong SCD initiatives focus on structural change. They emphasize development rather than growth, and they prioritize natural capital. Challenging power addresses structural power, legitimacy, agenda setting, framing, etc.	Move toward structural change	Strong SE initiatives strive for structural change in order to address community needs. These efforts derive from a vision of a more human, co-operative, and just economy. Humanized markets, socially directed enterprises and coalition building.
Strong SCD initiatives provide goods and services in ways that balance social, economic, and environmental goals. They aim for equity and justice, rejecting both the waterbed (some go up, some go down) and drawbridge (some safe inside the castle walls and others outside and in danger) politics of sustainability.	Engage in market-based activity	Strong SE initiatives engage in market-based provision of services and products, but they alter the criteria of exchange. They fashion new markets based on goals of affordability, social justice, and environmental sustainability. They re-localize the economy but are increasingly global in their perspective.
Strong SCD initiatives focus on building capacity for self-sufficiency and decentralization.	Focus on capacity building	Strong SE initiatives focus on building capacity for social and community-based ownership. Their activities build the collective assets of a community as well as co-operative models for scaling up.

Sustainable community development	Strong/Strong criteria	Social economy
Strong SCD initiatives focus on large-scale impacts. They address change at a range of nested scales: local, regional, national, and global. They recognize the need to partner with municipalities and regions to acquire needed resources.	Aim for scaling up and out	Strong SE initiatives focus on market activities that reduce dependence on the state. They are outward looking. They seek to develop networks, including strong municipal linkages, to scale up and scale out.
Strong SCD initiatives build broad coalitions and partnerships. They integrate small and family businesses with social economy organizations of various sizes.	Become part of network	Strong SE initiatives are values driven. They build broad coalitions, federations, and partnerships.
Strong SCD initiatives strive to change or subvert regulatory barriers. They are innovative. They seek new sources of capital for local green initiatives.	Challenge regulatory barriers	Strong SE initiatives create demand for innovative change. They then supply that demand as a way to get around obstructive power. They seek new forms of local capitalization and investment finance.
Strong SCD initiatives strive to ensure social justice, inclusion, and democratic governance. To measure success, they use socio-ecological indicators and new forms of accounting.	Strive for social inclusion	Social inclusion

The contributors to this volume are committed to research that advances the work of social economy and sustainability practitioners. We are enthusiastic about the potential of a convergence of these two fields, but our enthusiasm should not be misread as naïveté. We are well aware of the challenges of socio-economic transition and of the economic imperatives of capitalist accumulation that pressure firms (even well-meaning co-operatives, credit unions, and social enterprises) to reduce costs and generate surpluses in ways that often result in social exploitation and environmental decline (Meiksins Wood 2002). Although we are attentive to these pressures and tensions, we avoid what J. K. Gibson-Graham calls "capitalocentrism"—seeing capitalism as an all-pervading presence—since it leaves "little emotional space for alternatives" and can stifle one's imagination for political change (2006, xxii).

Many writers have struggled recently with the tension between the building of alternatives and the pressure of capitalism on those organizations that attempt to do so (Alperovitz 2011; Bajo and Roelants 2011; Curl 2012; Lewis and Conaty 2012; Lutz 2002; Murray 2010; Smith and Seyfang 2013). Each of the pockets of resistance to that pressure which are highlighted in this book arises out of a desire by people in particular places to do things fairly and sustainably. These organizations, and the individuals who participate in them, take risks and extend the boundaries of what is possible. They frame problems and solutions in new ways. They offer hopeful narratives of alternative futures. They build networks, institutional supports, and movements, sometimes with the help of the state (especially at the municipal and regional levels). They explicitly incorporate concerns about social and ecological sustainability in their endeavours. More and more, they federate and seek to enter multistakeholder coalitions to regulate or alter structures of provision and market pressures. Their existence provides a promising counternarrative to the dominance of capitalist logic. They open up new spaces for others to creatively reframe how we relate to each other and to the environment in ways that reflect strong sustainability and strong social economy approaches.

The many social economy organizations introduced in this book are consistent with sustainability in terms of not only what they do but how they do it. They provide robust, tested models of alternative ownership and control—models that animate the values of democracy, participation, and co-operation. They promote values grounded in commitment to a moral economy, an economy based on goodness, fairness, and justice—values that motivate people to co-operate in changing and building their own communities (Cannan 2000; Lewis and Conaty 2012). Social economy organizations develop relationships based on reciprocal, democratic, and co-operative principles. They live out their commitment to global justice, which they believe is essential to a just transition to sustainability. Their plurality and diversity help us to imagine not only how to "take back the economy" (Cameron and Wright, 2014; Gibson-Graham, Cameron, and Healy 2013) but also how to organize regionally and globally to transform it democratically.

Agyeman, Julian, and Bob Evans. 2004. "'Just Sustainability': The Emerging Discourse of Environmental Justice in Britain?" *Geographical Journal* 170 (2): 155–64.

Aleklett, Kjell, Mikael Höök, Kristofer Jakobsson, Michael Lardelli, Simon Snowden, and Bengt Söderbergh. 2010. "The Peak of the Oil Age: Analyzing the World Oil Production Reference Scenario in World Energy Outlook 2008." *Energy Policy* 38 (3): 1398–1414.

Allen, Patricia, ed. 1993. *Food for the Future: Conditions and Contradictions of Sustainability.* New York: John Wiley.

Alperovitz, Gar. 2011. *America Beyond Capitalism: Reclaiming Our Wealth, Our Liberty, and Our Democracy.* 2nd ed. Tacoma Park, MD: Democracy Collaborative Press; Boston, MA: Dollars and Sense.

Amin, Ash, Angus Cameron, and Ray Hudson. 2002. *Placing the Social Economy.* London and New York: Routledge.

Amyot, Sarah, Rupert Downing, and Crystal Tremblay. 2010. "Public Policy for the Social Economy: Building a People-Centred Economy in Canada." Public Policy Paper Series No. 3, June. Victoria, BC: Canadian Social Economy Research Partnerships, University of Victoria.

AtKisson, Alan. 2011. *The Sustainability Transformation: How to Accelerate Positive Change in Challenging Times.* London, UK: Earthscan.

Bajo, Claudia Sanchez, and Bruno Roelants. 2011. *Capital and the Debt Trap: Learning from Cooperatives in the Global Crisis.* London, UK: Palgrave Macmillan.

Barnosky, Anthony D., Elizabeth A. Hadly, Jordi Bascompte, Eric L. Berlow, James H. Brown, Mikael Fortelius, Wayne M. Getz et al. 2012. "Approaching a State Shift in Earth's Biosphere." *Nature* 486 (7 June): 52–58.

Block 1912 Collective. 2007. "Power and the Politics of Sustainability." In *Power and Resistance in Canada: Critical Thinking About Canadian Social Issues*, edited by L. Samuelson and W. Antony, 357–78. Halifax and Winnipeg: Fernwood.

Bouchard, Marie J., ed. 2013. *Innovation and the Social Economy: The Québec Experience.* Toronto: University of Toronto Press.

Bridger, Jeffrey C., and A. E. Luloff. 1999. "Toward an Interactional Approach to Sustainable Community Development." *Journal of Rural Studies* 15: 377–87.

Brundtland Commission. 1987. *Our Common Future: Report of the World Commission on Environment and Development.* Oxford: Oxford University Press.

Büchs, Melina, Graham Smith and Rebecca Edwards. 2011. "Low Carbon Practices: A Third Sector Research Agenda (TSRC Working Paper 59) 1–21. Retrieved from http://www.birmingham.ac.uk/generic/tsrc/documents/tsrc/working-papers/working-paper-59.pdf

Cameron, Jenny, and Sarah Wright. 2014. "Editorial: Researching Diverse Food Initiatives: From Backyard and Community Gardens to International Markets." *Local Environment* 19 (1): 1–9.

Cannan, Crescy. 2000. "The Environmental Crisis, Greens and Community Development." *Community Development Journal* 35 (4): 365–76.

Carson, Rachel. 1962. *Silent Spring*. New York: Houghton Mifflin.

Connelly, Sean. 2010. "Seikatsu Consumer Coop: Scaling-Up Food System Transformation?" Port Alberni, BC: BC-Alberta Social Economy Research Alliance.

Connelly, Sean, Sean Markey, and Mark Roseland. 2011. "Bridging Sustainability and the Social Economy: Achieving Community Transformation Through Local Food Initiatives." *Critical Social Policy* 31 (2): 308–24.

———. 2012. "We Know Enough: Achieving Action Through the Convergence of Sustainable Community Development and the Social Economy." In *The Economy of Green Cities: A World Compendium on the Green Urban Economy*, edited by Richard Simpson and Monika Zimmermann, 191–203. Dordrecht, Netherlands: Springer.

Curl, John. 2012. *For All the People: Uncovering the Hidden History of Cooperation, Cooperative Movements, and Communalism in America*. 2nd ed. Oakland, CA: PM Press.

Dale, Ann. 2001. *At the Edge: Sustainable Development in the Twenty-First Century*. Vancouver: University of British Columbia Press.

Davidson, Debra J., and Mike Gismondi. 2011. *Challenging Legitimacy at the Precipice of Energy Calamity*. New York: Springer.

Edwards, Andres R. 2005. *The Sustainability Revolution: Portrait of a Paradigm Shift*. Gabriola Island, BC: New Society.

Fairbairn, Brett. 2009. "A Rose by Any Name: The Thorny Question of Social Economy Discourse in Canada." Occasional Paper Series: Canadian Perspectives on the Meaning of the Social Economy, No. 1. Victoria, BC: Canadian Social Economy Research Partnerships, University of Victoria.

Fontan, Jean-Marc, and Eric Shragge, eds. 2000. *Social Economy: International Perspectives and Debates*. Montréal: Black Rose Books.

Gertler, Michael E. 2006. "Synergy and Strategic Advantage: Co-operatives and Sustainable Development." Saskatoon, SK: Centre for the Study of Co-operatives, University of Saskatchewan.

Gibson-Graham, J. K. 2006. *A Postcapitalist Politics*. Minneapolis: University of Minnesota Press.

Gibson-Graham, J. K., Jenny Cameron, and Stephen Healy. 2013. *Take Back the Economy: An Ethical Guide for Transforming Our Communities*. Minneapolis: University of Minnesota Press.

Gismondi, Mike, and Kailey Cannon. 2012. "Beyond Policy 'Lock-In'? The Social Economy and Bottom-Up Sustainability." *Canadian Review of Social Policy* 67: 58–73.

IEA (International Energy Agency). 2008. *World Energy Outlook 2008*. Paris: IEA.

———. 2010. World Energy Outlook 2010. Paris: IEA.

Johnston, Josée, Mike Gismondi, and James Goodman. 2006. "Politicizing Exhaustion: Eco-Social Crisis and the Geographic Challenge for Cosmopolitans." In *Nature's Revenge: Reclaiming Sustainability in an Age of Corporate Globalization*, edited by Josée Johnson, Mike Gismondi, and James Goodman, 13–35. Peterborough, ON: Broadview Press.

Jones, Van 2008. *The Green Collar Economy: How One Solution Can Fix Our Two Biggest Problems*. New York: Harper Collins.

Keiner, Marco. 2004. "Re-emphasizing Sustainable Development—The Concept of 'Evolutionability.'" *Environment, Development and Sustainability* 6: 379–92.

Lewis, Mike. 2006. "Mapping the Social Economy in BC and Alberta: Towards a Strategic Approach." BALTA Working Paper Series. Port Alberni, BC: BC-Alberta Social Economy Research Alliance.

Lewis, Mike, and Pat Conaty. 2012. *The Resilience Imperative: Cooperative Transitions to a Steady-State Economy*. Gabriola Island, BC: New Society.

Lewis, Mike, and Dan Swinney. 2008. "Social Economy and Solidarity Economy: Transformative Concepts for Unprecedented Times?" In *Solidarity Economy: Building Alternatives for People and Planet*, edited by Jenna Allard, Carl Davidson, and Julie Matthaei, 28–41. Chicago: Changemaker.

Lionais, D., and H. Johnstone. 2009. "Building the Social Economy Using the Innovative Potential of Place." In McMurtry, *Living Economics*, 105–28.

Lutz, Mark. 2002. *Economics for the Common Good: Two Centuries of Economic Thought in the Humanist Tradition*. London: Routledge.

McDonald, Jeff. 2005. "Critics: Nation's Dominant Food Bank Cares More About Bottom Line Than Feeding Poor." *Union-Tribune* (San Diego), 18 August.

McMurtry, J. J. 2009a. "Introducing the Social Economy in Theory and Practice." In McMurtry *Living Economics*, 1–34.

———. ed. 2009b. *Living Economics: Canadian Perspectives on the Social Economy, Co-operatives, and Community Economic Development*. Toronto: Emond Montgomery.

McMurtry, John. 2002. *Value Wars: The Global Market Versus the Life Economy*. London: Pluto Press.

Meadows, Donella H., Dennis L. Meadows, Jørgen Randers, and William W. Behrens III. 1972. *The Limits to Growth: A Report for the Club of Rome's Project on the Predicament of Mankind*. New York: Universe Books.

Mebratu, Destra. 1998. "Sustainability and Sustainable Development: Historical and Conceptual Review." *Environmental Impact Assessment Review* 18 (6): 493–520.

Meiksins Wood, E. 2002. *The Origin of Capitalism: A Longer View*. London: Verso.

Millennium Ecosystem Assessment. 2005. *Ecosystems and Human Well-Being: Synthesis*. Washington, DC: Island Press.

Murray, Robin. 2010. "Cooperation in the Age of Google: A Review for Co-operatives UK." Manchester: Co-operatives UK.

Neamtan, Nancy. 2009. "Social Economy: Concepts and Challenges." *Universitas Forum* 1 (3): 1–5.

Neamtan, Nancy, and John Anderson. 2010. "Enterprise Development." Paper prepared for the National Summit on a People-Centred Economy, Carleton University, Ottawa, 31 May–1 June.

O'Riordan, Tim. 2007. "Faces of the Sustainability Transition." In *The SAGE Handbook of Environment and Society*, edited by Jules Pretty, Andrew S. Ball, Ted Benton, Julia Guivant, David R. Lee, David Orr, Max J. Pfeffer, and Hugh Ward, 325–35. London: SAGE.

Pearce, John. 2003. *Social Enterprise in Anytown*. London: Calouste Gulbenkian Foundation.

Pearsall, Hamil, and Joseph Pierce. 2010. "Urban Sustainability and Environmental Justice: Evaluating the Linkages in Public Planning/Policy Discourse." *Local Environment: The International Journal of Justice and Sustainability* 15 (6): 569–80.

Polèse, Mario. 1999. "From Regional Development to Local Development: On the Life, Death, and Rebirth (?) of Regional Science as a Policy Relevant Science." *Canadian Journal of Regional Science* 22 (3): 299–314.

Poppendieck, Janet. 1999. *Sweet Charity? Emergency Food and the End of Entitlement*. New York, NY: Penguin Press.

Quarter, Jack, Laurie Mook, and Ann Armstrong. 2009. *Understanding the Social Economy: A Canadian Perspective*. Toronto: University of Toronto Press.

Rees, William E. 1990. "The Ecology of Sustainable Development." *The Ecologist* 20 (1): 18–23.

———. 1991. "Economics, Ecology and the Limits of Conventional Analysis." *Journal of the Air and Waste Management Association* 41 (October): 1323–27.

———. 1995. "Achieving Sustainability: Reform or Transformation?" *Journal of Planning Literature* 9 (4): 343–61.

Restakis, John. 2006. "Defining the Social Economy: The BC Context." Paper presented at the BC Social Economy Roundtable, Vancouver, January.

———. 2010. *Humanizing the Economy: Co-operatives in the Age of Capital*. Gabriola Island, BC: New Society.

———. 2011. *The Co-operative City: Social and Economic Tools for Sustainability*. Vancouver: British Columbia Co-operative Association.

Robinson, John. 2004. "Squaring the Circle? Some Thoughts on the Idea of Sustainable Development." *Ecological Economics* 48 (4): 369–84.

Robinson, John, and Jon Tinker. 1997. "Reconciling Ecological, Economic and Social Imperatives: A New Conceptual Framework." In *Surviving Globalism: The Social and Environmental Challenges*, edited by Ted Schrecker, 71–94. New York: St. Martin's.

Rockstrom, Johan, Will Steffen, Kevin Noone, Asa Persson, F. Stuart Chapin III, Eric F. Lambin, Timothy M. Lenton et al. 2009. "A Safe Operating Space for Humanity." *Nature* 461 (24 September): 472–76.

Roseland, Mark. 2012. *Toward Sustainable Communities: Solutions for Citizens and Their Governments*. 4th ed. Gabriola Island, BC: New Society.

Rusbridger, Alan. 2015. "The Argument for Divesting from Fossil Fuels is Becoming Overwhelming." *The Guardian*, March 16. http://www.theguardian.com/environment/2015/mar/16/argument-divesting-fossil-fuels-overwhelming-climate-change.

Shove, Elizabeth. 2010. "Beyond the ABC: Climate Change Policy and Theories of Social Change." *Environment and Planning* 42 (6): 1273–85.

Shove, E. and N.Spurling, eds. 2013. *Sustainable Practices: Social Theory and Climate Change*. London and New York: Routledge.

Smith, A., and G. Seyfang. 2013. "Constructing Grassroots Innovations for Sustainability." *Global Environmental Change* 23 (5): 827–29.

Smith, Graham. 2005. "Green Citizenship and the Social Economy." *Environmental Politics* 14 (2): 273–89.

Sneddon, Chris, Richard B. Howarth, and Richard B. Norgaard. 2006. "Sustainable Development in a Post-Brundtland World." *Ecological Economics* 57 (2): 253–68.

Srinivasan, U. Thara, Susan P. Carey, Eric Hallstein, Paul A. T. Higgins, Amber C. Kerr, Laura E. Koteen, Adam B. Smith et al. 2008. "The Debt of Nations and the Distribution of Ecological Impacts from Human Activities." *Proceedings of the National Academy of Sciences* 105 (5): 1768–73.

Urry, John. 2011. *Climate Change and Society*. London: Wiley.

Williams, C. C., and A. C. Millington. 2004. "The Diverse and Contested Meanings of Sustainable Development." *Geographical Journal* 170 (2): 99–104.

Wittman, Hannah, Mary Beckie, and Chris Hergesheimer. 2012. "Linking Local Food Systems and the Social Economy? Future Roles for Farmers' Markets in Alberta and British Columbia." *Rural Sociology* 77 (1): 36–61.

2 The Green Social Economy in British Columbia and Alberta

Mike Gismondi, Lynda Ross, and Juanita Marois

> *It should be axiomatic that an enterprise which has social purpose will have a clear positive environmental policy, for to be environmentally irresponsible is to be socially irresponsible. (Pearce 2003, 43)*

In this chapter, we describe, in broad brush strokes, what the BC-Alberta Social Economy Research Alliance (BALTA) mapping team has learned about social economics and green or environmental social economy organizations in Canada's two westernmost provinces. Because the social economy is challenging to define, it is also challenging to measure. Its emergent and rapidly evolving qualities add to the complexity of designing an appropriate net to capture its scale and scope. In order to apprehend the richness and diversity of the social economy sector in our two provinces, the BALTA team used a mapping survey, described below, to gather data from a variety of social economy organizations.

One intriguing finding in the data gathered by the BALTA team provided the seeds for this volume: a large number of social economy organizations declared that they were serving an environmental purpose. As John Pearce suggests in the statement quoted above, segmented definitions of social economy groups blur in reality. The hard lines of social, economic, environmental, and cultural—tick boxes in our survey—did an injustice to the integrated way in which many of these organizations see themselves doing their work and delivering value to their communities. But before delving into the details of the BALTA survey and our findings, we provide some contextual history for the social economy in Alberta and British Columbia.

Alberta has led all provinces in Canada in growth over the last twenty years (Alberta 2011). The export boom in Alberta continues to attract workers and investment from around the globe, especially in the petrochemical and energy industries, and Alberta now has the fastest-growing population in Canada. As a major supplier of petroleum resources, Alberta has been eager to spread its economic philosophy of neoliberalism across the nation, a goal in part realized by the election of the federal Conservative Party and an Albertan prime minister in 2006. Looking to Alberta to promote a social economy movement like that in Québec (described in chapter 1) might therefore seem a fond but futile dream.

Despite rapid growth, quick profits, and high wages for some Albertans, however, poverty and inequity persist in the province. Alberta is not homogeneous, despite cultural tropes of cowboy hats and oil rigs. In their "Introduction" to *Writing Off the Rural West* (2001), Roger Epp and Dave Whitson describe two Albertas: one sociogeographic region and set of peoples inside the economic boom, and the other outside. They argue that wealth and power is concentrated along the Highway 2 corridor and the cities of Calgary and Edmonton, in resource cities like Fort McMurray and Grande Prairie, and in the recreational settlements along the southwestern Rocky Mountain corridor; meanwhile, people in eastern rural Alberta and parts of the north and south, as well as in the poorer neighbourhoods of the cities, are struggling in what Epp later describes as "outer Alberta" (2006, 729). A recent report published by the Parkland Institute on disparity in Alberta confirms those patterns. Diana Gibson (2012, 7) found that economic inequality is increasing, with "Alberta's top 1 percent . . . by far the wealthiest in the nation, while at the bottom Alberta has the most intense poverty." Her analyses of Alberta's booming cities and industrial countryside help explain the need for the social economy in Canada's richest province. Ecological conditions are also deteriorating, as expansion in the tar sands, shale gas, and conventional oil and gas industries continues, with especially negative effects on ecosystems and First Nations downstream from Fort McMurray, home to the world's largest industrial megaproject.

But many Albertans seem determined to cash in on their place in a global free trade marketplace. Raising concerns about the negative impacts of the current boom on the poor or the environment is seen as meddling with people's personal rights to seek prosperity. Nevertheless, there is evidence that many other Albertans are resisting neoliberal, get-rich-quick economic clichés and are fighting for ecological and economic futures that are just and sustainable (Davidson and Gismondi 2011). Indeed, progressive politics, which has deep historical roots in the province, has generated many and varied collective responses by Albertans to poverty and economic and environmental precariousness.

The prairie west has always been a unique region of Canada. Alberta was founded in 1905, almost forty years after Canadian confederation in 1867. The region was shaped economically by grain farming and was politically dominated by federal land and immigration policies in its early decades. Gerald Friesen (1999) describes Alberta as the noisiest province—tempestuous and loud, with money in its pockets. Early on, Alberta's settlers and governments struggled, subordinated in part to eastern elites. Many Albertans carry resentment and animosity towards Ottawa's politicians and federal regulators, feelings brought forward from these early decades of the 1900s, when eastern Canadian bankers and politicians controlled private credit, loans and public investment, immigration, and resources in the western provinces. That resentment and protest against Ottawa became entrenched in the 1980s following the crash of Alberta's first oil boom. Increasing oil production and rising oil prices had created a thriving petrochemical refining and manufacturing sector and thousands of spin-off jobs in Alberta's construction and support service sectors. Real estate and business in the cities of Edmonton and Calgary were booming. Oil dollars filled the provincial coffers, and public spending expanded public sector services and jobs. Alberta had joined the twentieth century. But when the global oil crisis of the 1970s took oil prices even higher, Liberal prime minister Pierre Trudeau imposed a National Energy Program (NEP) to keep Alberta's politicians from raising oil prices to world rates and to maintain lower gas costs for eastern Canadian consumers. The federal government's actions killed the boom. The economy and the oil industry had gone bust by the mid-1980s. People lost companies, jobs, and homes. Many migrated out of the province. New grievances against Ottawa joined the old ones. Memories of the NEP and its effects persist, and the resentment is widespread across Albertans. In the 1990s, Ralph Klein, then Alberta's premier, became expert at using the memory of the NEP to whip up public resistance to federal environmental reviews of Alberta's resource projects. Well into the 2000s, Klein blunted public discussion of environmental issues like climate change; First Nations' and farmers' concerns about the Oldman River dam; and public concerns about business and housing expansion in Banff and Jasper National Parks, coal mining near Hinton, forestry and pulp and paper expansion in northern Alberta, gas exploration in the foothills, and the growth of the tar sands industry.

Paralleling Alberta's defiance of federal power has been an enduring socio-cultural set of images of the independent, self-reliant, go-it-alone Albertan (farmer, rig worker, oil businessman), which in turn has reinforced a widely held ideology that unbridled individualism, markets, and businesses are the solutions to poverty, social inequality, and even environmental protection, rather than government policy and programs (Filax 2008). The Conservative Party, which ruled the province from the late 1960s to 2015, wove this mythic individualism into its brand of prairie neoliberalism. In the 1990s, Premier Ralph Klein disguised government support for large corporations and private investors with folksy tales of his support for the self-reliant farm family, independent rig worker, or urban oil company entrepreneur, while gutting the environment department, cutting and curtailing public services, and privatizing lucrative government sectors (Taft 1997).

Nevertheless, a stream of progressive agrarian populist politics with deep historical roots in Alberta continues to flow in the province. Critics counter the roughneck and cowboy images by explaining that Alberta's individualism grew out of frontier communities, forged in the era of collaborative prairie settlement and homesteading. It was strong family and community co-operation that ensured the survival of those early settlers and rural communities against isolation, hostile weather, and difficult agricultural and economic conditions. Individualism, from this perspective, is rooted in community values. In those early days, collective responses by Albertans (to provide rural electrification, farm and fuel supply, and local financial capital) operated to offset the power of banks and corporations, "plutocratic economic parasites of Central Canada" (Epp 2006, 742). The co-operative movement took root in the prairies in the early 1900s as a democratic populist movement, and Albertans elected the United Farmers of Alberta (UFA) political party to govern the province (1920–35). The UFA founded the Alberta Wheat Pool in 1923, at the behest of co-operative farmers who realized the need for state support to confront private capital. But the Co-operative Commonwealth Federation would emerge in Saskatchewan, not Alberta, where the UFA political movement was displaced by Social Credit rule (1935–70), a more conservative than progressive force in Alberta and Canadian politics (Finkel 2006).

Social Credit's platform of support for struggling farmers, especially its concept of non-interest social dividends and its efforts to escape the control of central Canadian financiers, appealed to the broad Alberta population struggling out of the Depression. In 1938, Social Credit created Alberta Treasury Branch, a provincially controlled and owned financial institution that competed with private banks, as well as credit unions. The ideas behind the bank blended a Christian critique of capitalism with popular protest against commercial bankers in Toronto and Montréal, who prevented credit provision for many Albertans (Whalen 1952). Alberta Treasury Branch remains a Crown corporation today. Left-wing popular opinion is that it is a conservative counterweight to credit unions. That said, it maintains some 635,000 customers and $33 billion in assets, operating across Alberta as ATB Financial. Ralph Klein tried to privatize ATB (at the same time as he privatized the Alberta Liquor Control Board) as part of his neoliberal downsizing of the state in the 1990s. He was prevented by his own Tory rural caucus. ATB enjoyed public goodwill (Bird 2012) because during the recession of the 1980s, the corporation had protected many small businesses and oilfield contractors while the banks were calling loans and foreclosing. In an age of global mismanagement, ATB remains a well-managed, Alberta-owned Crown asset. If we seek financial sustainability to fund a green transition in Alberta, a publicly owned financial house with a progressive mission and supportive past practice in rural communities is a promising asset. Politics and a struggle for state power will have to come first, but the institution is already in place.

Similarly, Alberta credit unions (including a number of francophone *caisses populaires* in rural francophone communities like St. Paul and those in the Peace River country) also began providing alternative credit and community support in the mid-1930s. In 2013, the credit union system served members in more than two hundred branches across the province and had over $21.6 billion in assets (Alberta Central 2013, 3, 20). The Conseil de développement économique de l'Alberta, which serves the province's francophone population, also remains prominent in community development. And today, over 65 percent of Albertans are members of co-operatives.[1] Individualism co-exists with collectivity in the UFA agricultural, building, and fuel co-operative networks, as well as in more than 550 other member-owned Alberta co-operatives like grain pools and consumer co-ops, feedlots, gas and energy co-operatives, seed-cleaning plants, First Nations enterprises, and social housing co-operatives (www.acca.coop). Critics suggest, however, that we not overstate the depth of Albertans' co-operative commitment. They make note of pressures on the sector to become more competitive, reduce workforce, and even demutualize (Quarter, Mook, and Armstrong 2009). Writing about the late 1990s, Roger Epp (2006) describes the end of rural Alberta being the centre of political

---

1 Paul Cabaj, ACCA director. Speech at 2012 International Year of Cooperatives Gathering of Alberta Cooperatives, Red Deer, Alberta. Author's notes. Canada's 8,500 co-operatives and credit unions have more than 17 million members, and 4 in 10 Canadians are members of at least one cooperative (Canada, 2012, 15).

life in Alberta, along with the eclipse of many organizing and co-operative skills embedded in rural communities. But where Epp sees an eclipse, we see a stubborn legacy of co-operative frameworks and ideals resurfacing today in rural/urban collaboration around local food, conservation, alternative energy, and other environmental concerns. These also include promising alternative community finance models such as the new-generation co-operatives Westlock Terminals and the Battle River Railway, and the opportunity development co-operatives in Sangudo and Crowsnest Pass. Other indications of a progressive framework of values in Alberta are evident: continued state support for new and old forms of co-operation and credit unionism, considerable public membership in small and large co-operatives (more so in user services than production), and a rise of interest in co-operation in cities, especially among youth. It's not the united protest and glory of Alberta's past, but neither is it an empty field. Rebuilding a politics on these foundations is possible.

Alberta's Aboriginal peoples also have a history of participation in the social economy through innovative partnerships created to address their unique community needs. For example, the challenge of adequate housing for First Nations communities throughout Canada requires community-based responses because of the specifics of property ownership under First Nations treaty rights. Peace Hills Trust, a fully owned trust company founded in 1980 by the Samson Cree Nation, offers a First Nations response to housing problems that is created through common ownership and real estate equity limitations based on the Indian Act (Schwamborn 2010). Likewise, in response to the overrepresentation of Aboriginal people in Alberta's court system, Native Counselling Services of Alberta (NCSA) was established in 1970 with the objective of providing court-worker assistance to Aboriginal people in conflict with the law. Today, NCSA's services range from the provision of family and community wellness programs that shape restorative and social justice models to the full operation of the Stan Daniels Healing Centre, a federal Community Correctional Centre with a Section 81 designation.

Alberta's Métis people, who have faced a different set of barriers, have often been left outside of mainstream programs. Addressing this issue are the Métis Capital Housing Corporation (MCHC) and its sister corporation, the Métis Urban Housing Corporation (MUHC), both of which are owned by the Métis Nation of Alberta. MUHC was incorporated in 1982 to provide "affordable, adequate, and appropriate rental housing for low- and moderate-income Métis and Native families within the urban centres of Alberta" (Métis Nation 2007). Building on the

success of this endeavour, MCHC is now working to increase Métis home ownership, one example being MCHC's recently completed Boyle Renaissance project
in east downtown Edmonton, which contains 150 affordable units with district
energy provided by Enmax Corporation (Wodzynska 2014). There has also been
much pan–First Nations and Métis protest, including civil resistance, against
environmental destruction in various regions of the province.

It is this active and progressive history of Alberta co-operatives, credit unions,
trusts, non-profit organizations, and social groups (ethnic, First Nations, Métis,
religious, rural, and urban) that provides the context for current social economy
initiatives in the province, to which we will return following an introduction to the
social economy in British Columbia.

THE BRITISH COLUMBIA CONTEXT

Since its beginnings as a province, British Columbia has had a strong economic
base of natural resource industries, especially fisheries, orcharding and agriculture, forestry, and mining. But BC's economy is also cyclical and has resulted in
winners and losers, rich and poor classes, strong cities and weak small communities, and rural hinterlands. Today, many BC communities are suffering from crises
related to fluctuating resource prices, the collapse of fisheries, a declining forestry
industry, the overharvesting of resources and ecological degradation, and foreign
ownership of natural resource industries. Since the 1970s, a politics of confronta-
tion has created divisions between urban and rural people, pro-development and
pro-environment groups, and First Nations and settler communities. The recent
mountain pine beetle crisis decimated interior forest stands and threatened the
future of many of BC's non-metropolitan local economies (Nikiforuk 2011). Large
disparities of wealth can be seen between, for example, small communities in
rural and northern regions versus the lower mainland, as well as between social
classes within cities like Vancouver. Although British Columbia experienced near-
universal provincial growth during the long boom of the postwar period (with
the exception of First Nations communities), political and economic restructuring has created tremendous intraprovincial variability and inequality: "greater
income disparity, homelessness, and poverty are evident to anyone who walks
the streets of Vancouver, Victoria, and even smaller communities" (Cohen and
Klein 2011, 58).

As in Alberta, the social economy in British Columbia comprises many strands,
including traditional community economic development (CED) practice, a strong

co-operative movement, some progressive municipal initiatives, social enterprises, charities and foundations, and unions. One unique aspect of BC has been the strength of the province's First Nations, who have never been subject to treaty and who remain economically sovereign over their traditional territories. Since the 1970s, First Nations' local control over education and the economy has evolved, with land claims issues remaining a central motivating force underlying demands for community control of resources and economic opportunity. On the co-operative side, there is also a long history of Aboriginal co-ops within fisheries in British Columbia, especially with respect to harvesting; industrial fish processing co-operatives have been less successful. In terms of CED, Aboriginal development corporations are community owned and are often resource based. In the 1980s, the federal Canadian Aboriginal Economic Development Strategy sought to increase community capacity and community investment in First Nations. This generated interest in joint ventures between Aboriginal and non-Aboriginal people, a trend that continues to expand and evolve today.

Since the mid-1970s, British Columbia has also had a long evolution of Community Futures Development Corporations (CFDCs). In BC, these organizations have maintained a focus on lending and entrepreneurial development, with some social enterprise and social co-operatives in the mix. These development corporations have ranged from relatively conservative to more progressive. In rural areas, they remain important, proactive, and community based. Community Futures have also been involved in the development of community infrastructure. For example, the City of Revelstoke, located in the Columbia District of BC, has been active in addressing local business growth, unemployment, and the boom-and-bust cycles in the forest industry. Revelstoke municipal authorities established a community forest tenureship in the 1990s to support local wood milling, manufacturing, and value-added processing. Social-public partnership—that is, collaboration between social economy organizations and municipalities—is an important strand of strong sustainability revisited throughout this book.

Co-operatives and credit unions also have a long history and prominent presence in BC's society and economy. (See chapter 10 on credit unions in British Columbia and Alberta.) Religious, ethnic, and other co-operatives have played key roles in agriculture, fisheries, and forestry, as well as in the provision of services such as housing and elder care. (See *Stories of BC Co-op Movement* at http://www.uvic.ca/research/centres/cccbe/resources/galleria/index.php). Recently, the British Columbia Co-operative Association has drawn attention to the networks of green co-operatives providing alternative transport, housing, social, and food services in Canadian cities (Restakis 2010). On the financial side, Coast Capital Savings and Vancity credit unions are long-time supporters of the social economy and are exploring innovations in affordable and attainable housing and green building. In addition, one of Canada's largest consumer co-operatives, Mountain Equipment Co-op (MEC), has its head office and warehousing divisions in British Columbia. (MEC is also popular in Alberta and has outlets across Canada). As a retail co-operative, MEC tries to build and operate its facilities with minimum ecological impact and dedicates 1 percent of gross sales to supporting environmental causes. Further, MEC has established sustainability and value-based supply chain standards with both international suppliers and local sustainability initiatives. Some critics see MEC's mission of encouraging outdoor recreation and nature exploration as increasing the impact of humans on wild nature. Others are critical of its contribution to consumerism and its displacement of small local outdoor-equipment stores. MEC, nevertheless, provides an example of a progressive, global-scale, Canadian co-operative operating within a worldwide consumer society and capitalist economy. In collaboration with international groups, MEC is leading and encouraging retail companies to take up sustainability indicators, green procurement, fair workplace standards, and conservancy and stewardship initiatives (Ponto 2008; Quarter, Mook, and Armstrong 2009).

Enterprising Non-Profits (ENP), an emergent force in Canada's social economy, is a collaborative program that began in 1997 in Vancouver with support from the United Way and the Vancouver Foundation. The program "promotes and supports social enterprise development and growth as a means to build strong non-profit organizations and healthier communities" (VCF 2014). ENP grew rapidly throughout the province and now has affiliate sites across the country that are introducing innovative social purchasing models. A recent survey of social enterprises in British Columbia and Alberta indicates the wide range of their work and shows that an increasing number of such enterprises are involved in environmental work (Elson and Hall 2010). Social enterprises, which are now found worldwide, use commercial approaches to market their services and products and use profits to grow the enterprise (in terms of both impact and employment) and to extend their social and ecological missions.

Finally, one weakness in the social economy in both Alberta and British Columbia is the lack, across all sectors, of supporting infrastructure, which appears somewhat narrow in focus. There is a need for more systematic cross-sector alliance building and fiscal support along the lines of Chantier de l'économie sociale in Québec (Lewis and Conaty 2012). In the conclusion of this book, we return to a discussion of the role of government support and the building of system-wide supports needed to strengthen and expand the social economy network in western Canada.

MAPPING SURVEY METHODOLOGY

It wasn't until the mid-1990s that the term *social economy* began to be widely used, and it started in Québec. Since that time, Québec has led the country in the development of the sector (Bouchard 2013). But even by 2008, comparatively little discussion about the social economy sector—its actors, contributions, or impacts—had taken place in western Canada. In January of that year, the BALTA group undertook a five-year project to begin to fill the information gap. A preliminary profile of the size and scope of the sector in BC and Alberta was undertaken using existing data from such sources as *The Canadian Nonprofit and Voluntary Sector in Comparative Perspective* (Hall et al. 2005), other government studies, and various reports by non-government organizations. The resulting BALTA report provided evidence for the important roles of non-profit and voluntary organizations and co-operative businesses in employment and revenue generation, non-market housing, social enterprise, and the provision of local and regional social services. It also identified financial, philanthropic, and other intermediary groups that sustain and support the social economy. In particular, it acknowledged the significant presence of the co-operative model in western Canada and its role in consumer, energy, farming, housing, and non-financial services, alongside strong financial co-operatives and credit unions (Sousa and Hamdon 2008).

To learn more about social economy organizations in Alberta and British Columbia, the BALTA team implemented a mapping survey (Affolderbach, Gismondi, and Soots 2008). Using definitions from Restakis (2006) and Pearce (2003) to help identify which groups to survey, we sought information from co-operatives, credit unions, non-profit and volunteer organizations, charities and foundations, service associations, and community and social enterprises in both provinces. Drawing on Lewis (2006), we paid particular attention to those social economy organizations that use market mechanisms to generate revenue and pursue explicit social objectives. We believed that revenue generated by trading services and products in the market by organizations in the third sector is, as Pearce (2003, 25) argues, an important but largely under-recognized economic contribution to society—a contribution that provides social economy organizations with fiscal resilience and with a democratically controlled means to expand their programs.

For-profit enterprises were included in our survey only if surpluses were mutually shared by members in a collectively owned structure, such as in co-operatives or collectives. We excluded from our survey hospitals, universities, government organizations, and conventional capitalist firms such as sole proprietorships, partnerships, and investor-owned or publicly traded companies. The overall goal of the BALTA survey was strategic:

> We are interested in achieving more than merely setting out a baseline of actors in the social economy. For example, can mapping help us capture the characteristics of the social economy that are often rendered invisible quantitatively but are of crucial importance to achieving durable results? How do we capture data useful to policymakers? What kinds of questions are of importance to practitioners, which if answered could lead to improvements in the development of a new generation of practitioners? How can the research relevance of the mapping be maximized by producing a comparative base of accessible data from which more effectively honed research questions might be posed? (Lewis 2006, 2)

To further define our population in line with national survey efforts, we drew on the methodology of the Canada Research Chair in Social Economy research group, who used the following criteria when profiling social economy organizations: (1) economic activity through the production of goods or provision of services, (2) social rules prohibiting or limiting distribution of surpluses among members, (3) voluntary association of persons and/or of collective bodies, and (4) commitment to democratic governance processes (Bouchard, Ferraton, and Michaud 2006). With the collaboration of practitioners and umbrella groups in Alberta and BC, we developed a contact list for the survey of 1,600 social economy organizations (Affolderbach, Gismondi, and Soots 2009).

From the outset, a number of us in BALTA had been intrigued by certain social economy organizations doing key environmental work in our two provinces. While groups working on the environment were recognized in Canada's national voluntary sector survey (Hall et al. 2005), and in some survey work in Québec and the Maritimes, the BALTA team decided to explore the relationship between the social economy and environmental work more deeply. Our emphasis on environment is linked to increased public concern about resource extraction and the export of oil and gas, minerals, and forest products in both provinces, and the equally strong concern for conservation and ecosystem health and its links to life and livelihood. We formulated specific questions about environmental goals and activities in order to capture any evidence of the green social economy. As Lewis (2006, 16) explains:

> To better understand the extent to which the social economy in the region is engaged directly in environmental restoration and protection through social enterprise is, in my view, a strategic design issue. Given the cross-cutting nature of [the issues of] climate change, peak oil, and local and regional environmental degradation, the extent to which social enterprise is conscious of and practically engaged in activities that promote solutions is of real value.

The question in the back of our minds was whether environmental conservation should be understood as just one more mission alongside such goals as poverty alleviation, job training, and affordable housing provision, or whether the relationship between environmental and social sustainability is in fact more intertwined and will only be achieved with transformative change and a paradigm shift in thinking. This entire book explores this question. As Lewis (2007, 2) argues: "At the end of the day, . . . the belief that re-embedding social goals into the heart of our economic life is crucial, and that placing both into a proper and durable relationship within the ecological limits of our planet is our most present and urgent meta-priority."

MAPPING SURVEY FINDINGS: HIGHLIGHTS

The BALTA mapping project analysis is based on completed surveys from 478 social economy (SE) organizations, 33 percent from Alberta and 67 percent from BC. While we cannot claim that our findings represent the social economy sector, given the sampling method and size, an interesting portrait of the social economy in these provinces has begun to emerge from the information gathered. The following highlights from the BALTA mapping survey findings indicate the importance of the sector not only to the provinces' economic well-being but also to the well-being of their people and communities.[2]

---

2 For more details of the BALTA mapping project and survey results, go to "Mapping Results, Reports, and Papers" under the "Research" tab at the BALTA website (http://www. socialeconomy-bcalberta.ca/research/mapping-results-reports-papers.php). For the final report, see Gismondi et al. (2013).

- SE organizations are purposeful.
  - Almost 90 percent of organizations reported having an explicitly stated social purpose or mission guiding their work. Most frequently, these missions are related to education and training, the provision of basic needs, health, housing, human rights, and family services.
  - A significant proportion (26%) also reported having an environmental purpose or mission, and the majority of these focus their activities on conservation and protection, along with resource management.
- SE organizations help to build social capital in communities.
  - Almost half of the organizations service their local communities: cities, towns, and regional areas.
  - Almost three-quarters of the organizations also provide support to each other.
  - Over 75 percent of profits generated by the surveyed SE organizations are invested back into growing the organization and its services.
- SE organizations are active in the economy.
  - Annual operating budgets reported by SE organizations in the two provinces total over $638 million, while the capital budgets exceed $1.19 billion.
  - Annual revenue totals $2.62 billion, of which $1.95 billion is generated through participation in the market economy.
- SE organizations participate in a variety of work sectors.
  - Over 40 percent of the SE organizations described their "primary" work to be in the services sector
  - The focus of the remaining groups ranges from agriculture, forestry, fishing, and mining to arts and culture, housing, environment, and business.
- SE organizations provide numerous employment opportunities.
  - Collectively, the surveyed organizations have more than 12,500 full-time and 4,500 part-time employees.
  - In addition, the respondents provide 971 seasonal and 2,111 contract opportunities.
  - A total of 1,694 individuals from traditionally under-represented social groups are employed by 109 SE organizations.

The mapping survey asked respondents if they have an explicitly stated social and/or environmental mission. Twenty-six percent of the respondents indicated that their organization has an environmental mission. We will refer to this group as environmental social economy (ESE) organizations throughout the following discussion. The data provided by these 124 organizations form the basis for this initial portrait of ESE organizations in Alberta and British Columbia. Again, while we cannot claim representativeness, given the sampling method and size, the respondents provided important information about the ethos and activities of their organizations. For a full report of the findings from the ESE organizations within the BALTA Mapping Survey, see Gismondi, Ross, and Marois (2014).

Environmental Missions

Reinsertion of social and/or environmental goals into economic decision-making is a defining characteristic of social economy organizations. Thus, we asked respondents to choose, from a list of fifteen pre-defined items, all of the areas that best describe their establishment's "environmental mission or scope of activities." An additional "other" category was included to allow participants to elaborate on a mission or activity not found in the original list. As shown in figure 2.1, the ESE organizations reported a broad range of missions/activities, the most frequently identified ones being conservation and protection, resource management, alternative business practices, health, agriculture and food, and pollution prevention.

Of the multiple missions and activities listed for their organizations, participants were next asked to specify one primary category. Of the forty-five Alberta ESE organizations that specified a primary category for their environmental mission, conservation and protection, health, resource management, and agriculture and food were noted most frequently (see figure 2.2). There was also a relatively large "other" group whose environmental missions covered a range of activities not specified in the list of primary categories offered. The sixty responding ESE organizations in British Columbia provided a varied list as well (see figure 2.3). Excluding the "other" category, conservation and protection, alternative business practices, agriculture and food, and sustainability were most frequently noted.

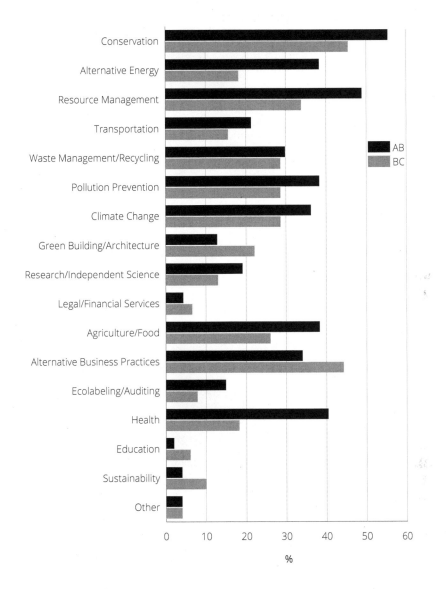

Figure 2.1 Environment-related activities of ESE organizations in Alberta and BC

Notes: N=47 (Alberta); N=77 (BC). Percentages do not total 100% because many of the organizations surveyed identified multiple environmental missions. The conservation category covers both conservation and protection.

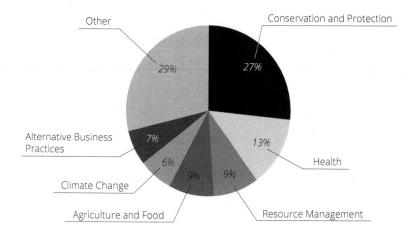

Figure 2.2 Primary environmental mission for Alberta ESE organizations

Notes: N = 45. "Other" combines categories selected by less than 5% of the organizations and/
or were unspecified. These categories are alternative energy (4.5%), transportation (2%), waste
management and recycling (2%), pollution prevention (4.5%), green building/architecture
(2%), legal/financial services (2%), sustainability (4.5%), and unspecified (7%).

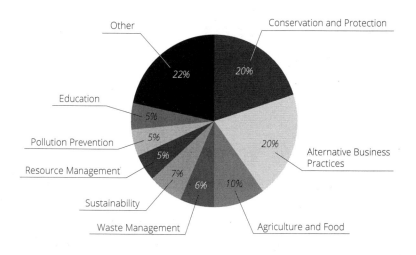

Figure 2.3 Primary environmental mission for BC ESE organizations

Notes: N – 60. "Other" combines categories selected by less than 5% of the organizations
and/or were unspecified. These categories are transportation (2%), climate change (3%),
green building/architecture (3%), research/independent science (2%), co-labeling/auditing/
monitoring (2%), health (3%), and unspecified (7%).

Social Missions

Most ESE organizations (93.5%) also had a social mission. In both Alberta and BC, social mission was defined most frequently by participation in the education and health sectors and through provision of basic needs.

We next asked respondents to choose a primary social mission. Alberta ESE organizations most frequently chose target groups and environment as their primary social mission (see figure 2.4). Although fair trade and sustainability were listed as separate categories, they could also be interpreted as environmental. In British Columbia, excluding "other," the ESE organizations most frequently chose target groups, education, and environment to define their primary social mission (see figure 2.5).

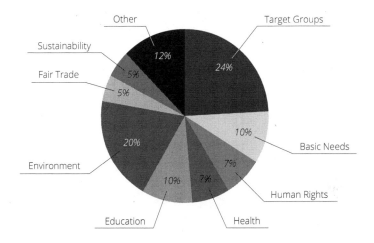

Figure 2.4 Primary social mission for Alberta ESE organizations

Notes: N = 41. "Other" combines categories selected by less than 5% of the organizations. These categories are housing (2%), legal/financial services (2%), family services (2%), arts and culture (2%), and other (2%).

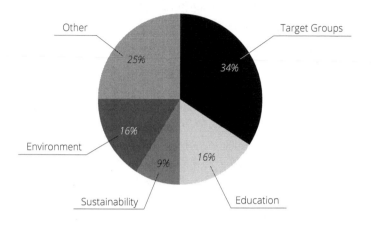

Figure 2.5 Primary social mission for BC ESE organizations

Notes: N = 56. "Other" combines categories selected by less than 5% of the organizations. These categories are human rights (1%), health (3%), basic needs (4%), family services (1%), fair trade (3%), housing (1%), and other (3%).

Organizational Structure

In addition to identifying the missions and activities of ESE organizations, the mapping project team explored the relationships among each organization's mission, age, structure, size, and ways of interacting with the community. The following descriptions emerged.

The ESE organizations tended to be younger than SE organizations in general. While the average age of the latter was 28.7 years in Alberta and 25.9 years in BC, the average age of ESE organizations was 25 years in Alberta and 21 years in BC. Figure 2.6 shows the growth of ESE organizations from 1914 to 2010. The most senior ESE organization currently operating in Alberta was incorporated in 1914; the most junior, in 2007. In British Columbia, the oldest ESE organization was incorporated in 1943; the newest, in 2010. A dramatic increase in the number of ESE organizations occurred in Alberta starting in 1998 and in BC starting in 1994.

The majority of ESE organizations in Alberta and British Columbia identified their legal form as a non-profit organization (45% and 51%, respectively) and/or a non-profit society (45% and 29%). In their study of social enterprises in Alberta and British Columbia, Peter Elson and Peter Hall (2010) reported a similarily high proportion, with 73.9 percent of their respondents with environmental missions reporting having a "non-profit legal structure." Interestingly, a number of ESE organizations surveyed for the BALTA mapping study in British Columbia (21%), but not in Alberta (4%), identified themselves as for-profit organizations or corporations. Given these structures, it is not surprising that in both Alberta and British Columbia, the majority of ESE organizations reported that they invested their profits back into their organizations (64% and 79%, respectively), while another 17 percent in each province reported donating to other community organizations.

Figure 2.6 Growth of ESE organizations in Alberta and BC from 1914 to 2010

Notes: N=44 (Alberta); N=76 (BC)

In terms of accountability to a defined constituency, almost two-thirds of all ESE organizations indicated that they had a membership base. Membership numbers across the various ESE organizations ranged from 20 to 2.8 million in Alberta and from 4 to 392,000 in British Columbia. A greater proportion of Alberta organizations (75%) than BC organizations (56%) reported having a membership base. While the mapping study found a median of 210 and 142 members in Alberta and

British Columbia ESE organizations, respectively, the average calculated in Elson and Hall's social enterprise study was 484 members (2010).

The social economy literature, particularly on community economic development, frequently emphasizes the local scale of operations within social enterprises, or what is often called "local embeddedness." Place-based connections are seen as a key factor in success but also as a limiting factor for the scaling up of operations. John Loxley and Laura Lamb (2007, 202), however, emphasize the importance of making business relationships with others in the larger economy. For example, the purchase by an expanding community development enterprise of goods or services produced by smaller marginal social economy organizations, or social enterprises, would be a backward linkage. Whereas, the sale by the community enterprise of a service or commodity to a larger community development firm like a province wide Food Coop or Cooperative Gas Bar would be a forward linkage. Thinking of business relationships as dynamic is a way to conceive of local embeddedness as nested in a larger system.

The results of our survey confirmed both the local and multi-levelled focus of social economy organizations. Most frequently, ESE organizations in both provinces provided services to the local communities and neighbourhoods, cities and towns, and regional areas where they were located (see figure 2.7). Despite this local focus, the ESE organizations in general reported a larger geographic focus than was reported by SE organizations as a whole, with proportionally more ESE organizations serving their provincial, national, and international communities. As figure 2.7 illustrates, in both British Columbia and Alberta, ESE organizations frequently served national and international communities. This finding is not surprising given that environmental issues cross political and geographic boundaries.

In addition to addressing environmental problems, ESE organizations tend to develop linkages and networks that enhance the social capital of an area and benefit the social economy. Social capital refers to attitudes that are based on neighbourliness, trust, and cohesion and that facilitate positive exchanges and effective collaboration (Logue 2006). This network-building characteristic was illustrated in our survey, with 81 percent of Alberta organizations and 88 percent of BC organizations stating that they provide support to other organizations. Figure 2.8 summarizes the types of support, along with the proportion of organizations providing that support. Note that the highest proportion of organizations provide support in the form of networking, capacity building, advocacy and promotion, and research and education.

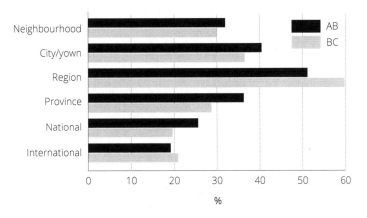

Figure 2.7 Geographic Range Served by ESE organizations in Alberta and BC

Notes: N=47 (Alberta); N=77 (BC). Percentages do not total 100% because many of the organizations surveyed indicated that they serve more than one type of geographical area.

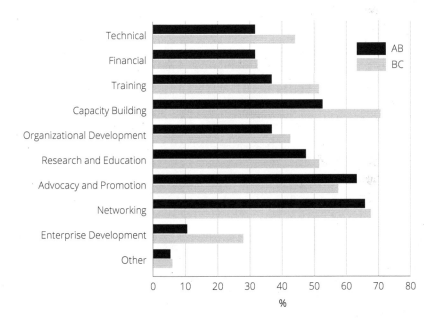

Figure 2.8 Type of support given by ESE organizations in Alberta and BC to other organizations

Notes: N=38 (Alberta); N=68 (BC). Percentages based on valid N (i.e., only those organizations indicating that they provide support to other organizations). Percentages do not total 100% because many of the organizations surveyed identified multiple support activities. "Other" includes, for example, "housing" and the "provision of food."

Work Areas, Employment, and Financial Profiles

The BALTA mapping project also explored the work sectors in which the ESE organizations participated, and the survey responses covered a broad range. The largest proportion of Alberta ESE organizations defined their primary work sector as involvement in services (35%), followed by 24 percent in the environment sector (conservation, resource management, transportation, research, and climate change) and 17 percent in the field of natural resources (agriculture, fishing, forestry, mining). As in Alberta, the largest proportion of ESE organizations in British Columbia defined their primary work sector as involvement in services (30%). Next largest was the environment (19%), followed by arts and culture (14%). Further work sector details for the ESE organizations in both provinces can be found in table 2.1.

Table 2.1 Primary work sectors

Work Sector	Alberta		BC		Total	
	%	N	%	N	%	N
Agriculture, forestry, fishing, mining	17.4	8	6.5	5	10.6	13
Finance/insurance	2.2	1	6.5	5	4.9	6
Arts and culture	2.2	1	14.3	11	9.8	12
Environment	23.9	11	19.5	15	21.1	26
Housing	4.3	2	–	–	1.6	2
Sales						
Retail	6.5	3	1.3	1	3.3	4
Wholesale	2.2	1	2.6	2	2.4	3
Services						
Social	15.2	7	15.6	12	15.4	19
Professional	6.5	3	10.4	8	8.9	11
Technical/scientific	2.2	1	–	–	.8	1
Administrative	–	–	–	–	–	–
Public	2.2	1	1.3	1	1.6	2
Health	8.7	4	2.6	2	4.9	6

Work Sector	Alberta		BC		Total	
	%	N	%	N	%	N
Education						
Teaching/education	6.5	3	9.1	7	8.1	10
Training	–	–	2.6	2	1.6	2
Business						
Manufacturing	–	–	1.3	1	.8	1
Construction	–	–	–	–	–	–
Transportation/storage	–	–	1.3	1	.8	1
Real estate	–	–	1.3	1	.8	1
Catering/hosting	–	–	–	–	–	–
Communications	–	–	1.3	1	.8	1
Waste management	–	–	–	–	–	–
Recreation/tourism	–	–	1.3	1	.8	1
Other	–	–	1.3	1	.8	1
Totals	100	46	100	77	100	123

Within these diverse sectors, responding ESE organizations employ more than 7,500 people in paid positions and create an additional 7,400 volunteer opportunities. Small organizations dominated the survey respondents, with 26 percent of Alberta ESE organizations and 54 percent of those in British Columbia reporting fewer than five full-time employees. Since the question about number of employees and volunteers was not answered by all respondents, the summaries provided here probably underestimate the total numbers of people employed in full-time, part-time, seasonal, contract, and freelance positions, as well as the number of volunteers across both provinces. Further employment details for the ESE organizations in both provinces can be found in table 2.2.

Table 2.2 Employment in Alberta and BC: Number of organizations and jobs

	Alberta		British Columbia		Total	
	Orgs.	Jobs	Orgs.	Jobs	Orgs.	Jobs
Full-time	25	227	56	5625	81	5852
Part-time	16	77	38	786	54	863
Seasonal	11	85	19	325	30	410
Contract	14	69	36	398	50	467
Target group	12		21		33	
Volunteers	25	2628	45	4773	70	7401

In addition to employing numerous people, ESE organizations in both provinces make significant financial contributions to the economy. Annual operating budgets reported total over $122.2 million, while capital budgets exceed $903.5 million. Note that only 68 percent of Alberta participants and 78 percent of BC respondents were able to provide fiscal information about their organization's actual operating budget. Even fewer Alberta (38%) and BC (29%) participants were able to provide dollar amounts to describe their organization's actual capital budgets. Therefore, the sums provided underestimate the total dollar amounts related to the organizations that responded to this survey, especially with respect to actual capital budgets.

Median figures (mid-point of the distribution) and sums (total across all organizations) for both the operating and capital budgets were calculated for BC and Alberta ESE organizations. In Alberta, the median operating budget was $338,404 (range = $900–$3.3 million), and in British Columbia, it was $248,566 (range = $950–$21.7 million). In addition, Alberta and BC organizations show total operating budgets of $25.7 million and $96.5 million, respectively. The median capital budgets for Alberta (range = $3000–$18.2 million) and BC (range = $200–$850 million) were calculated at $45,544 and $116,445, respectively. The responding organizations reported total capital budgets of $19.5 million in Alberta and $884 million in BC.

An obvious follow-up question to the size of the budgets was the sources of revenue to fuel these budgets. Most ESE organizations depend on a number of revenue sources. The most frequent sources of revenue reported in both provinces are sales of goods and services, government grants, donations, and memberships and subscriptions (see figure 2.9). Again, not all organizations were able to answer this question, so the percentages underestimate the numbers of ESE organizations receiving income from any particular source.

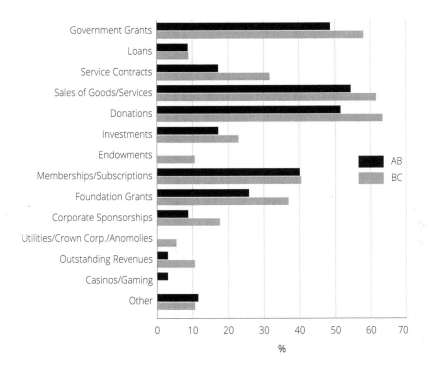

Figure 2.9 Sources of revenue for ESE organizations in Alberta and BC

Notes: N=35 (Alberta); N=57 (BC). Percentages do not total 100% because organizations surveyed indicated multiple revenue sources.

Annual revenue figures for ESE organizations were calculated by summing the dollar amounts from each of the categories noted in table 2.3 below—government grants, loans, service contracts, and so on. Figure 2.10 depicts the proportions of Alberta ESE organizations with total revenues within various ranges. As shown by the chart, the largest proportion of organizations surveyed (and who could also provide revenue information) reported revenues less than $20K. Significant proportions of Alberta ESE organizations reported total revenue in the ranges of $20K to $100K, $100K to $500K, and $500K to $1 million.

Table 2.3 Revenue: ESE organizations in Alberta and BC

		Alberta			British Columbia		
		N	Median	Sum	N	Median	Sum
Sales Revenue	Service contracts	6	$64.5 K	$3.6 M	18	$100 K	$22.1 M
	Sales of goods/ services	19	$20 K	$244 M	35	$80.7 K	$29.7 M
	Memberships/ subscriptions	14	$4 K	$3.2 M	23	$1.6 K	$481 K
Subtotal				$250.8 M			$52.3 M
Sources of Finance	Donations	18	$42.5 K	$45.8 M	36	$28.3 K	$55.7 M
	Government grants	17	$43 K	$3.7 M	33	$80 K	$21.6 M
	Investments	6	$3.8 K	$167.9 K	13	$6 K	$24.4 M
	Loans	3	$15 K	$177 K	5	$100 K	$1.0 M
	Endowments	0	N/A	N/A	6	$285 K	$2.2 M
	Foundation grants	9	$70 K	$1.6 M	21	$29.6 K	$1.6 M
	Corporate sponsorship	3	$5 K	$134.7 K	10	$34.2 K	$1.3 M
	Utilities/Crown corporations	0	N/A	N/A	3	$24 K	$75 K
	Outstanding revenues/ anomalies	1	N/A	$41.1 K	6	$70 K	$154 K
	Casinos/gambling	1	N/A	$57.8 K	0	N/A	N/A
	Other	4	$57 K	$1.5 M	6	$17.5 K	$1.8 M
Subtotal				$53.2 M			$109.8 M
Total Revenue		35		$303.5 M	57		$162.1 M

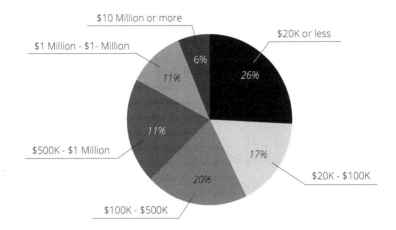

Figure 2.10 Total revenues of ESE organizations in Alberta

Notes: N = 35

As figure 2.11 shows, the largest proportion of BC organizations surveyed (and who could also provide revenue information) reported revenues between $100K and $500K, with another significant proportion reporting revenues between $1 million and $10 million.

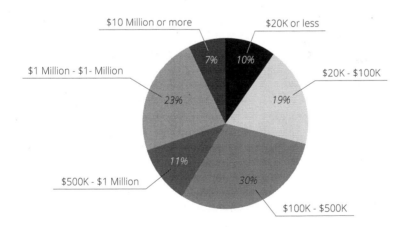

Figure 2.11 Total revenues of ESE organizations in BC

Notes: N = 57

ESE organizations in the two provinces reported a total of $303.1 million in sales revenue, $250.8 million in Alberta and $52.3 million in BC. Fifty-seven percent of Alberta and 73 percent of BC organizations earned at least a portion of their income through market-based or business activity (i.e., through the provision of goods and/or services). Figure 2.12 provides a summary of the proportion of ESE organizations in Alberta and British Columbia who reported involvement in various types of market-based activities.

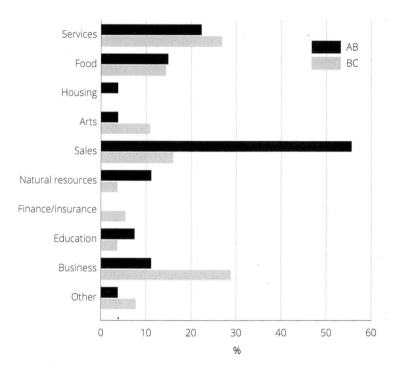

Figure 2.12 Market-based activities of ESE organizations in Alberta and BC

Notes: N=93 (Alberta); N=201 (BC). Percentages do not total 100% because many of the organizations surveyed identified multiple market-based activities.
*The categories include the following:
Services—social, professional, technical, scientific, administrative, public, health care, employment, personal, business, and consulting
Food—service/catering, production, and distribution
Housing—accommodation, housing, and property management
Arts—arts and culture, gallery arts, theatre, and performing arts
Sales—retail and wholesale
Natural Resources—agriculture, forestry, fishing, and mining
Business—production/manufacturing, construction, transportation/storage, real estate, etc.
Other—unspecified and unclassifiable data

The 124 ESE organizations that completed the BALTA mapping survey provided much information for the discussion that occurs in the following chapters of this book. These organizations show that seeking to achieve a social good through enterprise activity and being environmentally responsible can be compatible. The assertion that being engaged in socially conscious and challenging work is enough—that adding in the component of environmental responsibility is too much—is false. These ESE organizations are functioning with intertwined missions, proving that truly integrated development—development that balances social, economic, and environmental goals—is possible. To deepen our understanding, we conducted follow-up interviews with some of the directors of these organizations and found that many of them were operating with a "triple bottom line"—a commitment to a social mission, environmental sustainability, and financial self-sufficiency.

The social economy provides an approach to socio-economic activity that not only is consistent with sustainability but also provides alternative ownership and control models. It animates the values of democracy, participation, and co-operation while engaging people in the processes of local social change and community building (Cannan 2000). Social economy organizations also forge associative links with the state, which is one of the features of strong sustainability. Note, for example, the significant number of government contracts for environmental services that are delivered by ESE organizations. These relationships between government and ESE organizations lay the groundwork for scaling out co-operative multistakeholder strategies to address environmental problems.[3]

The social economy mobilizes people to act in the interests of eco-social justice based on reciprocity and co-operation. It builds community capital. The social economy can also serve to reinforce the notion that sustainability is a process and not a fixed outcome. Indeed, what Cressy Cannan (2000, 371) says about community development can also be applied to the social economy: it "tends to see some of its processes as goals—participation is both a means and end, for the participative society is one in which all can have a voice, where discrimination has been addressed, and where the capacities associated with effective participation continue to develop."

---

3 Figure 2.9 shows that between 48–58% (depending on province) of ESE organizations receive government grants; and between 18–32% (depending on province) of ESE organizations receive service contracts.

As this book argues, however, the depth, or strength, of sustainability and social economy initiatives is crucial. Initiatives at the strong end of the continuum have the best potential to be transformative; the weaker endeavours merely slow the decline.

REFERENCES

Affolderbach, Julia, Mike Gismondi, and Lena Soots. 2008. "Research Decisions in Mapping the Social Economy in Alberta and British Columbia." BALTA Mapping Working Paper No. 2. Port Alberni, BC: BC-Alberta Social Economy Research Alliance.

———. 2009. "Research Decisions in Mapping the Social Economy in Alberta and British Columbia." Port Alberni, BC: BC-Alberta Social Economy Research Alliance.

Alberta. 2011. *Highlights of the Alberta Economy 2011*. Edmonton: Government of Alberta.

Alberta Central. 2013. *Alberta Central Annual Report*. Calgary: Alberta Central. https://www.albertacentral.com/Annual-Reports/5322_1029_ALB_2013-Annual-Report_Book_Digital.aspx.

Bird, M. 2012. "Privatizing the Crown: The Exceptional Fate of Alberta's Liquor Control Board." *American Review of Canadian Studies* 42 (3): 329–42.

Bouchard, Marie J., ed. 2013. *Innovation and the Social Economy: The Québec Experience*. Toronto: University of Toronto Press.

Bouchard, Marie J., Cyrille Ferraton, and Valérie Michaud. 2006. "Database on Social Economy Organizations: The Qualification Criteria." Working Papers of the Canada Research Chair on the Social Economy No. R-2006-03.

Canada. 2012. *House of Commons Report: Status of Cooperatives in Canada, Report of the Special Committee on Cooperatives*. 41St Parl. Blake Richards, Chair. September.

Cannan, Crescy. 2000. "The Environmental Crisis, Greens and Community Development." *Community Development Journal* 35 (4): 365–76.

Cohen, Marjorie Griffin, and Seth Klein. 2011. "Poverty Reduction in British Columbia? How 'The Best Place on Earth' Keeps People Poorest." *Canadian Review of Social Policy* 65–66: 58–73.

Davidson, Debra J., and Mike Gismondi. 2011. *Challenging Legitimacy at the Precipice of Energy Calamity*. New York: Springer.

Elson, Peter R., and Peter V. Hall. 2010. "Strength, Size, Scope: A Survey of Social Enterprises in Alberta and British Columbia." BALTA Project C16. Port Alberni, BC: BC-Alberta Social Economy Research Alliance.

Epp, Roger. 2006. "Two Albertas: Rural and Urban Trajectories." In *Alberta Formed, Alberta Transformed*, edited by Michael Payne, Donald Wetherell, and Catherine

Cavanaugh, 726–46. Edmonton: University of Alberta Press; Calgary: University of Calgary Press.

Epp, Roger, and Dave Whitson, eds. 2001. *Writing Off the Rural West: Globalization, Governments, and the Transformation of Rural Communities.* Edmonton: University of Alberta Press.

Filax, Gloria. 2008. "Race-ing Alberta-ness." *The Ardent Review* 1 (1): 50–54.

Finkel, Alvin. 2006. "The Social Credit Revolution." In *Alberta Formed, Alberta Transformed*, edited by Michael Payne, Donald Wetherell, and Catherine Cavanaugh, 491–514. Edmonton: University of Alberta Press; Calgary: University of Calgary Press.

Friesen, Gerald. 1999. *The West: Regional Ambitions, National Debates, Global Age.* Toronto: Penguin Books/McGill Institute.

Gibson, Diana. 2012. *A Social Policy Framework for Alberta: Fairness and Justice for All.* Edmonton: Parkland Institute.

Gismondi, Mike, Lynda Ross, and Juanita Marois. 2014. "Mapping the Social Economy in British Columbia and Alberta: Data Summary Report—Organizations with Environmental Missions." Port Alberni, BC: BC-Alberta Social Economy Research Alliance.

Gismondi, Mike, Lynda Ross, Juanita Marois, Julia Affolderbach, Lena Soots, and Ashley Smith. 2013. "Mapping the Social Economy in British Columbia and Alberta: Final Report." Port Alberni, BC: BC-Alberta Social Economy Research Alliance.

Hall, Michael H., Cathy W. Barr, M. Easwaramoorthy, S. Wojciech Sokolowski, and Lester M. Salamon. 2005. *The Canadian Nonprofit and Voluntary Sector in Comparative Perspective.* Toronto: Imagine Canada.

Lewis, Mike. 2006. "Mapping the Social Economy in BC and Alberta: Towards a Strategic Approach." BALTA Mapping Working Paper No. 1. August. Port Alberni: BC-Alberta Social Economy Research Alliance.

———. 2007. "Constructing a Sustainable Future: Exploring the Strategic Relevance of Social and Solidarity Economy Frameworks." Port Alberni: BC-Alberta Social Economy Research Alliance.

Lewis, Mike, and Pat Conaty. 2012. *The Resilience Imperative: Cooperative Transitions to a Steady-State Economy.* Gabriola Island, BC: New Society.

Logue, John. 2006. "Economics, Cooperation, and Employee Ownership: The Emilia Romagna Model—in More Detail." Kent, OH: Ohio Employee Ownership Center. http://community-wealth.org/content/economics-cooperation-and-employee-ownership-emilia-romagna-model-more-detail.

Loxley, John, and Laura Lamb. 2007. "Economics for CED Practitioners." In *Doing Community Economic Development*, edited by John Loxley, Jim Silver, and Kathy Sexsmith. Halifax and Winnipeg: Fernwood and Canadian Centre for Policy Alternatives.

Métis Nation. 2007. "Metis Urban Housing." Métis Nation of Alberta. http://www.
albertametis.com/Affiliates/Affiliates-Programs-Urban.aspx.

Nikiforuk, Andrew. 2011. *Empire of the Beetle: How Human Folly and a Tiny Bug Are
Killing North America's Great Forests*. Vancouver: Greystone Books.

Pearce, John. 2003. Social Enterprise in Anytown. London: Calouste Gulbenkian
Foundation.

Ponto, Jason. 2008. "Is Mountain Equipment Co-op a Social Enterprise? Using the
Genuine Wealth Model to Assess MEC's Place in the Social Economy." Master's
thesis, Centre for Interdisciplinary Studies, Athabasca University.

Quarter, Jack, Laurie Mook, and Ann Armstrong. 2009. *Understanding the Social
Economy: A Canadian Perspective*. Toronto: University of Toronto Press.

Restakis, John. 2006. "Defining the Social Economy: The BC Context." Paper prepared
for the BC Social Economy Round Table, Vancouver, January. http://www.uvic.
ca/research/centres/cccbe/assets/docs/publications/practitioner/Restakis_
DefiningSocialEconomy.pdf.

———. 2010. *Humanizing the Economy: Co-operatives in the Age of Capital*. Gabriola
Island, BC: New Society.

———. 2011. "The Co-operative City: Social and Economic Tools for Sustainability."
Vancouver: British Columbia Co-operative Association. http://www.bcca.coop/
sites/bcca.coop/files/The_Co-operative_City_June_11.pdf.

Schwamborn, Julia. 2010. "Background Brief: Peace Hills Trust Company." Vancouver:
UNBC Community Development Institute.

Sousa, Jorge, and Evelyn Hamdon. 2008. "Preliminary Profile of the Size and Scope
of the Social Economy in Alberta and British Columbia." Port Alberni, BC: BC–
Alberta Research Alliance on the Social Economy.

Taft, Kevin. 1997. *Shredding the Public Interest: Ralph Klein and Twenty-five Years of
One-Party Government*. Edmonton: University of Alberta Press.

VCF (Vancity Community Foundation). 2014. "Social Enterprise Development."
Vancity Community Foundation. http://vancitycommunityfoundation.ca/s/social_
enterprise_development.asp?ReportID=465681.

Whalen, H. 1952. "Social Credit Measures in Alberta." *Canadian Journal of Economics
and Political Science* 18 (4): 500–17.

Wodzynska, Zuzanna. 2014. "Boyle Renaissance." *Award: Architecture/Design/
Construction*, February, 79. http://www.metiscapital.ca/Portals/0/News/255439-
February%202014_selected-pages.pdf.

3

The Role of the Social Economy in Scaling Up Alternative Food Initiatives

Mary Beckie and Sean Connelly

Food—what we eat, where we get it, how it's produced and distributed—can act as a catalyst for social, economic, and environmental transformation. The essential and multifunctional nature of food gives rise to a number of crucial and overlapping societal goals including aims related to nutrition, health, culture, community building, social equity, local economic development, and ecological integrity. Thus, food creates both an important platform for developing an integrative approach to sustainable community development and the strategic cross-sector collaboration needed to foster this transformative approach.

In this chapter, we describe and analyze collaborative innovations emerging from the social economy that are contributing to community transformation through the resocialization and relocalization of food. The case studies presented below— Edmonton's Good Food Box, the Rimbey Farmers' Market, and the New City Market local food hub in Vancouver—render visible some specific nodes at the intersection of the social economy and nascent alternative food systems. There are a growing number of alternative food initiatives that are influencing changes in the ways in which food is produced, distributed, and consumed. They provide an alternative work-in-progress narrative to conventional, industrial, and globalized agri-food systems and are drawing on social economy strategies to achieve their goals. The challenges they face in scaling up these innovations so as to increase their individual impacts and contribute to the development of a more comprehensive (field to plate to waste) alternative food system underline the essential role of social values and social infrastructure (collaboration, strategic alliances, and networks) in building the physical infrastructure that is also needed to realize the strong sustainability and strong social economy potential of alternative food systems.

A key similarity between strong sustainability and strong social economy approaches to social, environmental, and economic problems is the turn to the local, with emphasis on place-based and community-based responses to local and global problems. The fundamental characteristic that links alternative food initiatives to strong sustainability and strong social economy approaches is the overlap of the spatial concept of local with the values and principles of embeddedness, the rooting of food products and systems in a particular place and social context, where "local" becomes a strategy for values-based transformation of the food system. Attempts to embed food systems in particular locales reflect a key strategy behind the alternative food movement's goal of creating shorter value chains that reconnect consumers and producers (Goodman 2003; Winter 2003) and thus provide opportunities for generating the reciprocity, trust, transparency, and accountability that are critical to developing a more ecologically sustainable and socially just food system.

As Branden Born and Mark Purcell (2006) demonstrate, the localness of a food system should not be seen as having any inherent qualities—it is merely a strategy that can be applied by any group of actors to advance particular agendas. For this reason, local food initiatives benefit from explicit linkages to the value-based commitments of strong approaches to social economy and sustainable community development. Local food initiatives have the potential for broader transformation, but proponents need to be aware of and closely tied to the politics of alternative food systems (Guthman 2008a). Much of the focus of the local and alternative food movement is based on the need to pay the full costs of the environmental, social, and economic impacts of food, but if this movement is to contribute to food security and social justice, participation must be universal (Guthman 2011). Without attention to the underlying values of the local food movement, the localization of consumption and production risks being limited to the fetishization of local food for wealthier consumers. Such localization is based on principles that correspond more to weak sustainability and weak social economy approaches (as discussed in chapter 1).

The case studies of alternative food initiatives presented in this chapter provide insight into some of the challenges and successes in creating a sustainable local food system. Opposing the status quo of the conventional, globalized food system is a daunting David-and-Goliath task, yet the fact that these alternative food initiatives exist, are growing in number, and are part of broader global food security and sovereignty movements whose goal is to remake the food system (Larder, Lyons, and Woolcock 2014) illustrates the "politics of possibility in the here and now" (Gibson-Graham 2006, xxvi). These seemingly small initiatives can be seen as local sites of the transformation of global politics (Gibson-Graham 2006). Before launching into the description and analysis of these cases, we provide a brief background on the conventional industrialized food system, the rise of alternative agri-food initiatives, and the role of the social economy.

EMERGING ALTERNATIVES TO THE GLOBALIZED FOOD SYSTEM

Over the past century, significant scientific, economic, and political efforts have modernized and industrialized agriculture and the entire food system. Improvements in technology and technique have been nothing short of revolutionary, but much of this progress has come at the expense of ecosystems and communities. Agriculture now has the largest and most wide-ranging environmental impacts of any human activity, including loss of soil, water quality, biodiversity, and natural habitats (Millenium Ecosystem Assessment 2005). The conventional agri-food system is also heavily dependent on fossil fuels, from production to processing and distribution, producing approximately 25 percent of global greenhouse gas emissions (Foley et al. 2011). Within the context of climate change and a finite supply of fossil fuels, the ability of the industrial food system to provide global food security now and into the future is a topic of growing concern. As oil prices rise, so does the cost of food; currently, at least one billion people around the world are food insecure (FAO 2011). There are also growing concerns about food health and safety due to the prevalent use of pesticides, growth hormones, antibiotics, and preservatives in increasingly standardized and processed food.

The structure and viability of family farms and farming communities have also been severely affected by industrialized agriculture (Douglas 2010; Epp and Whitson 2001). Local control over production processes and markets is decreasing, while dependence on industrial inputs and long-distance markets intensifies. As agriculture and food have become increasingly drawn into the global economy, there has been a steady withdrawal of many interventionist policies and programs that once supported agriculture (Wiebe and Wipf 2011). The role of the nation-state in shaping agriculture development is diminishing with the implementation of liberalized trade arrangements; food is big business, and global markets and transnational agribusiness corporations are now key players affecting change in the food system (Heffernan and Constance 1994; Juillet, Roy, and Scala 1997). As a result of this shift, farmers are earning a declining share of the food dollar, while the cost of production continues to rise, driving many farmers into debt and bankruptcy (Qualman 2011). These structural conditions cause farmers to become chained to the "agricultural treadmill": they respond to worsening economic returns by further intensifying production through high-cost scientific and technological inputs in search of production efficiencies at greater scales (Ward 1993).

Much has been published recently to expose the sustainability challenges of the conventional food system. Such documentaries as *Food Inc.* (2008) and *Supersize Me* (2004) and books like Michael Pollan's *In Defence of Food: An Eater's Manifesto* (2008) and *The Omnivore's Dilemma: A Natural History of Four Meals* (2006) argue persuasively that reliance on a globalized and industrialized food system is eroding the ecological integrity, nutritional value, safety, sovereignty, and security of our food system. Initiatives exploring alternative approaches to food production, distribution, retailing, and consumption have blossomed in recent years, as evidenced by the exponential growth in farmers' markets in North America over the past ten years (FMC 2009; USDA 2011). Some participants in these and other alternative food initiatives take their cue from the hundred-mile diet or the organic movement, motivated by health concerns or issues such as peak oil and climate change, or by the community benefits associated with relocalizing economic activity, preserving farmland, and supporting local farmers and farming communities.

As part of the evolving response to the conventional food system, social economy entities and activities have emerged within the local food movement that are contributing to the "re-socialization" and "re-spatialization" of food (Sonnino and Marsden 2006, 183). The numerous examples include food banks, collective kitchens, community gardens, community supported agriculture (CSA), farmers' markets, good food boxes, and local food hubs. Through a long and rich history, the social economy has demonstrated a capacity to respond to social need through groups of citizens acting in collaborative and democratic ways to achieve common goals (Defourny and Develtere 1999; Moulaert and Ailenei 2005; Pearce 2003). For example, the development of the agricultural economy of western Canada relied on co-operatives, which provided the collective infrastructure to get farmers' products to markets and ensured that farmers received fair prices for their products and had access to machinery, equipment, and financing at fair rates (Faucher 1947). However, these social economy initiatives also struggled with the tensions involved in maintaining organizational stability and pursuing broader transformational change; in some cases (e.g., grain marketing), they were unable to achieve their objectives without state support (Lipset 1950).

For contemporary producers, alternative food initiatives offer several important benefits over the conventional supply chain, such as immediate payment and higher revenues (Verhaegan and Van Huylenbroeck 2001), as well as independence and greater control over production and marketing (Hunt 2007). The "quest for fresh products" has made farmers' markets and other alternative food venues popular with consumers (Sanderson et al. 2005, 6), who also seek "attributes not found in globally produced commodity goods"—such qualities as "authenticity and a sense of local community" (Hunt 2007, 54). Consumers point to a variety of ethical and environmental considerations influencing their purchasing of locally produced food, including "concerns about farmland protection" and "small farm viability" (Brown and Miller 2008, 20), interest in supporting "organic conditions and animal welfare" (Holloway and Kneafsey 2000, 286), and issues around food safety, food security, and diversity (Sanderson et al. 2005).

Typical of the social economy, relationships and linkages among public, private, and social economy sectors are being strengthened and expanded in alternative food initiatives, and reciprocity and mutual benefits are being achieved through the integration of a broad range of social, economic, and environmental objectives. In part because of these relationships, many see these alternative food initiatives as new consumption spaces defined by the interactions of local, ethical, and environmental discourses involving networks of producers, consumers, and institutions (Holloway and Kneafsey 2000). From this perspective, alternative food systems are considered "a means of taking back control from the multinationals and contributing to local community revitalization" (Sanderson et al. 2005, 12). In contrast to a corporately controlled global food system, social economy and alternative food initiatives are often self-organizing, locally embedded, and locally controlled (Feagan and Morris 2009), responding in size and character to local supply and demand, and are "conditioned by local community norms, values and culture" (Lyson, Gillespie, and Hilchey 1995, 108).

By mobilizing public resources and resources generated by the marketplace as well as through voluntary involvement, the social economy strives to build relationships that are linked by a common purpose and to create new knowledge and benefits for its members or the community as a whole (Fonteneau et al. 2010). The social economy, however, is not without its challenges and shortcomings. Moulaert and Ailenei (2005) identify sustainable financing, fluctuating government and institutional support, and higher-level organizational development as prevalent challenges for the development of this sector. Amin, Cameron, and Hudson (2002) critique social economy players who fail to uphold the guiding principles and goals of this sector and in some cases embrace the larger capitalist system. A similar analysis can be applied to alternative food initiatives.

Despite growing interest in alternatives to the conventional food system, the scale of production and distribution focused on supplying local demand constitutes only a small percentage of total food sales, and conventional retailers remain the primary source for food acquisition, whether local or imported (Alberta 2008; FMC 2009; Smithers, Lamarche, and Joseph 2008). In addition to scale, a number of other constraints limit the role of local and alternative food initiatives within the larger food system, including scope (range of products, particularly in a northern climate), accessibility and convenience, physical infrastructure (storage, processing), and organizational capacity. Issues related to affordability, social exclusion, gender, and labour practices have also raised concern about the values and goals shaping the development of alternative food initiatives (Allen 2008; Delind 2011; Guthman 2008b; Hinrichs 2003). The key challenge facing the local food movement is how to evolve to the point of transforming rather than merely informing the food system—from farm to plate to waste. Achieving this goal will require strategies and innovations that meet both quantitative and qualitative objectives, that build the "social and physical infrastructure" (Connelly, Roseland, and Markey 2011) needed to scale up and scale out community-oriented food projects such as farmers' markets and community supported agriculture (Beckie, Huddart Kennedy, and Wittman 2012; Friedmann 2007; Johnston and Baker 2005; Wittman, Beckie, and Hergesheimer 2012).

In the three case studies that follow, we highlight the successes and challenges of scaling up alternative food systems based on greater convergence of the social economy and sustainability. Our starting point is the recognition that in order to scale up, a rebuilding of the infrastructure to support local and alternative food systems is required and that this infrastructure has both social and physical components.

THE GOOD FOOD BOX, EDMONTON

The provincial capital of Edmonton and the surrounding rural municipalities in northern Alberta (also known as the Capital Region) constitute a metropolitan population of over a million. Like the rest of the province, this region is characterized by a dry continental climate with warm summers and cold winters. The productive black prairie soils of the area support viable large-scale crop and livestock operations. There is also a concentration of market gardens in the peri-urban area surrounding Edmonton; most notable is the northeast area of the city, which supports a number of successful small-scale fruit and vegetable operations due to a unique microclimate that creates an extended growing season similar to that in the southern-most parts of the province.

The Good Food Box (GFB) program emerged at a time when there was considerable local-level organizing in opposition to redevelopment of agricultural land in the northeast part of the city between 2006 and 2010. The non-profit organization Greater Edmonton Alliance (GEA) was successful in leading a broad-based citizen's movement focused on preserving the last tract of agricultural land within the city limits, raising awareness of problems with the existing food system, and linking food and land-use policy for city planners, politicians, and the broader public. The movement—which included farmers in northeast Edmonton, faith-based organizations, local businesses, and citizens—was successful in ensuring that any future planning and development for the northeast sector of the city recognize the value of its agricultural characteristics—including micro-climate, soil capabilities, and moisture content—and their contribution to sustainable food and agriculture systems for Edmonton (City of Edmonton 2010). Widespread public concern for local agriculture in the Capital Region encouraged the City of Edmonton to develop a local food and agriculture strategy (see Beckie, Hanson, and Schrader 2013). The GFB program was able to build on the emerging enthusiasm for local food and to effectively link concerns over redevelopment with the local food system more generally.

GFB organizers recognized that a key strategy for farmland preservation was to increase the viability and profitability of local farmers and to raise the awareness of the potential for local food for consumers (GEA, 2010). Yet there were three key barriers to achieving both goals: lack of collaboration across the food chain, limited consumer access to and awareness of local food, and limited distribution opportunities for producers. The conventional food system provides little incentive for collaboration. Growers, consumers, institutional buyers, processors, and restaurant owners have few opportunities to interact, and personal relationships and connections have been eclipsed by the pursuit of efficiencies and economies of scale. As one local producer put it (interview with authors, Edmonton, February 2, 2010), "Producers need to work together to create a sense of interdependency rather than competition so that the significant costs, risks and benefits of investing in local food infrastructure can be shared." In other words, it is trust, reciprocity, and collaboration that are critical for rebuilding the food system.

Consumers' limited access to and awareness of local food options was a challenge for rebuilding the food system. Beyond the weekly farmers' markets, there are few alternative venues for convenient access to local food in the Capital Region. As a result, consumers committed to supporting local food systems find themselves shopping at supermarkets in the middle of the week. Likewise, local farmers and producers have limited options for marketing their goods to local customers. For example, while selling at the farmers' market provides direct access to consumers, it also takes the farmer off the farm at critical points of the growing season. In addition, the lack of local food wholesalers makes it difficult to access the restaurant industry. Chefs wishing to source local food often have to buy from multiple producers in order to get the volume required, and they face challenges in addressing other parameters such similar quality, size, shape, flavour, and consistency.

The distribution of local food is fragmented and underdeveloped within Edmonton, and the Good Food Box program was seen as a way to build connections between farmers and the consumers who want to buy the product; it could provide an alternative to supermarkets while also maintaining a connection to the social and environmental values that gave rise to interest and concern about local-food issues in the Edmonton region. As one GFB customer stated (interview with authors, Edmonton, January 27, 2010):

> I think most of the people I know that have joined up with the GFB did it as much for the good food as for the political reasons because they didn't want it to fail. Right now we are hoping to try and reach out to people who maybe aren't that, who just want the convenience and I think you still have to be a little bit convinced that it's good because you don't get to choose your vegetables and choices are made for you.

The GFB was set up as a social enterprise in 2009. It was designed to increase the availability of locally produced food for all families in the Edmonton area beyond the weekly farmers' markets. The objectives of the project were to provide convenient access to affordable fresh produce to Edmonton residents, to provide fair market value to producers, to expand marketing and distribution for producers beyond the farmers markets, to be accessible to all, and to create jobs for low-income residents. The pilot project ran for six continuous weeks of delivery in 2009 and was expanded to the entire growing season for the two years following. The idea at the proposal stage was to evolve into a fully independent co-operative (GFB organizer, interview with authors, Edmonton, January 26, 2010).

The project was originally designed for 110 participants, but when a call for interest was put out, more than a thousand people signed up. The project delivered 236 bags of fresh produce per week, 31 of which were subsidized for low-income clients of the Edmonton Food Bank. Customer surveys at the end of the year indicated that 88 percent of participants were extremely or very satisfied with the quality of the produce and the price. When asked why they participated, the primary response was to support local farmers (63%) and the secondary response was to support local food security (53%), demonstrating a values-based commitment to local food that goes beyond food as a commodity (GFB organizer, interview with authors, Edmonton, January 28, 2010).

The GFB was expanded for the 2010 and 2011 seasons to include a pre-order purchasing website that connected consumers to all of the products that were available at the farmers' markets, increasing convenience for consumers and increasing sales of food products outside the mainstream food system, primarily to suburban residents. While it was no longer run explicitly as a social enterprise (the grant for subsidizing low-income access was not renewed), the local non-profit organization dedicated to supporting independent and local businesses in the Edmonton area that began managing the program donated 1 percent of total sales to the Mennonite Central Committee. Although the GFB was still committed to organic and sustainable production, it was no longer limited to locally sourced products; rather, it had expanded to businesses that operate locally, in part as a result of the difficulty in obtaining year-round access to a range of products in a northern climate. The program expanded to cater to niche foodie and middle-class markets, with prices that reflect those demographics. For example, consumers were able to purchase prepared meals, seafood, meats, seasonings, chocolates, breads, and vegetables, in addition to the standard range of products available during the growing season (GFB employee, interview with authors, January 28, 2010).

Moving to online pre-order sales and expanding product offerings for middle-class suburban consumers not only provided the opportunity to scale up connections between local producers and consumers but also yielded a critical mass that made further infrastructure investments viable. For example, securing warehousing space with cold storage, more delivery trucks, and additional labour would not have been feasible based on the numbers involved with the GFB project alone, and without that critical infrastructure, it was impossible to expand the GFB program so as to include more participants and neighbourhoods (GFB employee, interview with authors, 28 January, 2010). However, to cover the costs of scaling up, there was increasing pressure to prioritize higher-revenue boutique options over functions and options that improve equitable access to local food. The online ordering included offerings such as precooked frozen meals as well as seafood and chocolate, which were obviously not local but were provided by local businesses. These tensions resulted in some of the original GFB members leaving the program and running their own bulk-buying clubs out of their kitchens because they did not feel that the GFB program was paying enough attention to the values and politics of local food.

The GFB ceased operations in 2012, as it was not generating enough revenue to justify the expenses. Attempts to expand the customer base in the suburban market based on convenience were unable to compete with the convenience and price of the mainstream food system. Meanwhile, the values of the social economy and sustainability that created the interest and rationale for the GFB initially were no longer emphasized as strongly. The demise of the GFB can be explained in part by the project attempting to scale up too quickly, paying too much attention to building the physical infrastructure for local food, and not cultivating the social infrastructure required to build a long-lasting movement around the social, political, and environmental issues associated with where our food comes from.

Meet Your Maker
Sean Connelly

FarmFolk CityFolk, a Vancouver-based non-profit organization that focuses on creating a local, sustainable food system, runs a number of projects that seek to provide access to and protection of farmland, to support local growers and producers, and to engage citizens in addressing local food issues. The organization has been particularly effective at building relationships, networks, and trust all along the food value chain, thus contributing to both the physical and social local food infrastructure (MYM 2014). They bring together representatives from hundreds of local food businesses for workshops, speed-dating roundtables, resource information sessions, and a delicious local food potluck lunch. Meet Your Maker provides an on-the-spot opportunity for networking and contracting among local food producers, processors, distributors, and commercial buyers. MYM events develop and solidify relationships between food producers and retail buyers and chefs. It has resulted in new business contacts, immediate sale contracts, and education on the challenges that both producers and buyers face in advancing local food. Over $1 million in contracts has been generated since the inaugural event in 2008.

MYM (Meet Your Maker). 2014. "Meet Your Maker." FarmFolk CityFolk. http://www.farmfolkcityfolk.ca/events/meet-your-maker-3/.

Located along the corridor between Edmonton and Calgary, the region of Central Alberta is characterized by a strong agricultural heritage that continues to support a viable, rural-based economy. The towns and their surrounding farming communities have a combined population of approximately fifty thousand. During the summer months, thousands more are drawn to the many lakes and other recreational amenities of the region: Sylvan Lake, for example, received over 760, 000 tourists in 2014 (CMBAC 2014). This influx of activity, paired with the region's rich resource base, significantly shapes the local economy and creates employment and income opportunities. Unlike the many agricultural communities in the prairie region that are declining due to out-migration, the communities within this region have remained relatively stable and economically viable. Black prairie soils are prevalent here, and large-scale crop and livestock operations are the mainstay of the regional economy. However, vegetable and fruit production is increasing, as is the direct marketing of fresh produce through seasonally operated farmers' markets; there are currently twelve farmers' markets operating in this region. Similar to other regions of Alberta and the rest of Canada, these farmers' markets are predominantly non-profit or co-operative organizations; as such, they are agents of the social economy. The following case study focuses on the farmers' market in the town of Rimbey.

Describing itself as a "community on the move," the town of Rimbey (population 2,496) is located in Ponoka County, within close proximity to three large lakes (Pigeon Lake, Gull Lake, and Sylvan Lake) and within 150 kilometres of Alberta's three largest cities (Calgary, Edmonton, and Red Deer). Rimbey has a stable economy, supported by well-established agricultural and oil and gas industries, and provides most essential services to the town and surrounding farming population of approximately twelve thousand. While strong local economies can be an important factor in the development of viable farmers' markets, this is not always a given. As will be discussed below, the success of farmers' markets ultimately depends on local leadership and the embeddedness of the market in the community and the region.

The Rimbey farmers' market was established in the late 1980s, but by 2006, it was on the verge of shutting down, with only seven vendors remaining (Gail Rondeel, interview with the authors, Rimbey, April 8, 2008). A number of factors influenced the market's decline including lack of leadership, vision and direction; a poor location; fading interest and support from the town; and a reputation "for being such a terrible market" (Gail Rondeel, interview with the authors, Rimbey, April 8, 2008) within close proximity to a number of other, highly successful markets in the region. In 2007, however, the market experienced a dramatic turnaround with a new market manager and board of directors, and forty-two vendors. By mid-summer, a number of other new vendors had signed up. Within a short period of time, the Rimbey market succeeded in becoming a "great reason to get up on Saturday mornings"—a rallying call that has become the market's slogan.

The market manager explained that the market's renewed success began with the transition away from the for-profit model under which it was previously operating and towards an emphasis on contributing to the social aspects of the community. She emphasized that a locally embedded market generates a unique community atmosphere not typically offered in the conventional food retail sector:

> I wanted to make the market a community event where people wanted to go on a Saturday morning, where they wanted to do their shopping, where they wanted to go meet for coffee, meet their friends. If you can make the market a really fun place to be, which is something that is lacking in our society . . . well, I think this is why farmers' markets are so important. We have people coming to the market and dancing. We have older senior couples actually ballroom dancing at the market. All this stuff gives a real sense of community. (Gail Rondeel, interview with the authors, Rimbey, April 8, 2008)

Hiring a small bus to pick up seniors, having a volunteer band play each market day, providing family-directed entertainment, and garnering support from local businesses through donations (such as doughnuts and coffee) are other innovative ways in which a spirit of community has been brought back into the Rimbey market. Rather than being in competition with local businesses, the market has drawn people to the town. The market's leadership has also made efforts to make the market environmentally friendly. People are encouraged to bring their own shopping bags and coffee cups and efforts are made to get children and youth involved. Every fourth Saturday is an "environmental solutions day," with a focus on local best practices and "green" inventions. This market is not about "bigger is better"; rather, it focuses on community needs and values. In fact, the manager plans to limit the number of vendors at the market to "keep its community atmosphere" and to avoid the hectic frenzy of some of the larger, tourist-oriented markets. Unlike those markets, Rimbey's market has a predominantly local customer base, which shapes what vendors sell and what social and educational activities are included. The market is also viewed as an opportune entry point for expanding and diversifying production in the area and increasing residents' access to local foods: for example, a contract has been secured with the seniors' lodge for fresh vegetables sourced from market vendors, and there are plans to partner with the 100 Mile Kitchen, another local food initiative, to offer classes at the market on canning and preserving food.

The success of the market is largely due to strengthened relationships with local community organizations and town administration: for example, the market partnered with the Rimbey Historical Society and is now located on their grounds and has access to buildings and infrastructure at a reasonable cost. The market has also developed better linkages with other markets clustered in Central Alberta. The region has a strong network of experienced managers who network with one another, sharing tips on market development and potential new vendors and investigating ways to share costs and resources such as using a joint promotional campaign. Market managers in the region also collaborate to arrange market days and hours in order to avoid competition and overlap. This coordination enables the development of a "market circuit," making it possible for customers and vendors to attend multiple markets during the week. For example, Innisfail Growers, based in this region, is a partnership of five family farms that sell fresh vegetables at thirteen different markets in central, northern, and southern Alberta, on every day of the week except Monday. This kind of collaboration and reciprocity is typical of the social economy. When vendors and customers are given more market options, and when vendors can expand production to meet greater demand and can enter into new market relations, the entire supply chain is strengthened. But participation in the cluster of markets of Central Alberta not only fosters the development of individual firms and markets; it also creates a collective competitive advantage through expanded horizontal and vertical linkages among public, private, and social economy sectors, facilitating a scaling up and scaling out of regional food networks as a whole while retaining the authenticity of the market experience.

The Rimbey market thus provides a good example of the benefits of investing in social infrastructure for the scaling up of alternative food initiatives. The commitment to building relationships among community partners, responding to local needs and values, and the farmers' market creating a unique atmosphere that cannot be replicated by the conventional food system have all contributed to the success of this initiative. The regional clustering of farmers' markets has also provided a valuable mechanism for scaling up and scaling out the social and environmental benefits without having to make a major investment in physical infrastructure, such as would be required for the development of a regional food

hub. Hence, clustering can be an important and useful strategy for scaling alternative food initiatives; however, without subsequent development of physical infrastructure (e.g., storage, processing, distribution), challenges of scale, scope, and
impact remain. While offering an alternative to the conventional food system and
generating important environmental, health, and social impacts for the local community, the Rimbey market and other markets in the region still play only a minor
role in terms of total regional food sales.

THE NEW CITY MARKET LOCAL FOOD HUB, VANCOUVER

Metro Vancouver, situated in the Fraser River Delta region of the Pacific coast,
comprises twenty-two municipalities and one treaty First Nation. With a population of over two million, it is one of the most densely populated metropolitan
areas of Canada. The moderate oceanic climate of the BC Lower Mainland, with
its extended growing season, rich soil, and flat terrain, enables diverse agriculture
production, ranging from a variety of horticultural crops (vegetables, fruits, ber-
ries, nuts, and flowers) to dairy and livestock operations. Increasing population
density has driven up land prices in recent years, causing farm sizes to decrease,
but the productive farmland in the province is, to a large extent, protected as the
British Columbia Agricultural Land Reserve.

In 2005, the Vancouver Coastal Health Authority released the Vancouver Food
System Assessment (Barbolet et al. 2005), which identified investment in local-
food infrastructure as a key component to creating a more just and sustainable
local food system. Drawing on experiences in other jurisdictions, the report indicated that social enterprises and supportive policies could drive this reinvestment
on a system-wide basis. The report catalyzed action by local food organizations
in Vancouver to further explore the potential of social enterprises in initiating
change across the local food system. One organization that emerged was Local
Food First (LFF), a multistakeholder, collaborative initiative whose mission was to
build and strengthen a just and sustainable local food system. Throughout 2007,
LFF hosted and engaged in a range of interviews, workshops, and community
consultations with farmers, food-based businesses, development organizations,
funders, and government to identify the key leverage points for reorienting the
local food system along sustainability principles.

These various research, partnership development, engagement, and outreach
activities confirmed the need to rebuild the systems and value chains related to
local food so that farmers could have more direct access to the growing local food

market. There is no shortage of small-scale local food initiatives in Vancouver. Urban farming, community gardening, and multiple farmers' markets and Good Food Box programs exist throughout the region. At all points along the food system, there are examples of small innovative solutions to reorienting the food system to respond to social, economic, health, and environmental concerns. However, as in Edmonton and Rimbey, the challenge was how to connect and scale up these initiatives so that they would have a more significant impact.

The recurring barrier to each proposed initiative was the lack of coordination across the local food value chain and the lack of physical and social infrastructure to support increased food security across the region. A critical component of that missing infrastructure is the need for a new, permanent home for the Winter Farmer's Market in Vancouver. As a result, in 2009 LFF began to focus its energies on rebuilding the local food infrastructure based on a proposed New City Market (NCM) local food hub. The idea was that the need for a permanent home for the Winter Farmers' Market could serve as the catalyst to bring together all aspects of the food chain and provide a physical space where consumers, producers, retailers, and restauranteurs could address common challenges that prohibit the scaling up of their individual initiatives.

The food service industry—restaurants, cafeterias, caterers, and so on—was identified as a key component for shifting consumption towards local food and providing a stable source of sales for producers. However, food service actors raised concerns about reliability of supply and the absence of a local food distribution system to make that food more accessible. From a producer perspective, the lack of collaboration and coordination among farmers in terms of what to grow and the absence of facilities for processing and prepping food were key barriers to increasing supply for the food service industry. Without local food infrastructure in place—such as wholesale and retail marketing, office space, cold storage, small-scale processing facilities, and distribution systems—the start-up costs for new food enterprises committed to an alternative food system are too prohibitive for any one enterprise to undertake. As one producer stated (interview with authors, Vancouver, February 5, 2008):

> We all need a localized distribution system if we want to expand production and access to local food. It only makes sense to do it as a shared system, where producers can collaborate to share and address the risks. For example, the movement to shared distribution requires producers to think of the bigger picture in terms of advancing a more resilient food system. It is not a question of seeing each other as competition and conflicts between

individual producers, but rather an opportunity to increase options and connections to consumers.

The key challenge from an economic development perspective was how to address the issue of scale while still maintaining the connection to the values-based appeal of alternative food systems. How do you get producers, consumers, and everyone in between working together to justify all the dedicated elements of infrastructure necessary for an alternative food system? Building the NCM was seen by proponents of alternative food systems in Vancouver as a means to build partnerships and social capital around local food issues, which would in turn support broader capacity building to scale up the alternative food movement through the development of the physical infrastructure.

The NCM was envisioned as a physical space that could strengthen connections between consumers and producers, provide functions that model all aspects of a local food system, and supply the infrastructure necessary for making local food more accessible for consumers and improving the viability of local farming in terms of fair wages and working conditions. Key functions envisioned for the NCM include wholesale and retail food sales, processing and food preparation facilities, cold storage and warehousing services, and office space for local food organizations (HB Lanarc Consultants 2010). The project is still in the predevelopment phase, but negotiations are underway with the City of Vancouver to identify potential sites, explore different business and governance models, and lay the groundwork for the capital campaign.

Over a hundred different stakeholders came together to contribute to visioning exercises regarding the role and function of the NCM. There is considerable support from the City. As one participant stated (interview with authors, Vancouver, January 10, 2010): "The local food hub is a great idea. You don't have to sell it to the planning department—they are behind it because it addresses so many areas they are concerned with. But to work with the City in getting access to land, the department of real estate needs to see the business plan. They want to know, how will this make money?"

In addition, the NCM is an attractive proposition for property developers, who see the potential to add value to their developments through association with the NCM. However, in the excitement of securing land and capital for what promised to be an innovative food hub, proponents ran the risk of focusing exclusively on the physical components of the NCM and neglecting the equally important social aspects that have made the Rimbey markets a success. Working on the business case limited options, as the focus was on the physical infrastructure and how it could be used by individual stakeholders (i.e. what would you pay per square foot for cold storage). The process was criticized for failing to sufficiently bring local food system stakeholders together to imagine how the food system infrastructure might be used differently (Kimmet, 2011). The NCM is now a project of the Vancouver's Farmers Market Society, where the proposed functions of the NCM are being modeled at existing markets to explore how they might be organized and to build support with the goal of transitioning the farmers markets from a temporary, weather dependent event towards a permanent network of community-based food distribution system that could be housed in the NCM when it is built (Vancouver Farmers Market, 2013).

The success of the NCM will ultimately depend not simply providing the missing food system infrastructure, but also on innovative governance and business models that ensure that the infrastructure is used to foster relationships among food system actors and to promote greater consumer awareness of local food. Scaling up local food system infrastructure based on activities that make the most sense from an economic standpoint runs the risk of simply replicating the mainstream food system on a local basis. Careful attention must be paid to alleviating the tensions between business case planning, on the one hand, and commitment to the values and activities that can bring about structural changes in our food system, on the other.

CONCLUSION

The case studies described above provide three different examples of local food initiatives operating within the social economy. In various and unique ways, these initiatives have attempted to build capacity through innovative strategies emerging from collaborative relationships. Some of these relationships, such as producer partnerships and farmers' market clusters and circuits, are horizontal in nature, while others, such as those involving organizational and physical infrastructure development, public procurement, and expansion into other market options, also involve vertical linkages to public and private sectors. However, the case studies also illustrate some particular challenges associated with moving from visionary ideals of strong sustainability and strong social economy approaches to transforming local food systems to on-the-ground projects in competition and in cooperation with the conventional food system. Despite some laudable successes, the major challenge for these and other alternative food initiatives remains: how to access the resources (both social and physical) required to scale up their impact without sacrificing the commitment to strong social economy and strong sustainability that distinguishes them from the conventional food system.

Securing the investments (in terms of resources, time, commitment, and trust) needed to scale up local production and consumption can result in efforts that are, due to risk management concerns, incremental and relatively uninvolved in politically contentious issues such as equity, redistribution, and solidarity. The challenges, costs, and risks of scaling up reduce the potential for structural change as limited resources are directed to filling gaps and meeting the conditions for basic business viability. For example, in order for New City Market to access City-owned land, a business plan was required by the City of Vancouver. Although that is a reasonable requirement, prioritizing social justice is not a common feature of business plans or development pro forma practices. If we agree that we need to transform the local food system to make it both more sustainable and more just, we cannot be limited to and bound by the economic constraints of the existing food system, which views food purely as a subsidized commodity. Social economy strategies provide a means of addressing what Smith and Seyfang (2013, 827) refer to as the "dilemma of scale" by providing alternative means of organizing, such as the regional clustering of farmers' markets, that provide the benefits of scaling up collaboration while avoiding the risks associated with capital investment, capture, and instrumentality. Resolving the tensions between activities that make the most sense from an economic standpoint and those that are required for deep structural changes in human-environment interactions is clearly a difficult and complex process that requires an integrated approach. Reflective practice, which is emphasized in some research on alternative food movements (Guthman 2008b; Lockie 2009), may help to resolve these tensions. Futhermore, placing those efforts within the framework of strong sustainable community development and strong social economy can lead to initiatives that enhance well-being through the development of different forms of community capital—social, human, cultural, physical, economic and natural (Roseland 2012)—and not just through quantitative measures of growth, wealth, and consumption. In each of the case studies profiled here, emphasis was placed on co-operation and coordination as part of the solution to the context-specific challenges of innovation and as a way to contribute to a growing global movement that is attempting to remake the food system (Larder, Lyons, and Woolcock 2014).

A second dimension of the pursuit of both sustainability and social justice as illustrated by the cases above concerns behavioural dimensions of change. Food security, food sovereignty, justice, and sustainability are goals identified by the alternative food movement, yet these are extremely complex social and political issues that are dependent upon underlying community values (Feagan and Morris 2009). In Alberta and British Columbia, local food initiatives have emerged out of a commitment to values-based transformation which recognizes that the conventional food system is not environmentally sustainable, is socially unjust, and is not economically viable in a full-cost sense. However, as noted in the discussions of the Good Food Box project and the New City Market local food hub, moving from conceptual planning to actual implementation can result in shifting priorities as a pragmatic response to get projects funded and engaged with a broader cross-section of the population. Linking concepts of food security and food justice to other local social and political issues creates the foundation for broader coalitions and capacity building, which can then be applied to developing the social infrastructure needed to support local food.

Despite commitments to strong social economy and strong sustainability, the Good Food Box and the New City Market local food hub show that difficulties and tensions result from values-based commitment to structural change (strong) and incremental implementation (weak). Investments in physical infrastructure can aid in scaling up the impact and reach of alternative food initiatives. However, these investments are insufficient on their own. A strong social infrastructure— one that maintains and reinforces underlying values and goals and gives rise to collaboration, coalition building, and partnering—is a necessary foundation for building the physical infrastructure (for production, storage, distribution, and retail) required for a robust and resilient local food movement.

Critical engagement and dialogue by citizens is fundamental to supporting the iterative process of reflection and action needed to develop a values-based strong social infrastructure. Nourishing the social foundation of alternative food systems while making strategic investments in physical infrastructure can catalyze transformative change that matches the goals and values of strong sustainability and strong social economy.

REFERENCES

Alberta. 2008. "Local Market Expansion Project: Alternative Agricultural Markets in Alberta, 2008." Edmonton: Alberta Agriculture and Rural Development. http://www.assembly.ab.ca/lao/library/egovdocs/2008/alard/172446.pdf.
Allen, Patricia. 2008. "Mining for Justice in the Food System: Perceptions, Practices, and Possibilities." *Agriculture and Human Values* 25 (2): 157–61.

Amin, Ash, Angus Cameron, and Ray Hudson. 2002. *Placing the Social Economy.* London and New York: Routledge.

Barbolet, Herb, Vijay Cuddeford, Fern Jeffries, Holly Korstad, Susan Kurbis, Sandra Mark, Christiana Miewald, and Frank Moreland. 2005. *Vancouver Food System Assessment.* Vancouver: Centre for Sustainable Community Development, Simon Fraser University; City of Vancouver, Department of Social Planning; and Environmental Youth Alliance. http://www.sfu.ca/content/dam/sfu/cscd/PDFs/ researchprojects_food_security_vancouver_food_assessment%20(short).pdf.

Beckie, Mary A., Lorelei L. Hanson, and Deborah Schrader. 2013. "Farms or Freeways? Citizen Engagement and Municipal Governance in Edmonton's Food and Agriculture Strategy Development." *Journal of Agriculture, Food Systems, and Community Development* 4 (1): 15–31.

Beckie, Mary A., Emily Huddart Kennedy, and Hannah Wittman. 2012. "Scaling Up Alternative Food Networks: Farmers' Markets and the Role of Clustering in Western Canada." *Agriculture and Human Values* 29 (3): 333–45.

Born, Branden, and Mark Purcell. 2006. "Avoiding the Local Trap—Scale and Food Systems in Planning Research." *Journal of Planning Education and Research* 26 (2): 195–207.

Brown, Cheryl, and Stacy Miller. 2008. "The Impacts of Local Markets: A Review of Research on Farmers Markets and Community Supported Agriculture (CSA)." *American Journal of Agricultural Economics* 90 (5): 1296–302.

City of Edmonton. 2010. *The Way We Grow: Municipal Development Plan, Bylaw 15100.* http://www.edmonton.ca/city_government/documents/PDF/MDP_Bylaw_15100. pdf.

CMBAC. 2014. Economic Impact Assessment of Sylvan Lake Tourism. December, 2014 http://sylvanlake.ca/uploads/Sylvan_Lake_Tourism_EIA_-_Final_Report.pdf

Connelly, Sean, Mark Roseland, and Sean Markey. 2011. "Bridging Sustainability and the Social Economy: Achieving Community Transformation Through Local Food Initiatives." *Critical Social Policy* 31 (2): 308–24.

Defourny, Jacques, and Patrick Develtere. 1999. "Origines et contours de l'économie sociale au Nord et au Sud." In *L'économie sociale au Nord et au Sud*, edited by Jacques Defourny, Patrick Develtere, and Bénédicte Fonteneau, 25–56. Brussels: De Boeck.

Delind, Laura B. 2011. "Are Local Food and the Local Food Movement Taking Us Where We Want to Go? Or Are We Hitching Our Wagons to the Wrong Stars?" *Agriculture and Human Values* 28 (2): 273–83.

Desmarais, Annette Aurélie, Nettie Wiebe, and Hannah Wittman, eds. 2011. *Food Sovereignty in Canada: Creating Just and Sustainable Food Systems.* Halifax and Winnipeg: Fernwood.

Douglas, David J. A., ed. 2010. *Rural Planning and Development in Canada.* Toronto: Nelson.

Epp, Roger, and Dave Whitson. 2001. "Introduction: Writing Off Rural Communities?" In *Writing Off the Rural West: Globalization, Governments and the Transformation of Rural Communities*, edited by Roger Epp and Dave Whitson, xiii–xxxv. Edmonton: University of Alberta Press.

FAO (Food and Agriculture Organization of the United Nations). 2011. *The State of Food and Agriculture, 2010–11: Women in Agriculture—Closing the Gender Gap in Development*. Rome: FAO. http://www.fao.org/docrep/013/i2050e/i2050e.pdf.

Faucher, Albert. 1947. "Cooperative Trends in Canada." *Annals of the American Academy of Political and Social Sciences* 253: 184–89.

Feagan, Robert B., and David Morris. 2009. "Consumer Quest for Embeddedness: A Case Study of the Brantford Farmers' Market." *International Journal of Consumer Studies* 33 (3): 235–43.

FMC (Farmers' Markets Canada). 2009. *National Farmers' Markets Impact Study*. Brighton, ON: FMC.

Foley, Jonathan A., Navin Ramankutty, Kate A. Brauman, Emily S. Cassidy, James S. Gerber, Matt Johnston, Nathaniel D. Mueller et al. 2011. "Solutions for a Cultivated Planet." *Nature* 478 (20 October): 337–42.

Fonteneau, Bénédicte, Nancy Neamtan, Fredrick Wanyama, Leandro Pereira Morais, and Mathieu de Poorter. 2010. *The Reader 2010—Social and Solidarity Economy: Building a Common Understanding*. Turin: International Training Centre of the International Labour Organization.

Friedmann, Harriet. 2007. "Scaling Up: Bringing Public Institutions and Food Service Corporations into the Project for a Local, Sustainable Food System in Ontario." *Agriculture and Human Values* 24 (3): 389–98.

Gibson-Graham, J. K. 2006. *A Postcapitalist Politics*. Minneapolis: University of Minnesota Press.

Goodman, David. 2003. "The Quality 'Turn' and Alternative Food Practices: Reflections and Agenda." *Journal of Rural Studies* 19 (1): 1–7.

Greater Edmonton Alliance. 2010. "The Way We Eat." www.greateredmontonalliance. com/wayweeat.pdf

Guthman, Julie. 2008a. "Bringing Good Food to Others: Investigating the Subjects of Alternative Food Practice." *Cultural Geographies* 15 (4): 431–47.

———. 2008b. "Neoliberalism and the Making of Food Politics in California." *Geoforum* 39 (3): 1171–83.

———. 2011. "'If They Only Knew': The Unbearable Whiteness of Alternative Food." In *The Food Justice Reader: Cultivating a Just Sustainability*, edited by A. H. Alkon and J. Agyeman, 263–82. Cambridge, MA: MIT Press.

HB Lanarc Consultants. 2010 (April). *New City Market: A Food Hub for Vancouver—Visioning Report*. Vancouver: Vancouver Famers Markets, Local Food First, and Vancouver Food Policy Council. http://www.refbc.com/sites/default/files/

NewCityMarket-Food-Hub-for-Vancouver-Visioning%20Workshop%20Report-April2010.pdf.

Heffernan, William D., and Douglas H. Constance. 1994. "Transnational Corporations and the Globalization of the Food System." In *From Columbus to ConAgra: The Globalization of Agriculture and Food*, edited by Alessandro Bonnano, Lawrence Busch, William Friedland, Lourdes Gouveia, and Enzo Mingione, 29–51. Kansas City: University of Kansas Press.

Hinrichs, C. Clare. 2003. "The Practice and Politics of Food System Localization." *Journal of Rural Studies* 19 (1): 33–45.

Holloway, Lewis, and Moya Kneafsey. 2000. "Reading the Space of the Farmers' Market: A Preliminary Investigation from the UK." *Sociologia Ruralis* 40 (3): 285–99.

Hunt, Alan R. 2007. "Consumer Interactions and Influences on Farmers' Market Vendors." *Renewable Agriculture and Food Systems* 22 (1): 53–66.

Johnston, Josee and Lauren Baker. 2005. "Eating Outside the Box: FoodShare's Good Food Box and the Challenge of Scale." *Agriculture and Human Values* 22 (3): 313–25.

Juillet, Luc, Jeffrey Roy, and Francesca Scala. 1997. "Sustainable Agriculture and Global Institutions: Emerging Institutions and Mixed Incentives." *Society and Natural Resources* 10 (3): 309–18.

Kimmet, Colleen. 2011. "Doubts Lace Excitement over Vancouver's Local Food Hub." *The Tyee*. October 24. http://thetyee.ca/News/2011/10/24/New-City-Market-Doubts/

Larder, Nicolette, Kristen Lyons, and Geoff Woolcock. 2014. "Enacting Food Sovereignty: Values and Meanings in the Act of Domestic Food Production in Urban Australia." *Local Environment* 19 (1): 56–76.

Lipset, Seymour M. 1950. *Agrarian Socialism: The Coöperative Commonwealth Federation in Saskatchewan, a Study in Political Sociology*. Berkeley: University of California Press.

Lockie, Stewart. 2009. "Responsibility and Agency Within Alternative Food Networks: Assembling the 'Citizen Consumer.'" *Agriculture and Human Values* 26: 193–201.

Lyson, Thomas A., Gilbert Gillespie, Jr., and Duncan Hilchey. 1995. "Farmers' Markets and the Local Community: Bridging the Formal and Informal Economy." *American Journal of Alternative Agriculture* 10 (3): 108–13.

Millennium Ecosystem Assessment. 2005. *Ecosystems and Human Well-Being: Synthesis*. Washington, DC: Island Press.

Moulaert, Frank and Oana Ailenei. 2005. "Social Economy, Third Sector, and Solidarity Relations: A Conceptual Synthesis from History to Present." *Urban Studies* 42 (11): 2037–51.

Pearce, John. 2003. *Social Enterprise in Anytown*. London: Calouste Gulbenkian Foundation.

Qualman, Darrin. 2011. "Advancing Agriculture by Destroying Farms? The State of Agriculture in Canada." In *Food Sovereignty in Canada: Creating Just and Sustainable Food Systems*, edited by Annette Aurélie Desmarais, Nettie Wiebe, and Hannah Wittman, 20–42. Halifax and Winnipeg: Fernwood.

Roseland, Mark. 2012. *Toward Sustainable Communities: Solutions for Citizens and Their Governments*. Gabriola Island, BC: New Society.

Sanderson, Kim, Michael Gertler, Diane Martz, and Ramesh Mahabir. 2005. "Farmers' Markets in North America: A Background Document." Saskatoon: Community-University Institute for Social Research, University of Saskatchewan.

Smith, Adrian and Gill Seyfang. 2013. "Constructing Grassroots Innovations for Sustainability." *Global Environmental Change* 23 (5): 827–29.

Smithers, John, Jeremy Lamarche, and Alun E. Joseph. 2008. "Unpacking the Terms of Engagement with Local Food at the Farmers' Market: Insights from Ontario." *Journal of Rural Studies* 24 (3): 337–50.

Sonnino, Roberta, and Terry K. Marsden. 2006. "Beyond the Divide: Rethinking Relations Between Alternative and Conventional Food Networks in Europe." *Journal of Economic Geography* 6 (2): 181–99.

USDA Agricultural Marketing Service. 2011.

Vancouver Farmers Markets. 2013. *Vancouver Farmers Markets Annual Report 2013*. Vancouver: Vancouver Farmers Market Society.

Verhaegen, Ingrid, and Guido van Huylenbroeck. 2001. "Costs and Benefits for Farmers Participating in Innovative Marketing Channels for Quality Food Products." *Journal of Rural Studies* 17 (4): 443–56.

Ward, Neil. 1993. "The Agricultural Treadmill and the Rural Environment in the Post-Productivist Era." *Sociologia Ruralis* 33: 348–64.

Wiebe, Nettie, and Kevin Wipf. 2011. "Nurturing Food Sovereignty in Canada." In *Food Sovereignty in Canada: Creating Just and Sustainable Food Systems*, edited by Annette Aurélie Desmarais, Nettie Wiebe, and Hannah Wittman, 1–19. Halifax and Winnipeg: Fernwood.

Winter, M. 2003. "Embeddedness, the New Food Economy and Defensive Localism. *Journal of Rural Studies* 19 (1): 23–32.

Wittman, Hannah, Mary Beckie, and Chris Hergesheimer. 2012. "Linking Local Food Systems and the Social Economy? Future Roles for Farmers' Markets in Albert and British Columbia." *Rural Sociology* 77 (1): 36–61.

4 Human Services and the Caring Society

John Restakis

In Canada, and in the industrialized global North generally, social care systems that took a century to build up have been deeply damaged by three decades of government retrenchment and neglect and by the catastrophic effects of free market ideas on public services. These systems constitute the complex fabric of publicly funded safety nets, from universal health care to unemployment insurance and services to the handicapped, that have been needed to offset the market failures in human services that are endemic to a capitalist system. The response of civil society and of the co-op movement in particular, to the deleterious effects of these free market ideas has, in turn, placed a spotlight on the relationship between sustainability, traditionally connected to the carrying capacity of environmental systems, and the functioning of systems for social care.

Transposing the traditional language of sustainability to the operations of social care systems has its challenges. The issues of growth and consumption, for example, have very different implications for these two fields. In the context of an economic model that depends on the depletion of natural resources, unlimited growth and consumption are by definition unsustainable, but this is not the case in the field of social care and the operations of the social economy. Unlike the capital economy, which, in the production and consumption of material goods, depletes the natural and social capital upon which it rests, the social economy, which is concerned with the production and consumption of human services, is characterized by activities that expand and replenish the social capital that sustains it. How, then, do we understand the question of sustainability with respect to human services, and in particular, with respect to social care? This is one question I address in this chapter.

A second question relates to the relative strength of different models for the provision of social care in terms of their potential to transform and strengthen the social economy and social care itself. In this framework, strong social economy approaches entail fundamental structural and institutional change; increased scale; the creation of deeper and more extensive social networks; greater scope for capacity building, both for organizations and individuals; and viable alternatives that challenge existing regulatory systems and power relationships. The approach outlined below is based on the democratization of social care systems and the strengthening of reciprocity and mutuality. It thus embodies an exceedingly strong model of sustainability within the particular context of the social economy and the social and economic principles upon which it rests.

In particular, what I want to explore in this chapter is the question of how the physiology of human services—their organizational and institutional set-up— either helps or hinders the production of human services that embody what I would call caring relationships: that is, human services that are based on actual relationships among persons as opposed to interaction between persons and impersonal systems. It is from this perspective that I interpret the notion of sustainability with respect to human services—that is, models of human service that have the capacity not only to provide social care but to do so in a manner that embodies and promotes care as an exchange of empathetic human relations. This perspective draws on my own interest in the transformative role of democracy in human services and raises fundamental questions concerning human dignity and the interplays of power.

Let me begin with a story.

In the winter of 2008, in the small town of Trail in the BC interior, Annie Albo lay dying with congestive heart failure in the Kootenay Boundary Regional Hospital. She was ninety-one years old. Her husband, Al, aged ninety-six, was also in the hospital—sick and exhausted from the worry and strain of caring for his wife. They had been married for seventy years.

One day, Annie was wheeled into her husband's room and told to say goodbye. She was being transferred to a nursing home in Grand Forks, roughly a hundred kilometres away. Hospital staff had already strapped Annie to a gurney, so she was not able to embrace her husband in the few moments before they took her away. They said their goodbyes. Annie Albo died alone two days later, on 19 February 2008. Al died thirteen days after that (Ballem 2006).

When the newspapers broke the story, a wave of outrage swept the province. Angry letters to the editor, withering television coverage, and an uproar in the BC legislature wrung an apology from the minister of Health and a promise to examine how such a heartless decision could be made. Nurses working at the hospital organized a petition calling for a public inquiry. According to Margaret Kempston, a registered nurse who worked at the hospital, the Albos' treatment was "horrible and disgusting," but she added that spousal separation "happens all the time." The final injury came to light when a government official confirmed that Trail's single palliative bed was in fact available when Annie Albo was separated from her husband and forced out of the hospital despite the frantic objections of her family. During the course of the examination concerning the conditions leading to the decision, senior managers at the Regional Health Authority refused to answer any questions, saying flatly that proper procedures had been followed. In the end, no one was found to be at fault, no accountability was forthcoming, no disciplinary action was taken. Nothing changed.

This heartbreaking story illustrates perfectly the tragic consequences and needless suffering caused by a dysfunctional human services system. Countless stories could be told of other seniors and other families who have endured similar distress and indignity in communities across Canada and the United States—and indeed, in every place where patients are powerless to influence bureaucracies that serve institutional interests rather than the interests of those they are meant to help. The story of Annie and Al Albo touched a raw nerve across the province. And it was not only empathy that prompted the outpouring of anger. It was also the unsettling question that the story raises in the minds of each of us: Could this happen to me?

Stories documenting the neglect and abuse of seniors have been a staple element in Canada's headlines and news hours for many years. They are depressingly familiar and just as shocking today as they were thirty years ago. What receives less attention is the pervasive anxiety and silent struggle that millions of seniors face daily as they contend with the challenges of aging with few supports at home, in their communities, or from government. These same fears of isolation, maltreatment, and neglect remain a constant presence in the lives of the vulnerable, whether they are people living with disabilities or those who have, for whatever reason, been left stranded at society's margins. They have reason to worry. Social care systems have been unravelling steadily over the last twenty years. The economic crisis that began in 2008 and the culture of accelerating government cutbacks and austerity have only deepened the worry.

Historically, the rise of social care in the advanced capitalist societies is inseparable from the advent of democracy, which in turn became possible only with the rise of an organized working class (Thompson [1963] 1980). A prime cause behind the struggle for democracy in the West was to establish a political system capable of distributing to the majority a share of the material security and prosperity that was the privilege of elites. Such a system only comes to be when there is a commensurate distribution of political power. Progressive social policy—the broad distribution of material security through public means—is a factor of democracy. Democracy is essential for the preservation of human services and the protection of the human and social dimension of social care itself.

The character of social care—its content, its manner of operation, and the distribution of its benefits—has remained relatively unchanged since the great wave of social reform after the end of World War II. It was at this time that the universal systems of social security, health insurance, family benefits, and public welfare were established (Ferrera 2005). And while it is true that the nature and extent of these social care systems varied greatly from one country to the next, and especially between northern Europe and North America, they shared essential common features—in particular, the rising importance of government as the provider of social welfare. But almost all the social policy reforms in Europe and North America since then have been centred on matters of redistribution—extending the coverage of social welfare systems to larger segments of the population (Ferrera 2005; Finkel 2006). The actual delivery of these services—the fundamental character of the relation between the state and the citizen—remained relatively unchanged until free market ideas began to influence public policy in the 1980s, beginning in Britain. Until then, publicly funded social programs were delivered almost exclusively by the state through centralized bureaucracies.

To be sure, these vast delivery systems succeeded in distributing benefits to unprecedented numbers of people. The quality of life for the large majority of people improved dramatically—more than in any previous period of history. Centralized bureaucracies were deemed essential for systems in which universal coverage required regulation, standardization of services, and equality of access. Their moral foundation, however, was based on notions of charity—the social responsibility of the state to care for its members. They were profoundly paternalistic systems in which the state provided and the citizen received. The legitimacy of the state rested on this social foundation. The essential character of this disempowering, and ultimately belittling, system was not to be altered until the 1980s, when, ironically, the state monopoly over social care was called into question by the adoption of free market principles into public services by Margaret Thatcher. This shift in the presumptive role of the state by the embrace of the free market

cracked a centuries-old mould that had fixed the citizen as a powerless dependent of the state in matters of social care. That citizens contributed to the cost of
these services through their taxes had little effect on the powerlessness that they
often experienced when actually using these services—particularly social welfare,
which carried with it the additional indignity of social stigma. It was a model
whose antecedents extend back to the Poor Laws of England, which stripped the
poor and the weak of their autonomy and social identity. And just as the adoption
of utilitarian, free market ideas dissolved the relations between the commercial
economy and society at the dawn of the industrial age, so too has the adoption
of these same ideas threatened to destroy the social content of care in the public
economy (Restakis 2010, chap. 1).

Multicultural Health Brokers
Juanita Marois

Multicultural Health Brokers (MCHB) is an Edmonton-based workers'
co-operative that seeks to provide health education and improve access
to health care services among the city's immigrant and refugee communities. The co-op has grown from its original twelve members in 1994
to fifty-four health brokers today, who together represent more than
twenty linguistically diverse cultural communities. Located in the inner-
city community of McCauley but active all across the municipality, the
co-op serves over two thousand families (approximately ten thousand
individuals). "We are guided by international cooperative principles of
social justice, community accountability and democratic governance,"
states executive director Yvonne Chiu, a founding member. "Our work
now covers the whole life stage of pre-natal to infants, children/youth,
adults, and the golden years—we have a program that supports isolated immigrant/refugee seniors" (Chiu 2012). Budgets have grown from
$115,000, in 1994, to over $2 million, and the organization has contracts
with Government of Alberta departments of health, children's services,
education, and employment.

Chui, Yvonne. 2012. Speech to Gathering of Alberta Cooperatives, Red Deer,
    Alberta. Multicultural Health Brokers Cooperative. 2015. http://mchb.org/

Today, social care is well on its way to being commodified in most Western nations. The desocializing dynamics of the Industrial Revolution that were, at least in theory, contained within the market economy have reached deep into the public systems that were once the preserve of the state. The colonization of the public domain by commercial interests in the late twentieth century is in many ways analogous to the enclosure of the commons in the eighteenth century. What were once public goods in the form of universally accessible human services are being steadily transformed into commercial goods accessible only to those who can afford to pay for them. What we are witnessing in the present day is a new enclosure of the commons: once again, common wealth is transmuting into private profit—a process that is, in large measure, driven by the continuing decline of opportunities for profit making in the market economy.[1] With governments as willing partners, the privatization of public goods and the monetization of social care now beckon as a new frontier from which profits might be wrung—from the provision of health care and clean water to the running of education systems and prisons.

As a result, a number of questions arise. Will civil society find the means to reclaim the social and collective foundations of the public systems that are being abandoned by government and annexed by capital? In an era in which free market ideas and the influence of capital reign supreme within government, can the state be trusted with public welfare? If not—and this is not merely hypothetical—what is the alternative? And finally, can social care be humanized? The sustainability of human services as exchanges of caring relationships is predicated on these questions.

In Canada, as in much of the industrialized West, most of the debate on the changing role of government has centred on government's retreat from the provision of public services, largely as a response to the deficits of the 1980s and 1990s and the rise of the neoliberal view that the private sector can do better. But changes in social policy and in the delivery of social care have also been fuelled by widespread public discontent with traditional delivery systems. People are fed up with the paternalism, inflexibility, and dehumanizing attributes of state bureaucracies (Finkel 2006). Stories like that of Annie and Al Albo have become all too familiar for far too many people. Combined with the burgeoning public deficits, this has provided a fertile context for the rethinking of public services.

When universal social care systems were first established at the beginning of the last century, first in western and northern Europe and later in North America,

---

1 See OECD, 2014, "Policy Challenges for the Next 50 Years".

social, cultural, and economic conditions were much different from those that would evolve in the wake of the unprecedented material prosperity generated by capitalism. Throughout most of the 1900s, large portions of Western society were still an accident or a sickness away from total ruin. Basic social security, health care, worker compensation—these programs were designed to provide a basic standard of care for large classes of people. The twentieth century was an era marked by a mechanistic industrial paradigm, an age of assembly line automation that paved the way for the service-based consumer society that has since come to replace it.

This transition to a post-scarcity society has brought with it some fundamental changes, chief among them being the accelerating individuation of society—the strange rise of the individual as someone who is defined solely by what he or she buys and the construction of personal identity as an extension of market forces (Elliot and Lemert 2009). Fuelled by the relentless message of the free market, this individualistic mindset has made choice in the marketplace a criterion of personal freedom and a symbol for consumer culture as a whole. Previously, in the mass industrial age, basic health care and universal social security reflected a model of social care that was geared to large classes of people who lacked these necessities. *Social needs were generalized.* In the post-scarcity era, in the fantasy age of unlimited personal consumption, needs have become specific and concrete, reflecting the precise needs and preferences of individuals, not classes.[2] With society awash in material goods, people now expect to be recognized and responded to as individuals with respect to social goods and human services. The growing failure of the system to do so provides one means of understanding a possible new future for civil society generally and co-operatives in particular.

The Cleaning Solution
Celia Lee and Kailey Cannon

Based in Vancouver, The Cleaning Solution was established in 2004 as a non-profit organization dedicated to employing individuals from the local community who have experienced mental illness and are now ready to re-enter the workforce. The organization provides environmentally

---

2 This formulation of general versus concrete characterizations of social needs is derived from Stefano Zamagni, a professor of economics at the University of Bologna. (Lecture, Bologna Summer Program for Co-operative Studies, 2009)

friendly cleaning services for medium-sized businesses, strata and apartment buildings, schools, churches, and government buildings. The Cleaning Solution benefited from a strong "incubating" relationship with the Canadian Mental Health Association (CMHA). In 2011, a performance snapshot document evidenced that The Cleaning Solution showed significant human, attitudinal, and revenue impacts (Demonstrating Value Initiative 2011). In 2014, TCS employed sixty-eight workers (up from five in 2004), who work ten to twelve hours per week (ENP Case Study 2014). Today the Cleaning Solution derives the bulk of its revenue from sales of services priced according to upper-middle market rates in the industry (The Cleaning Solution 2015). Its website reports an 85 percent retention rate for employees. The organization was recognized for a City of Vancouver award in 2012, receiving an honourable mention for Access and Inclusion.

Demonstrating Value Initiative. 2011. "The Cleaning Solution: Performance Snapshot." http://www.demonstratingvalue.org/sites/default/files/resource-files/TCS-2011_0.swf.
Enterprising Non-profits. 2014. "The Cleaning Solution Case Study." ENP, Vancouver, British Columbia.http://www.socialenterprisecanada.ca/web-concepteurcontent63/000024540000/upload/Toolkits/StrengtheingToolkit/TCS_CaseStudy_FINAL.pdf.
The Cleaning Solution. 2015. http://www.cleaningsolution.ca/.

The very notion of standardized systems of care that can be applied to all, regardless of personal preferences, has become something of an anachronism. The reaction against this type of universalism is rooted in the dubious belief that everyone's basic needs are now met and that we, as consumers, should be able to purchase public goods according to our choice, just as we acquire consumer goods. This belief renders us willing to overlook the dire conditions of many who still struggle in poverty or barely survive on social assistance.[3] Yet it is a point of view that has become characteristic of the consumer age—or at least of that

---

3 In Canada, despite a growing GDP and federal surpluses, the issues of poverty, homelessness, and hunger show no signs of abating. Between 1989 and 2005, food bank usage increased by 118 percent; in 2005, approximately 15 percent of Canada's children lived in poverty and rates of child poverty, a powerful indicator of broader social and economic conditions, had remained unaffected for fifteen years (CAFB 2005, 3, 5). In 2013, an average of 833,098 people used a food bank every month (Food Banks Canada 2013, 1).

segment of society that has the money to pay for alternatives and is not prepared to wait in line. This attitude is especially prevalent with respect to those public goods that are amenable to personal preferences and, most especially, to improvement in quality by the expenditure of disposable income: for example, health care, home care, services to the disabled, and public education. This shift in societal attitudes, combined with the inability—or unwillingness—of the state to respond to the change in public expectations, has been a key factor in opening the way for the commercialization of social care, for which there is a growing market. Another critical factor has been the failure of those forces that believed in universal public care to understand this change, to acknowledge its meaning and implications, and to provide progressive responses that were capable of addressing it.

What eventually arose was a twin movement: a push for more pluralistic and private models of care, based on a continuation of free market logic, and a contrary thrust towards non-commercial, social economy solutions. Both approaches call for more pluralism in how care is delivered and more choice on the part of the individual. They differ radically, however, on how this should be achieved, and this difference derives from profound differences in the perception of what social care is.

The privatization of social care is the familiar route of the free market approach. The socialization of care, however, is less well known and less documented. The fact that it is also less lucrative for private interests goes a long way towards explaining why so little attention has been paid to it. Another reason is that for three decades, a relentless campaign to discredit government and the very notion of public services was conducted through all available channels of the media and the academy by the think tanks and private sector promoters that championed the privatization of public goods. The clamour for privatization—particularly in health care—has not subsided. If anything it has grown. There is simply too much money to be made. Despite this, and despite the growing demand for individualized care, public opposition to privatization of universal systems has remained strong. But something is changing. A new interest has arisen in the role of civil society in public welfare and social care.

Over the past twenty years or so, the rise of social co-ops and other forms of social enterprise has gained considerable attention as the glow of privatized care has lost some of its original lustre. In Canada, the failures of privatization in areas such as home care and long-term care were widely reported throughout the 1990s. The ongoing crisis and general instability of the free market model has also undermined calls for its extension in the public sector (Mehra 2005; Roland 2008).

The emergence of social enterprise as a new, hybrid form of social care has been met with growing interest. Within the co-operative movement, the rise of social co-ops has been the most significant change to occur in thirty years. These are co-operatives whose purpose is the provision of social care, not only to their own members but also to the community as a whole. Their primary focus is on services to marginalized populations and to society's most vulnerable groups. This development signals a change in attitudes towards the market, on the one hand, and the role of government and the public sector, on the other. Privatization is not the only way the market can be used to reform social care. There is a social alternative that reflects a shifting perception of how civil society must now respond to changing times.

ON CIVIL SOCIETY AND THE SOCIAL ECONOMY

The term *civil society* has now entered—or more accurately, re-entered—the vocabulary of common political discourse. The concept has roots in the political and moral philosophy of the ancient Greeks and the democratic society in which it was first conceived. The stress on the moral life that was a central part of Greek philosophy was always bound up with the concept of civic duty and the pursuit of the just society (Plato 2007). For Plato, the ideal state is one in which people dedicate themselves to the common good; practice civic virtues of wisdom, courage, moderation, and justice; and perform the social and occupational role to which they are best suited. Aristotle (2000) held that the "polis," or city-state, was an "association of associations" and the social reality that made political life possible. For these thinkers, there was no distinction between state and society, and the idea of civil society as a political concept was profoundly influenced by the democratic institutions of Athens: civil society was made possible by the fact that individuals were not mere subjects of an absolute power but were independent actors with the freedom to form horizontal bonds of mutual interest with others and to act in pursuit of this common interest. This was the essence of citizenship, and the link between civil society and democracy was to remain a defining feature of the term. One subsector of civil society comprises those activities carried out by organizations that provide a vast range of goods and services through collaboration—by people working together to realize mutual, and collective, goals. It is this economic dimension of civil society that constitutes the social economy.

With the rise of interest in civil society and the social economy, the market view of society as composed of two sectors—the private and the public—is now being challenged. The notion of the social economy calls into question the narrow reading of economics as a dimension divorced from society. It enlarges classical economics to include the social relations that accompany and underlie the creation and distribution of wealth and situates economic behaviour within the wider compass of social reality (Mendell 2003).

For both of these conceptions—civil society and the social economy—the notions of reciprocity and mutuality are fundamental. They are also essential for understanding the means by which a new view of social care—a civil view—might be developed as a more humane alternative to current systems. And it is through the lens of reciprocity and mutuality that we might glimpse what it means to move from the paradigm of the corporatist welfare state to that of a caring society.

THE PRINCIPLE OF RECIPROCITY

Reciprocity is the social mechanism that makes associational life possible. Reciprocity rests on the expectation that a kindness will be returned, in a system of mutual obligation and voluntary exchange. When I willingly give something of value to someone, be it a material object or a favour of some sort, I do so on the assumption that the other person will at some point be willing to do the same for me, thereby acknowledging my gift. If, for example, my neighbour, Fred, asks to borrow my lawn mower, and I loan it to him, my expectation is that Fred will recognize that he now owes me a favour. If I subsequently ask Fred for something of roughly equivalent value, and he refuses, the basis of reciprocity falls apart. No more loaning of the lawn mower to Fred. Moreover, if Fred's failure to reciprocate forms a pattern and becomes known, his reputation will suffer and others will stop extending favours to him as well. The willingness to reciprocate is a basic signal of the *sociability* of an individual. Taken to an extreme, the complete unwillingness of individuals to reciprocate is tantamount to severing the bonds between themselves and other people. Reciprocity is thus a social relation that contains within itself potent emotional and even spiritual dimensions, elements that account for an entirely different set of motivations within individuals than those underlying behaviour in the classical sense of maximizing one's utility as a consumer.

Reciprocity and the promotion of mutual benefit animate a vast range of economic activities that rest on the sharing and reinforcement of interpersonal attitudes and values that constitute essential bonds between the individual and the human community. When reciprocity and mutuality find economic expression in the exchange of goods and services among people and between and within communities, the result is the social economy. Examples range from the the creation of "friendly societies" in the 1800s for the provision of various services, including burials, to the promotion of neighbourhood safety through organizations like Neighbourhood Watch today.

What is exchanged in reciprocal transactions is not merely particular goods, services, and favours but, more fundamentally, the expression of good will and the assurance that one is prepared to help others. This exchange is the foundation of trust. Consequently, the practice of reciprocity has profound social ramifications and entails a clear moral element. Reciprocity is a key for understanding how the institutions of society work. But it is also an economic principle with wholly distinct characteristics that embody social as opposed to merely commercial attributes. For one thing, the use of reciprocity increases both its value and the social capital on which it rests. Each instance of reciprocity strengthens the bonds of trust and mutuality that make it possible. An increase in the number and operations of social economy organizations like co-operatives and community service organizations raises the capacity of a community to care for its members. For the provision of humane systems of care, this capacity is at the core of sustainable social care.

Finally, reciprocity is egalitarian—its operation presupposes a direct relationship of equality between the individuals involved. It is very different from altruism and charity, where the giver may have no relation to the receiver and where there is a clear asymmetry of power. In the matter of social care, this equality of power has profound implications. And it is this egalitarianism that is characteristic of social co-operatives.

SOCIAL CO-OPERATIVES

The rise of social co-operatives represents a new frontier in the shifting boundaries of public, private, and commercial spheres. Pioneered in Italy during the 1980s, social co-ops embody the collectivist and co-operative traditions of the past, along with a new focus on individual choice and the use of market forces that until now have been hallmarks of neoliberal approaches to social policy. The blending of these elements makes social co-ops a kind of social experiment that places civil society at the forefront of social service reform. Based on models of care that embody the strengths and values of civil society, social co-ops offer an alternative to both state and market systems and are forging new roles for civil society and government. And while the debate in Italy concerning the role of the state has raged, as it has in all the Western democracies, the practical outcomes of social co-ops within Italy are indicators of where the future of social policy reform may ultimately lie.

In Italy, more than 14,000 social co-operatives now provide social services throughout the country. In 2008, they employed 317,000 individuals, including more than 40,000 disadvantaged persons (Carini and Costa 2013). This represented fully 23 percent of the non-profit sector's total paid labour force, even though the co-operatives constituted only 2 percent of non-profit organizations. The economic turnover of social co-ops in 2011 was over €8.9 Billion, with 402,900 employed and more than five million people using their services. (Carini and Costa 2013). From 2007 to 2011—the period when the financial crisis made itself felt—employment in Italy fell by 1.2 percent, while the number of employees in private enterprises decreased 2.3 percent (Censis 2012). In contrast, the number of employees in social co-operatives increased by 17.3 percent, with a growth of 4.3 percent in 2012 alone (Carini and Costa 2013). Today, social co-ops are a central aspect of Italy's social service system. In the city of Bologna, 87 percent of the city's social services are provided through municipal contracts with social co-ops.

In 1991, legislation was introduced to recognize and regulate the increasingly important role that social co-operatives were playing in the provision of social care in Italy. It was the first social co-op legislation in Europe. As described in Law 381/91, social co-ops have as their purpose "to pursue the general community interest in promoting human concerns and the integration of citizens." The social co-operatives in Italy aim to benefit the community and its citizens rather than to maximize benefits solely for co-op members. Italian legislation also acknowledges the affinity between public bodies such as municipalities and health boards, on the one hand, and social co-ops for the promotion of public welfare, on the other, and it emphasizes the possibility of collaboration between them. In consequence, an important symbiotic relationship has developed between these co-ops and the municipal bodies that are primarily responsible for contracting their services.

The establishment of social co-ops in Italy has resulted in improved access and a net increase in the variety and quality of social care (Borzaga and Depedri 2012; Thomas 2004). According to leaders within the social co-op movement in Italy,[4] this increase has not been at the expense of civil service jobs, which was a major concern of the public sector unions. Instead, the public services have been able to concentrate on areas where state regulation, oversight, and centralized information and distribution can benefit the system. Social co-ops focus on the front lines

---

4 Alberto Alberani, formal presentation to Bologna Summer Program for Co-operative Studies, Bologna, 2007.

of care where service design and relationships between caregivers and users are paramount in determining the quality of care, two examples being personal care for the elderly and the treatment of people with addictions. As a result, the relative cost of care in areas where social co-ops have been operating has declined while the quality of care has improved.[5] Job satisfaction among employees working in social co-ops is also higher than that reported in either the public or private sectors, despite the fact that wage rates are generally lower (Bacchiega and Borzaga 2003; Borzaga and Depedri 2005). Why is this so?

The reasons flow from the nature of social care itself and the ways in which co-op models require caregivers and users to make explicit and reinforce the human relations that underlie care. The principles of reciprocity, equality, and accountability are inalienable qualities of humane care. They are also organizational attributes of co-operative organizations. They are not, however, attributes of either state systems or private for-profit systems.

Free Geek
Kailey Cannon

A non-profit organization pursuing social and environmental goals, Free Geek Portland was founded in 2000. Since then twelve additional autonomous Free Geek organizations have sprung up in the United States, Toronto, and Vancouver. Free Geek has a dual mission: to reduce the impact of e-waste through refurbishing, reuse and recycling and to provide computer technology training to all people in the community at low or no cost (Free Geek Vancouver 2013). Its members are concerned about a widening "digital divide" (unequal access by the poor to computers and computer training) and an alarming increase of toxic e-waste destined for developing countries.

In a 2009 study, Free Geek Portland alone had provided more than fifteen thousand refurbished computers and had recycled two thousand tons of e-waste (Johnson 2009). Fosdick argues that refurbishing gets

---

5 Taking into account both the costs and benefits of social co-ops to the public sector (costs being public subsidies and fiscal advantages and benefits being taxes paid by both the employed workers and the co-operative and a decrease in the demand for social and health services by disadvantaged workers), public authorities save more than €5,000 per capita annually (Borzaga and Depedri 2013).

around the need for a new computer, and the chemicals and resources used to build it, which he estimates at ten times the products' weight (2012, 58). Most Free Geek groups generate enough revenue from sales of computers and parts in their thrift stores to be financially independent, but they occasionally receive donations and grants as well. Through its Adoption Program, Free Geek gives its clients the option of volunteering labour in exchange for a free computer. In Vancouver, the Free Geek Build Program requires a would-be purchaser to learn how to refurbish computers. They refurbish six in order to keep the sixth computer for free. Some Free Geek groups also have a special internship program through which they offer "skills training, letters of reference, professional feedback, and resume assistance" in exchange for interns' unpaid work. Others support the broader community through a Hardware Grant program and donate refurbished computers and equipment to nonprofit organizations.

Fosdick, Howard. 2012. "Computer Refurbishing: Environmentally Reducing the Digital Divide." *Bulletin of the American Society for Information Science and Technology* 38 (3): 58–62. https://asis.org/Bulletin/Feb-12/FebMar12_Fosdick. pdf.
Free Geek Vancouver. 2013. http://www.freegeekvancouver.org/index.html.
Johnson, Jim. 2009. "Free Geek, a Computer Recycler: Testing the Limits of Reproducing Worker-Managed Enterprises." *Grassroots Economic Organizing Newsletter* 2 (3). http://www.geo.coop/node/366.

THE CASE FOR A CO-OP APPROACH TO SOCIAL CARE

There are three compelling reasons to promote co-operative models for the delivery of social care. The first has to do with the nature of social care and the kind of models that are best suited to deliver that care. This concerns the question of relational goods. The second reason pertains to the relation of organizational structure to service design, delivery, and efficiency. The third reason is the need to humanize care through the socialization of its content and its manner of operation. The democratization of care is essential.

Relational Goods

The "discovery" of relational goods is one of the truly paradigm-shifting developments in recent economic analysis. Unlike conventional goods, relational goods can only be enjoyed jointly with others, not by an individual alone. A relational good is a kind of public good in that it is anti-rival—that is, unlike a rival good whose use by one consumer excludes its consumption by others, a relational good is freely available to all and the amount available is not reduced by its consumption (Weber 2004). As a consequence, participation in the consumption of relational goods actually benefits both the participant and others and increases the value of the good itself. Examples include the collective joy of an audience experiencing a musical performance, the generalized laughter at a comic film, and the surge of energy in a stadium when one side's team scores a goal. The greater the number of people who enjoy a relational good, the greater its utility. On a more intimate level, relational goods acquire value through sincerity, or genuineness—they cannot be bought or sold. Friendship and caring are relational goods, and they are their own reward. They are things whose sale would immediately destroy their worth.

In human services, relational goods are services that are characterized by the exchange of human relations. Because the quality of the personal relationship lies at the core of the exchange between the provider and the recipient, relational goods can be optimally produced only by the provider and recipient acting *together*. Beyond this, relational goods have also been defined as the value of the relationship itself, over and above the particular goods or services that are produced (Uhlaner 1989). These qualities are at the heart of social care. Reciprocity, the entering into a relationship of mutual benefit on the basis of equality, is the foundation for a type of care in which both caregiver and recipient share in the generation of care as a human relation, not as a purchased commodity or a charitable offering from the strong to the weak.

Consider, for example, care for a person with a disability. A reciprocal relationship offers recipients the means to determine how their care will be provided; they have a say in determining when the service would be offered, who the caregiver will be, what the content of the care will be, and how their personal preferences and needs can best be served. Reciprocity in social care entails sharing among equals: sharing of information, responsibility, and power. Reciprocity is the source of dignity for the user, vocational gratification for the caregiver, and mutual accountability for both. It is the mechanism by which a society makes manifest its internal solidarity and the mutual responsibility of its members. Without the democratization of care through the sharing of power and the reordering of relationships on the basis of equality, none of this is possible. Co-operative structures in which power is shared between provider and user make this possible.

Services such as education, health care, and care for people with disabilities are "social" because they are not merely commercial commodities. Based on social relations, they are wholly different from the for-profit exchange of commodities that characterizes commercial transactions. This is why referring to such services as "products" or to the recipients of social care as "clients" is so profoundly false. It is the unthinking impulse in a market society to commodify a human, and social, relation. Neither state bureaucracies, which depersonalize social service recipients, nor private sector firms, which instrumentalize recipients as a source of profit, can ever be suited to the provision of relational goods.

Organizational Structure

To be clear, I am not claiming that private sector firms are incapable of attending to the caring aspect of a social service. I am saying that the cultivation of the relational aspect of care, what is in essence its human factor, is not generally in their interest since it means investment in time, and therefore money, and a private firm's objective function is to maximize profits. The same problem of conflicting priorities undermines private firm investment in employee training and professional development. Although such investment tends to increase service quality, employment standards, and staff morale, it does not, at least in the short term, increase profits. In both cases—state and for-profit delivery—what suffers is the quality of a caring and reciprocal relationship, which is at the heart of the service being produced. This shortcoming of conventional delivery systems has little to do with the intentions that lie behind these models of social care. What is at issue is the faulty physiology of the structures and economic principles underlying the provision of care. Neither the redistributive economic logic of government nor the commercial exchange logic of the private sector can do justice to the reciprocity principle that is the basis of social and relational goods.

Organizational form is fundamental to the relationship between the content of social care and the systems that provide it. In state-delivered systems, social care is properly perceived as a civic right that should be available to all citizens equally. But equality in service delivery rarely translates into social care that is fair, or appropriate, or responsive to the unique needs of individuals. What is fair for all is often grossly unfair for individuals. Universal access through state systems requires that services be designed for application to large classes of users, not to individualized cases. Inflexibility, remoteness, and regimentation of care are a necessary consequence, along with the inevitable dehumanizing and impersonalizing effect of bureaucracy.

These characteristics of state-delivered services are well known, both academically and in the lived experience of countless individuals who have had to endure the inefficiencies and indignities of bureaucratic systems. An alternative to both private care and traditional government delivery is essential if the public nature of health and social care is to be protected and if these services are to be responsive to people's actual needs and preferences. With both the right models reflecting the inherent qualities of care as an exchange of relations among people and a public policy that promotes such an approach, the provision of care can be extended throughout society at a local, community level. In addition to radically transforming the provision of care, such an approach has the potential to transform society as well.

Co-op models for the production of health and social services have shown a remarkable capacity to provide new types of care at a cost and in a manner that blends the benefits of a public good with the choice and responsiveness usually associated with a private sector service. For example, social co-ops have played a major role in improving both the quality of home care and the working conditions, wages, and professional competence of home care givers. An outstanding North American example is Co-operative Home Care Associates in the South Bronx, which, according to the CHCA website, employs more than two thousand staff and generates $60 million in home care services annually. Some social co-operatives provide life-skills training and employment to people with intellectual disabilities, again simultaneously offering a public good and individual choice. In many such co-ops, individuals not only find meaningful employment; they also sit on the board of directors and, with support from personal advocates, have a say in how the enterprise is run. The effectiveness of these organizations is rooted in the structure of co-operatives as user owned and operated. Like public services, co-operatives have a mandate to serve the collective needs of member-owners. In the case of social co-ops, this aim extends to the community as a whole, but the scale of delivery is much smaller, and unlike government systems, the design and delivery of these services rests in the hands of co-op members. The operation of these control rights by members provides the choice with respect to service that is characteristic of the private market without the constraints associated with having profit as the primary goal.

In the case of health services, co-operatives have pioneered a patient-focused approach to health care that is a direct consequence of user control over the design and delivery of these services. Health co-ops in Canada provide community-based care to over one million Canadians. In BC, health co-ops now operate in Victoria,

Nelson, and Mission, with interest growing in other communities as well. These co-ops were started to provide communities with the kinds of health services that had been either withdrawn by the Province or never provided to begin with. Other key human services provided by co-ops include funeral care. Across Canada, there are thirty-nine funeral co-ops, with twenty-five of them located in Québec. Everywhere they operate, funeral co-ops provide exemplary service to their members at a considerably lower cost than private funeral services.[6]

In the provision of social care, social co-ops and other forms of social enterprise have increased the range of services available to citizens while simultaneously containing the costs for the provision of these services by the state. The co-op model has been most effective when it is developed as a complement to, not a substitute for, public services. In those places where social co-ops are most advanced, their proponents advocate strongly for government to continue playing a central role in the funding and regulation of public services.[7]

The case of social co-ops in Italy shows that the multistakeholder structure of social co-ops is a key factor in lowering costs, increasing service innovation, addressing market failures, and responding to the changing needs of individual users. The involvement of stakeholder groups in the production and delivery of services confers advantages that differentiate these co-ops from conventional non-profits, private firms, and government agencies (Bacchiega and Borzaga 2003).

Unlike non-profits and private firms, which are controlled primarily by those who receive monetary benefits from the organization (employees in non-profits and investors in private firms), social co-ops are controlled by a variety of stakeholders, allowing costs to be contained. The control rights exercised by consumers and volunteers moderate the distribution of profit and the rise of costs, and so social co-ops can provide services more efficiently. The involvement of consumers and volunteers in the delivery of services also lowers the cost of production. Moreover, the involvement of multiple stakeholders reduces the traditional

---

6 According to Alain Leclerc of the Federation of Funeral Co-ops, the average cost of a funeral in Québec is about $5,600, whereas a funeral arranged through a co-op generally costs less than $4,000 (presentation at BC Co-operative Association, 2011). For more information on funeral co-operatives in Québec, see Fédération des coopératives funéraires du Québec (http://www.fcfq.coop/en/funeral-cooperatives/). For an example of a funeral co-op in Alberta, see Serenity Funeral Service (http://www.serenity.ca).

7 This is the common position adopted by social co-op activists for example in Emilia Romagna and by the Lega Co-operative e Mutue and Confcooperative, the two largest co-operative federations in Italy.

asymmetries of information that compromise the efficient delivery of services in non-profits, welfare service models, and private firms. Consumer involvement, in particular, increases access to information, spurs innovation in service design, and raises the levels of transparency and accountability in the organization.

Social co-ops are better than government at coping with insufficient budgets, which is a key market failure of government services. Combining public and private funds that are used to capitalize services is a key strategy of social co-ops for distributing costs in a way that subsidizes those who are less able to afford the services. Forty percent of Italian social co-ops have introduced measures to distribute resources in such a way that users are not required to pay the full cost of services provided to them (Borzaga and Depredri 2012). Some services are provided free of charge to all users (48% of co-ops) or to the poorest users (36%). This extremely important distributive function—which has a profoundly beneficial effect on the community, both by lowering poverty rates and by saving costs to the state—is made possible by the unique organizational structure of the co-ops, by the high levels of trust they generate, and by their capacity to mobilize resources from volunteers, donations, and intrinsically motivated workers who donate overtime to the organization (Borzaga and Depredri 2012). The involvement of multiple stakeholders also limits the monopoly market control of government services and the attendant constraints on the ability of users to access services that actually reflect their preferences.

Since social co-ops are not as limited in how profits are distributed as are conventional non-profit organizations, which are prohibited by law from distributing profits to those who exercise control over the organization, they are better equipped to raise capital from members, funders, and other stakeholders. They are also able to provide a limited return on capital to investors and funders. These capital advantages make social co-ops more entrepreneurial and more able to finance innovation in service delivery or the development of new projects.

Finally, social co-ops play a powerful role in strengthening the social determinants of health in a community. The alleviation of poverty, the reduction of inequality and social alienation, the expansion of social solidarity and social capital, and the improvement of access to services among the vulnerable and marginalized are all measurably affected by the prevalence of social co-operatives (Borzaga and Depredri 2012).

Taken together, these structural features of the co-op model greatly increase its sustainability, not only because they reinforce a humane quality in the kind of social care provided but also because they strengthen the economic basis for its provision.

Democratizing Care

Social co-ops, like all co-operatives, are defined by the fact that they grant control rights to stakeholders and members. In this sense, they are distinct from non-profits that are essentially defined by the constraint on distribution of profits, as noted earlier. In a co-operative structure, it is the element of member control and ownership of the co-operative that defines both the culture and the operations of the organization. In those social co-ops where the service users are also members, the operation of control rights has the capacity to transform the user from being merely a passive recipient of care—an *object* of care systems—to being a protagonist in the design and delivery of the care—an active *subject* in the care relationship. Social care becomes a shared outcome between caregiver and care receiver. This element of personal control is fundamental to the reform of social care systems, particularly for those who are most dependent—people with disabilities, the poor, and the marginalized.

The reform of social care, its transformation into a humane system of social relationships, requires at minimum its democratization. This democratizing element is the central reason why co-operative forms of social care represent such a strong instance of sustainable human services—they embody the reciprocal nature of care while transforming the institutional structures that provide it.

SCALING AND THE PERILS OF SUCCESS

Since their inception, social co-operatives in Italy have been able to sustain a rate of growth and diversification that is a testament to the robustness and the innovative power of the model. The country's social co-ops have been able to develop both horizontal and vertical networks that have enabled them to greatly expand their capacity for service delivery at local, regional, and inter-regional levels. Through the development of multi-layered consortia, the co-ops have maximized their ability to lower operating costs, to distribute resources, to share knowledge, and to innovate in the design and delivery of services through their close affiliation with other co-ops and the diverse groupings of stakeholders that support them. Indeed, this is one of the characteristic features of the co-operative movement in Italy and a key factor in its continued growth when compared to the private sector (Menzani and Zamagni, 2010).

In absolute numbers, social co-operatives increased from a little over 2,000 before the passage of Law 381 in 1991 to nearly double (3,900) by 1996, and reached 7,363 in 2005 (Euricse 2009). This growth continued until at least 2008, when 13,938 social co-operatives were registered, with about 8,000 of these providing social services and 5,000 providing work integration (Andreaus et al. 2012). Therefore, about 20 percent of the social co-operatives that are currently active emerged before the law on social co-operatives was enacted. What is also interesting is that recent research shows a relatively positive economic situation among Italian social cooperatives despite the global economic and financial crisis. From 2008 to 2011 the co-operatives increased their overall turnover by 20.4% and their total assets by 28.4%. In addition, employment data shows a positive trend with a variation from 2008–2011 of nearly 10% (Carini and Costa 2013).

Nevertheless, the global financial crisis has taken its toll. The number of social co-operatives increased by only 324 in 2009 and 98 in 2010; meanwhile, 31 fewer co-ops were registered in 2011. This trend relates not only to the market crisis but also to the fiscal policies of the central government—which has decreased funding to local authorities, those ultimately responsible for the contracting of services to the co-ops—and to the need for social co-ops to merge in order to achieve economies of scale (Borzaga and Depedri 2012).

A number of issues are thus highlighted by these data. First, while social co-ops have flourished in Italy, their strength has been predicated on a combination of both intrinsic strengths and the public policies of government. The enactment of empowering legislation that recognizes and validates their social role is a key factor in their growth. The availability of public subsidies through supportive tax policies and the provision of public service contracts are essential to their operation. Unfortunately, this makes social co-ops extremely dependent on supportive government policy. If public funding for their services is cut, they suffer—as demonstrated in Italy by the decline in growth following the fiscal crisis in 2008.

Second, the need for increased scales of operation—often required by the scale of services demanded by public contracts—has generated the growth of both consortia and individual co-operatives, and this can be at odds with the need for close contact and interaction with members and users at local community levels. The charge has been made that the success and size of some social co-ops has alienated them from the kinds of interactions and community relations that are fundamental to the health of democratically governed organizations and the specific needs of the communities they are meant to serve. This, too, is a consequence of government policy, declining public funding, and the demands of surviving in a capitalist economy.

Finally, while state policies have provided social co-ops with both organizational and financial instruments that enable them to capitalize their operations, the model still relies on the use of public and private forms of capital that are subject to the vagaries of a capitalist economy. Perhaps this is unavoidable. But the exploration of social market models and non-capital forms of exchange that reflect and reinforce the co-operative and reciprocal nature of the social economy in general, and the mission of social co-ops in particular, is an issue that demands serious study if the social co-op form is to realize its potential.

BEYOND DEFENSIVENESS

Despite the role that social co-ops in Italy have played in social care reform in that country, for the most part, organizations within civil society as a whole have been very reluctant to engage government around the question of remaking social care. For two decades, this role has been controlled by private sector groups in the advancement of their own commercial interests, and—perhaps—as part of a genuinely held belief in the superiority of free market models. What this has meant is that civil society, and the political Left generally, has been placed in the position of defending a dysfunctional status quo. Labour, in particular, has been unwilling to countenance any move that can be construed as weakening the state role in public services—and by extension, compromising further the jobs of civil servants. In Canada, as elsewhere, the ripping up of collective agreements and the downsizing and subsequent loss of thousands of public sector jobs has taken its painful toll. Among its crippling effects is a fortress mentality on the part of organized labour. But the uncomfortable question must still be asked—if labour's interests, in Canada at least, are driven solely by the fact that the bulk of their members and dues payers are in the public sector, how can they be a force for a reform of social care that questions the received role of the state?

On the whole, the posture of the political Left and of those segments in civil society that have become active in this issue is defensive—they constitute a conservative force in opposition to change. Given the damage done to public services in the name of "reform" over the last two decades, this is understandable. But the continuing defence of the state monopoly model is untenable, short-sighted, and revealing of serious weaknesses. The short-term interest of labour is one issue. A second is the dependence of many civil society institutions on government.

Civil society, despite its formal distinctions from the state, remains a dependent sector—in many ways, a client sector of the state.

Too many non-profits and NGOs, and the leadership they employ, are kept in operation solely by government funding. For example, more than 50 percent of the cost for services provided by voluntary non-profit social welfare agencies in the United States is funded through government purchase-of-service arrangements. Government funds account for 65 percent of the Catholic Charities budget, over 60 percent of Save the Children, and 96 percent of Volunteers of America (Gilbert and Terrell 2005). The same is generally true in Canada. This absence of autonomy has undermined these organizations' capacity to represent, and fight for, the interests of civil society as a sector with its own interests apart from those of the state. At a time when government has all but erased the distinctions between private and public interests, state dependency threatens civil society's capacity to demand reform of public institutions in accordance with the values appropriate to those institutions and the public interest. Failure to take full measure of the issues at play and to show leadership on what is perhaps the defining question of public policy at the dawn of the twenty-first century has left the field precisely to those forces least concerned with the public interest.

In a move that should serve as a wake-up call for the Left, the case for a civil approach to human services is now being led by conservatives. The Big Society experiment now unfolding in Britain has become a central tenet of the Cameron government even as it slashes public funding for everything from health care and education to public transport and postal services, all in the name of austerity. Using arguments for increased user control, democratic accountability, service flexibility and innovation, and the empowerment of citizens and local communities, Big Society proponents are asking civil society to take up the challenge for the production of human services and a vast range of government programs. The intellectual case for this approach has been made by Phillip Blond, a former lecturer in philosophy and theology, who has argued that it is only conservative values that are capable of protecting the social bonds of community that are undermined both by the paternalism of the state and the rampant individualism of liberal ideology. His argument for an alternative to statism, on the one hand, and privatization, on the other, has provided intellectual cover to the Conservatives, who are now cutting public services while mouthing ostensibly progressive values. To support this approach, Blond rewrites economic and political theory to deny the role that both socialism and liberalism have played in the development of civil values, including an understanding of social care as a collective responsibility. He also conveniently glosses over the appalling historical record of political conservatism, particularly in Britain, as the primary obstacle to the emergence of public systems of care for the vulnerable (Blond 2009).

But the most disturbing question is this: Why is it that the civil case for the provision of social care has come from conservatives and the political Right? How is it that once again, the terms of this fundamental debate about social care have been set by those who have historically been least committed to it? Without question, progressive forces have once again been outflanked on a central point of public policy, and it is merely a question of time before the same progressive arguments for the reform of public services being used in Britain will be appropriated by the forces of conservatism in Canada and the United States.

Already, the Harper administration in Ottawa has undertaken a wholesale review of the charitable sector, including a rewrite of charity legislation to reflect a more "entrepreneurial" and market-driven approach to social giving. In his 2014 budget speech to Parliament, Finance Minister Jim Flaherty rationalized the introduction of additional restrictions on the operations of Canadian charities with the claim that the changes are intended to curb money laundering by foundations with ties to terrorist organizations (Fekete 2014). Not a scrap of evidence has been presented to justify this claim. Coupled with the selective auditing of those environmental groups that have opposed the government's oil policies, these actions further intensify the demonization of the charitable sector by the Harper government. As public confidence in government and the corporate sector plummets, Ottawa is vandalizing what remains of public trust in those civic institutions that are now the last outpost of civic values in this country. In this, the Harper administration is taking its cues from the Cameron government in Britain. And, as in Britain, those sections of civil society that have historically been most committed to improving social care for the most vulnerable are deeply skeptical of the outcomes—and for good reason. The Harper Conservatives were defeated in late 2015 by Justin Trudeau's Liberals, who campaigned on government trust in civil society groups.

Despite this, the sustainability of human services and what I have termed the "relational content" of care is deeply related to the emergence of new, civil forms of social care that complement public systems. Both forms are necessary. And for those who advocate for a more humane alternative to the status quo, it is not enough to demand that civil society play a larger role in the protection of existing social services. If alternative models are to be viable, new modes of social care that embody the attributes of reciprocity, accessibility, and accountability must be implemented. In this, Blond's (2009) diagnosis is correct. But what is lacking is the blend of organizational form and public policy that can combine empowering and socializing delivery models, on the one hand, with new economic and power-sharing relations with the state, on the other. What is needed is a new conception of market forces with respect to social care and relational goods. In this context, we can at least thank the British Tories for showing that this is possible, even if the underlying motives are suspect.

Civil society finally has to reflect upon and articulate civil solutions to the challenges of social care in a new era. This entails the liberation of civil society from its dependency on the state—the maturation of the sector as an independent social force—and the creation of a true civil economy for social and relational goods: that is, a social market suited to the unique operations and requirements of the social economy. Only in this way will the overwhelming power and influence of the capitalist market be brought into balance with civil values. An autonomous civil economy based on reciprocity and civil values would also make possible the political power necessary to negotiate a new social contract for a new age.

CONCLUSION

There seems little question that the potential impacts of the policies and practices outlined above—impacts related to structural change, market-based activity, scale, networking, and challenges to existing regulatory systems and capacity building—have profound implications not only for human services but for sustainability broadly conceived. The reconstruction of human services along civil lines entails a deepening of the relations among social economy organizations and a convergence of ideas and practices that are based on a long-term vision for humanizing social care by embedding the practice of reciprocity and expanding democratic control by citizens. For strengthening the social economy and for promoting social care systems that both sustain and enhance the human element of care (and that begin to introduce environmental factors related to care), a civil model of social care is fundamental. In this sense, the approach outlined here represents a strong social economy framework for interpreting the issue of sustainability with respect to human services. A focus on civil systems of social care that activate the key principles of reciprocity, mutuality, and democratic control results in the transformation of human services at a broad institutional level while simultaneously expanding the scale, coherence, and capacity of the social economy itself.

The critical question that remains is whether the key institutions of civil society and the myriad of organizations that compose the social economy can find common cause to advance a vision of social care that is both progressive and transformative. This poses a political challenge as much as a moral one. Effecting such change entails a radically different conception of civic rights, of the supportive role of the state in protecting those rights, and of the inherent and inalienable right of citizens to protect the collective public goods that have taken generations of struggle to achieve. And yet it is clear that the status quo is not working. If those who seek transformation are able to set the terms of the debate for change, they will win the day because as the poet said, "The Times They Are A-Changin'." But certainly not in the way we had hoped. Just look at Britain.

REFERENCES

Andreaus, Michele, Chiara Carini, Maurizio Carpita, and Ericka Costa. 2012. *La Cooperazione in Italia: Un'Overview*. Euricse Working Paper No. 27/12. Trento, Italy: European Research Institute on Cooperative and Social Enterprises.

Aristotle. 2000. *Politics*. Translated by Benjamin Dowett. Edited by Paul Negri. London, UK: Dover.

Bacchiega, Alberto, and Carlo Borzaga. 2003. "The Economics of the Third Sector: Toward a More Comprehensive Approach." In *The Study of the Nonprofit Enterprise: Theories and Approaches*, edited by Helmut Anheier and Avner Ben-Ner, 27–48. New York: Kluwer Academic/Plenum.

Ballem, Penny. 2006. Report to the Honourable George Abbott Minister of Health Re: Mrs. Frances Albo.

Blond, Phillip. 2009. "The Future of Conservatism." Speech to launch ResPublica, London, UK, 26 November. ResPublica. http://respublica.fatmediahost9.co.uk/item/speech-the-future-of-conservatism-dqac-zjyf.

Borzaga, Carlo, and Sara Depedri. 2005. "Interpersonal Relations and Job Satisfaction: Some Empirical Results in Social and Community Care Services." In *Economics and Social Interaction: Accounting for Interpersonal Relations*, edited by Benedetto Gui and Robert Sugden, 125–49. Cambridge: Cambridge University Press.

——. 2012. "The Emergence, Institutionalisation and Challenges of Social Enterprises: The Italian Experience." *CIRIEC-España, Revista de Economía Pública, Social y Cooperativa* 75 (August): 35–53.

——. 2013. "When Social Enterprises do it Better: Efficiency and Efficacy of Work Integration in Italian Social Cooperatives." In *Social Enterprise: Accountability and Evaluation Around the World*, edited by Simon Denny and Fred Seddon, 85–101. London and New York: Routledge.

CAFB (Canadian Association of Food Banks). 2005. *Time for Action: Hunger Count 2005.* Toronto: Canadian Association of Food Banks.

Carini, Chiara, and Ericka Costa. 2013. Exploring the Performance of Social Co-operatives During the Economic Crisis: The Italian Case. Euricse Working Paper n. 59/13.

Censis. 2012. "Primo rapporto sulla Cooperazione in Italia." Rome: Fondazione Censis, Centro Studi Investimenti Sociali. http://www.fondazionedallefabbriche.coop/wp-content/uploads/2013/06/Primo-Rapporto-Censis-sullacooperazione-in-Italia.pdf.

Elliott, Anthony, and Charles Lemert. 2009. *The New Individualism: The Emotional Costs of Globalization.* Rev. ed. London and New York: Routledge.

Euricse. 2009. "Observatory on Cooperatives and Social Enterprises in Italy." Trento, Italy: European Research Institute on Cooperative and Social Enterprises.

Fekete, Jason. 2014. "Budget Will Crack Down on Charities with Links to Terrorists, Organized Crime: Jim Flaherty." Postmedia News, February 7.

Ferrera, Maurizio. 2005. "Democratization and Social Policy in Southern Europe: From Expansion to 'Recalibration.'" Discussion paper. Geneva: United Nations Research Institute for Social Development.

Finkel, Alvin. 2006. *Social Policy and Practice in Canada: A History.* Waterloo, ON: Wilfrid Laurier University Press.

Food Banks Canada. 2013. Hunger Count 2013. Mississauga, ON: Food Banks Canada. http://www.foodbankscanada.ca/FoodBanks/MediaLibrary/HungerCount/HungerCount2013.pdf

Gilbert, Neil, and Paul Terrell. 2005. *Dimensions of Social Welfare Policy.* Boston: Allyn and Bacon.

ISTAT (Istituto Nazionale di Statistica). 2003. *Le cooperative sociali in Italia, anno 2003.* Rome: Istituto Nazionale di Statistica.

———. 2005. *Le cooperative sociali in Italia, anno 2005.* Rome: Istituto Nazionale di Statistica.

Mehra, Natalie. 2005. "Flawed, Failed, Abandoned: 100 P3s, Canadian and International Evidence." Toronto: Ontario Health Coalition. http://www.european-services-strategy.org.uk/outsourcing-ppp-library/contract-and-privatisation-failures/flawed-failed-abandoned-100-p3s-canadian-and-i/flawed-failed-abandon-p3.pdf.

Mendell, Marguerite. 2003. *The Social Economy in Quebec.* VIII Congreso Internacional del CLAD sobre la Reforma del Estado y de la Administración Pública, Panamá, 28–31 October.

Menzani, Tito, and Zamagni, Vera. 2010. "Cooperative Networks in the Italian Economy." *Enterprise and Society* 11 (1): 98–127.

OECD (Organisation for Economic Co-operation and Development). 2014. "Policy Challenges for the Next 50 Years." OECD Economic Policy Paper No. 9. OECD Publishing

Plato. 2007. *The Republic*. Translated by Desmond Lee. London, UK: Penguin Classics.

Restakis, John. 2010. *Humanizing the Economy: Co-operatives in the Age of Capital*. Gabriola Island, BC: New Society.

Roland, Gérard. 2008. "Private and Public Ownership in Economic Theory." In *Privatization: Successes and Failures*, edited by Gérard Roland, 9–31. New York: Columbia University Press.

Thomas, Antonio. 2004. "The Rise of Social Co-operatives in Italy." *Voluntas: International Journal of Voluntary and Nonprofit Organizations* 15 (3): 243–63.

Thompson, E. P. (1963) 1980. *The Making of the English Working Class*. London: IICA.

Uhlaner, Carole. 1989. "Relational Goods and Participation: Incorporating Sociability into a Theory of Rational Action." *Public Choice* 62: 253–85.

Venturi, Paolo, and Flaviano Zandonai, eds. 2012. *L'impresa sociale in Italia: Pluralità dei modelli e contributo alla ripresa*. Rapporto di Iris Network. Milan: Edizioni Altreconomia.

Weber, Steven. 2004. *The Success of Open Source*. Cambridge. MA: Harvard University Press.

Zamagni, Stefano. 2009. Lecture at the University of Bologna Summer Program for Co-operative Studies, Bologna, Italy.

5

Towards Sustainable Resource Management

Community Energy and Forestry in British Columbia and Alberta

Julie L. MacArthur

The social economy projects highlighted in this chapter illustrate both the potential and the challenges of uniting the social economy and environmental sustainability.[1] They demonstrate that community control of energy, electricity, and forestry through renewable energy co-ops, co-operative electricity distribution networks, and collective ownership of forest resources can provide the incentives and focus needed to achieve specific social and environmental goals and thus to strengthen the social economy–sustainability convergence. More importantly, they serve as models of sustainability and contribute to the capacity building and movement building that is required for a more sustainable future. However, these projects do not exist in isolation. Public austerity measures and the current focus on continental and global markets for resources does not provide a level playing field for those initiatives focused on serving local needs. In addition, the success of community-based initiatives can actually work against widespread implementation of sustainable practices that are rooted in the social economy. Success sometimes brings pressure to "demutualize"—that is, to change the legal form of the organization from a co-operative to a joint stock company. It can also result in large private enterprises "poaching" skilled workers from an organization, thus weakening the project's impact.

---

1 I would like to thank the anonymous reviewers for their thoughtful commentary on this essay. Any errors and omissions are, of course, my own.

Strengthening social, economic, and environmental sustainability in Canada requires reorienting the goals and mechanisms of natural resource governance. Global and national trends in energy and resource sectors suggest future insecurity for many Canadian communities. Some of these trends include increasing prices, ever-expanding demand, increasing energy-intensive extraction of "dirty" fuel sources such as the Athabasca tar sands, and a shift away from resource management for the public good and toward short-term profit (Cohen 2007; Gattinger and Hale 2010). These trends are particularly problematic because of both the centrality of energy and resource sectors to the Canadian economy and society and the contribution of these sectors to critical environmental challenges. Understanding if and how social economy initiatives are able to create new and more sustainable development paths in these sectors is therefore important.[2] The efforts of community-based actors to reorient resource governance along more sustainable and more socially just paths can tell us much about both social economy potential and governance issues in these technologically and financially challenging areas.

Local economic development and sustainable resource and energy governance are inextricably linked. Reliance on the extraction and distribution of primary commodities (or staples) like timber, oil, and gas rather than on higher-level processing has long been criticized as stunting Canadian economic development (Innis 1967, 1995; Mackintosh 1967). Non-local project ownership also has problematic economic impacts when raw materials are exploited in outlying areas (the periphery) for the economic development of an often urban and elite core. These processes can lead to rural underdevelopment and also to longstanding political conflicts and resentments. More recently, a focus on an extractive and ever-expanding materials economy has drawn criticism on environmental grounds (Paehlke 2008; Sheer 2007), especially with respect to the contribution of human activity to global climate change through the widespread combustion of fossil fuels. As a country with 0.5 percent of the world's population but 2 percent of the total global GHG emissions, Canada has a responsibility to current and future

---

2 Conceptualizations of the social economy vary. For brevity's sake I use "community-based," "local," and "social economy" project development interchangeably. This is because in the energy sector these projects are overwhelmingly local, based in specific towns or communities, and interested in community development. I do not mean to suggest that important tensions do not exist between communities, or actors within a given community, nor do I suggest that the social economy is always either small or local. For discussions on these topics see, for example, Amin (2009), Laville, Levesque and Mendell (2007), and McMurtry (2010).

generations to reduce its environmental impacts. Unfortunately, this challenge is not being taken up at the federal level and is only addressed in a piecemeal fashion at the provincial level. Canada is a laggard compared to other OECD countries in the development of new renewable sources of power such as solar and wind (Homer-Dixon 2009; Nikiforuk 2008; Paehlke 2008).

Clearly, then, there is a need to reassess the foundations of the Canadian economy and to create and implement alternative mechanisms that provide for greater stability for both humans and the environment that sustains them. The social economy provides institutional configurations that may help to overcome the thorny jobs-versus-environment dualism that dominates conversations about sustainability, particularly in western Canada. In the social economy, not only does the concept of "value" go beyond monetary returns, but a range of social concerns (rather than profit alone) drive development (McMurtry 2010). Work from a variety of academic disciplines has demonstrated that the social economy's heterodox modes of production and distribution can have clear and immediate impacts that enable more sustainable livelihoods (Hill 2002; Ostrom 1990; Ostrom, Schroeder, and Wynne 1994; Uluorta 2008). Canada's First Nations represent an especially important population for re-embedding resource control within the local community. Despite the fact that they have been practicing what we now call the social economy for many years, these communities continue to be socially and economically marginalized in Canada (Wuttunee 2010).

To date, very little work has been undertaken in British Columbia or Alberta to understand how, where, and with what effect communities are engaging directly in energy and resource sectors. This chapter begins to fill this gap by exploring how specific social economy projects and their proponents are attempting to address resource challenges and opportunities in innovative ways. With particular focus on renewable electricity, I profile key social economy initiatives in British Columbia and Alberta, identifying a range of contributions and models.[3] These projects are part of the social economy to the extent that their motivations often extend beyond profit (e.g., to local sustainability), frequently because they are geographically rooted in communities directly affected by resource development.

While specific communities in these provinces have made and continue to make contributions toward deepening sustainable community development,

---

3 The data reported in this chapter is taken from the 2009–10 BC-Alberta Social Economy Research Alliance B6 project, "Prospects for Socializing the Green Economy: The Case of Renewable Energy," led by Noel Keough and Paul Cabaj. A full summary of the project is available online at http://www.socialeconomy-bcalberta.ca/research/serc-2-research.php.

challenges abound. Scaling up these models in a globalized market economy is problematic given the heavy impacts of resource industries. A key contribution of this chapter thus lies in identifying factors that strengthen and deepen the social economy potential in these sectors. After describing the forces, both politico-economic and environmental, that provoke and facilitate community mobilization around resources, I explore the actors and structures of some key social economy resource initiatives in the two provinces. I conclude with an assessment of their strength in terms of socio-economic and environmental sustainability.

LINKING RESOURCES, GOVERNANCE, AND SUSTAINABILITY

Despite significant provincial and sectoral variation, resource management and development in Canada continues to progress along unsustainable paths. Clear evidence exists that ecosystem degradation is a threat not only to human life but also to long-term economic growth (Barnosky et al. 2012). Shifting to stronger social economy and sustainability models requires an understanding of the primary actors and the policy environments in key resource sectors. In oil, gas, forestry, and fisheries, private firms, regulated to varying degrees by federal and provincial public agencies, extract and develop resources for sale in international markets. In the electricity sector, public ownership and regulation play a much larger role.[4] Alberta and British Columbia differ significantly in how they govern the power sector. BC, like most Canadian provinces, has developed highly integrated and public electrical power systems. The different policy environments in BC and Alberta create different opportunities for and barriers to the involvement of community actors. For example, in British Columbia, a Crown corporation, BC Hydro, owns and operates most of the electricity system; in Alberta, by contrast, private actors operating for profit play the largest role.

In both provinces, key energy and resource policies continue to support large-scale resource exploitation rather than initiatives that aim for greater sustainability (either social or environmental). Examples, with a focus on exports, include the following:

- The multi-billion dollar Enbridge Northern Gateways Pipeline taking fossil fuel products from the Athabasca tar sands across British Columbia to Kitimat for export

---

4 This is changing, however. See, for example, discussions by Cohen (2007) and MacArthur (2016).

- The continued development of the Athabasca tar sands, along with associated water pollution, GHG emissions, and local health concerns
- The construction of high-voltage transmission lines for the export of electricity to the United States, with accompanying policy dispensing with the requirement for public-needs testing[5]
- In British Columbia, energy policies that limit the development of new public renewable-energy generation (e.g., wind and solar) and that shift new developments to the private sector[6]
- Continued approval for natural gas extraction through processes of hydraulic fracking, threatening water resources and human health

These developments are problematic since energy-related activities from the combustion of fuels and fugitive emissions are the largest source of GHG emissions in Canada. In 2013, these accounted for 81% of total Canadian GHG emissions (529 Mt for combustion and 59 Mt from fugitive sources) (Canada 2015, 18). Between 1990 and 2013, GHG emissions increased 18 percent from 613 megatonnes (Mt) of carbon dioxide equivalent to 726 Mt (Canada 2015, 18). The global financial crisis resulted in a drop in emissions at the national level between 2008 and 2010 due to manufacturing slow-downs and electricity conservation; however, emissions have been rising steadily again in recent years. National aggregate figures also mask large resource-based emission increases (since 1990) in Western Canadian provinces: 66 percent in Saskatchewan and 53 percent in Alberta (Canada 2015 25–26, Canada 2015b 58). Finally, land use changes through the conversion of GHGs sinks like forests and wetlands also have a significant impact on our overall emissions trends. The Canadian Greenhouse Gas National Inventory Report points out that "since 1990, 1.3 million hectares of forest have been lost in Canada. GHG emissions from forest conversion dropped from 19.2 Mt CO_2 eq in 1990 to 13.5 Mt CO_2 eq in 2013" (Canada 2015, 58). So, not only are we expanding our resource extraction, but are also generally reducing the land's ability to help mitigate the effects of these changes.

---

5 Projects like the Alberta-Montana tie line, for example, are controversial because the provincial government has stepped in to reduce the levels of consultation and oversight over the need for and approval of new projects. In this case, Enbridge is building a 345 km, $1 billion transmission line to connect Alberta's power grid to Montana's. This increases the reliability of the power system so that shortages in one area can be compensated through transfers from other locations, but it also facilitates export.

6 BC's 2010 Energy Policy removed the focus on energy self-sufficiency and shifted to export.

The lack of serious engagement in sustainable resource management on the part of governments is, in part, attributable to the concentrated power of key actors in the resource industries. The energy sector's centrality to modern society results in a considerable amount of political and economic power for its key players, who, by extension, constitute a powerful policy lobby. Four of the five largest multinationals in the world are oil companies. Annual exports of energy resources from Canada were worth in excess of $94 billion in 2010 (National Energy Board 2011, 2). Policy choices are also influenced by the problematic way in which we measure economic growth and judge government performance: these metrics are heavily weighted toward short-term profits and balanced books at key points in electoral cycles. The shift away from public development of new renewable-energy generation in British Columbia, for example, was justified on the basis of transferring both debt and risk to private actors, even though taxpayers pay the costs of incentivizing, co-ordinating, and monitoring new developments.

While state agencies and firms may have clear access to data on the scope and scale of natural resource wealth, the public is often unaware of the value or scale of the resources within their borders. This lack of knowledge causes communities to be unaware or slow to act when valuable land is leased or when resources are sold or developed (Walker 2008). The local share in profits is thus limited to securing a job at the mine or plant or to indirect benefits from royalties and taxes paid by private firms. In addition, the control of project siting, size, and approval often involves local authorities minimally, if at all, a trend that is increasing with pressure from resource companies to "streamline" project approvals at both provincial and federal levels (Canada 2012b). Social economy initiatives focused on human (social) needs, expanded notions of value, and (sometimes) more porous and democratic corporate governance structures have the potential to play a role in addressing these environmentally problematic policy initiatives.

In the last few years, the decentralization and devolution of resource management in Canada has received considerable attention (Krupa, Galbraith, and Burch 2013). This is evidenced both in the enthusiasm for social economy power (electricity) projects (Carson and Hardy 2009) and in BC's 2010 Community Forest Management Policy (Ambus and Hoberg 2011). Some analysts advocate decentralization, devolution, and localization (though not necessarily privatization) as a more efficient, effective, and democratic means of managing the commons (Rifkin 2002; Sheer 2007). Others raise serious questions about the efficacy, purpose, and legitimacy of doing so (Albo 2006; Ambus and Hoberg 2011; McCarthy 2005). One reason for concern is that when resource markets are opened up for private development, as they have been for independent power producer (IPP) projects, community and social economy actors capture a very small portion of this, even in provinces, like Ontario, with clear community-power policy supports (MacArthur 2016).

With regard to the power sector in particular, advocates of localization make a number of claims. First, given a system in which electricity is primarily generated in rural areas and the load centres are the cities, electricity often travels many hundreds of kilometres before reaching its final destination, and the further it travels, the more is lost in the process (Akorede et al. 2010). So by reducing the scale of generation and locating it nearer to load centres, less power is wasted via line-loss. Second, megaprojects—nuclear and hydro, for example—are generally located in relatively remote areas, which are often home to poor, Indigenous communities. Rather than distributing the burden of impact across a broader population, such projects place a disproportionate share of that burden on the people who dwell in these areas. For that reason, the decision to rely heavily on such projects for our supply of energy is inherently a political choice (Hoffman and High-Pippert 2009). Finally, the institutional configurations (closed networks) and high concentration of actors and generation sources in the power sector lead to a lack of democratic control. Elite groups maintain control, albeit oftentimes with a veneer of public consultation (Johnson 2008, 2011).

The continued controversy over Site C in British Columbia provides a clear example of these tensions. Federal and provincial approval has been granted for the building of a large (1,100 MW) dam that will flood prime farmland along the Peace River in northeastern BC. The dam will be the third dam on the Peace, and the electricity produced will be transmitted, as with the W.A.C. Bennett and Peace Canyon dams, to more populous areas of the province, as well as to Alberta and the United States. Despite long-standing local opposition to the project that successfully derailed it in the 1980s, the BC government, in 2010, announced a regulatory review for Site C in order to meet the forecasted increase in demand for electricity and in 2014 the project was given environmental assessment approvals and the province approved investments of 8.3 billion (BC Hydro 2014). The controversies that arise from these types of large developments support a move toward the development of power generation in more places, close to load centres, and away from the highly centralized (and public) power development models of the 1960s to 1980s.[7]

---

7 Of course, there are also significant issues of cost and efficiency raised by the ideal of distributed generation. This include the continued requirement for firm power sources, the

Social economy resource projects can take a number of forms across diverse sectors such as forestry, fisheries, oil, gas, and electricity. Actors engage in the social economy as a response to particular needs, and as a result, projects can cover any phase of development—distribution, production, marketing, or management— and can be run as either for-profit or non-profit organizations. BALTA's research in the energy sector identified a range of ownership types: educational non-profit societies, community-owned projects, partnerships with public or private actors, and First Nations projects.[8] Each of these makes specific contributions to community development and to sustainability more generally (Soots and Gismondi 2009), with some models being stronger than others in this regard. For example, partnership models, while common and helpful for overcoming financial and technical barriers, dilute the social economy depth of projects. Examples of these different models and their implications are examined in the following sections.

Given that the social economy itself is a very broad category, as is resource management, the potential variety of projects for analysis in this chapter was simply too vast to be covered comprehensively. The cases I chose to focus on have a significant degree of community involvement in at least one stage of development, either through the formation of co-operative associations or through partnerships between public agencies (municipalities), First Nations, and other actors. Co-operative forms are particularly well suited to heighten community development potential given their (relatively) democratic constitution (Restakis 2010; MacPherson 2009), institutional flexibility, and long history of community economic development in Canada and around the world. Gordon Walker and colleagues (2007, 79) highlight other important benefits of co-ops:

> Explicit involvement in or implicit exposure to community RE [renewable energy] projects gives "the public" a positive view of RE more generally, thus supporting RE technology diffusion at both smaller (micro household) and larger (macro utility) scales. Another possibility is that this route of support for new technologies creates a particular "niche," to use the language

---

environmental impacts and costs of systems management, and the impacts of power lines connecting hundreds or thousands of small generators.

8 These projects may or may not involve partnerships, but the specific powers, rules, and attributes of projects led by First Nations communities makes them distinct from other projects.

of sustainable transition management, within which creativity and innovation in the social organization of technology can occur (including different configurations and scales of technology and models of project development and ownership), the necessary support infra-structure can be developed and social learning can take place.

Social economy resource models are accompanied by potential environmental and socio-economic benefits (Hoffman and High-Pippert 2009; Loring 2007). However, as the Consumer Co-operative Refinery Limited (CCRL) experience demonstrates (see sidebar), social economy organizations are not inherently "green" or "small." Not all social economy projects in the energy sector, for example, focus on renewable fuels or electricity, but they are well suited to respond to the needs of particular communities. In the CCRL case, the need was local development and access to cheaper fuels. And as sustainability issues become more salient for communities, social economy actors are moving to respond.

The Co-op Refinery Complex
Julie L. MacArthur

The Co-op Refinery Complex (CRC) in Regina, Saskatchewan, formerly known as Consumers Co-operative Refinery Limited, is the oldest and largest co-operative in the energy sector in the country, and perhaps even the world (Fairbairn 1989). It began in the 1930s, when Saskatchewan farmers, frustrated with high oil prices, pooled their funds and bought a used refinery in Corpus Christi, Texas. After tearing the refinery apart and rebuilding it in Regina at a cost of $35,000, the farmers recouped that amount in the first year of operation (Interview with CRC Employee, June 2009). CRC has upgraded four times over the past eighty years of operation, most recently with a $2.66 billion expansion (Johnstone 2012). It is now capable of refining everything from light sweet crude to heavy Saskatchewan crude and tar sands bitumen into a finished product. This capacity is unique in Canada. CRC typically refines 100,000 barrels per day and employs more than eight hundred people on a permanent basis, with an additional thousand people employed or contracted as needed. The "savings" (a co-operative term for profits) are recycled back into Saskatoon-based Federated Co-operatives Ltd., of which CRC is a wholly owned subsidiary, and to Co-op retail store members across western Canada.

Fairbairn, Brett. 1989. Building a Dream: The Co-operative Retailing System in Western Canada, 1928-1988. Saskatoon, SK: Western Producer Prairie Books.

Johnstone, Bruce. 2012. "'Massive' $2.66B Expansion Project Complete at Regina Refinery." *The Leader-Post*, October 26.

Co-op Refinery Complex. 2014. "Operations." http://www.ccrl-fcl.ca/operations. html.

Wind Energy: Peace Energy and NaiKun

Peace Energy Co-operative (PEC) was incorporated as a co-operative in Dawson Creek, BC, in 2003. The organization's strategic objectives include: educating the community about renewable energy, facilitating the development of renewable resources, creating local development opportunities and economic self-sufficiency (PEC 2014). PEC was a driving force behind BC's first utility-scale wind installation, the Bear Mountain wind farm. This 102 megawatt (MW) project, a joint venture between Aeolus Power (Sidney, BC) and AltaGas (Calgary, Alberta), consists of thirty-four 3 MW turbines situated along the length of an eight-kilometre bluff overlooking Dawson Creek. Bear Mountain started producing electricity in late 2009, providing enough energy to power most of the South Peace region of British Columbia. The electricity is sold to BC Hydro through a twenty-five-year electricity purchase agreement with the utility.

The Bear Mountain wind project is an example of a social economy actor playing a key role in developing local support for a project and acting as a spokesperson for local interests. Initially, co-op members explored a small locally owned turbine project but ruled it out because they wanted to fully utilize the potential of the wind on a local ridge. The PEC formed a partnership with Aeolus Power, who then partnered with AltaGas to develop the project. The co-operative and Aeolus received a finder's fee for the site and their work. They also followed through on a negotiated option to buy a share in the revenue stream by raising $300,000 from their members. A confidentiality clause with AltaGas prevents the co-op from disclosing what the actual share is, but these funds guarantee the co-op a share for the life of the project and are helping PEC to become self-sustaining (MacArthur 2016).

The co-operative's role in developing the project began with securing an investigative use permit (IUP) for the Crown land on which the wind farm sits, allowing them to access the land for data gathering and testing. The wind resource was originally being monitored by BC Hydro for development. However, the Province's

2002 Energy Plan required the utility to cede new renewable development to the private sector. Once the land became available for private development, it attracted interest from international companies keen to move into the newly opened and relatively lucrative independent power producer (IPP) sector in the province. The 378-member co-operative set a $200 investment share in the wind project. It took the initiative to get a wind project developed on the site, with as much local participation as possible. As Steve Rison, a former director of the co-op, explained in an interview, a number of companies had also expressed interest in developing the site, and the idea of a partnership held appeal: "We thought, there's no way we're going to be able to raise enough locally to get into the big wind business, so we need a development partner with more expertise and access to bigger pockets. So we put together kind of a call for proposals and targeted some development companies."[9]

Other benefits, beyond direct investment returns for members, arose from the wind farm project. The co-op worked with the project developers to maintain hiking trails near the site and to use local labour whenever possible. According to Rison, "We pushed very hard that, when the contracts were awarded from construction and equipment hauling, we'd have local businesses participate so we could generate as much economic spinoff as possible." Yet another benefit of the Bear Mountain project for the co-operative was experience. As Rison put it, the experience "made us more confident to develop other projects, renewable energy, not necessarily wind. That capacity building is a good feature of local involvement." PEC is now looking into other projects, such as Centennial Green, a distributed heating and energy project in Dawson Creek. In 2012, the co-operative moved into the retail of small wind turbines and signed a memorandum of understanding with the local college (Northern Lights) to work on education, training, and renewable projects together. In 2013, PEC also completed its first solar installation on the Peace Co-operative building in Dawson Creek.

Another partnership, this one involving a First Nation, is in the approval process for a wind farm project on BC's coast. The NaiKun Wind Energy Group has proposed to build Canada's first (and the world's largest) offshore wind farm in the Hecate Strait between Haida Gwaii and Prince Rupert, with 110 turbines and a 39 MW installed capacity. Like the Bear Mountain project, NaiKun is a partnership; in this case, however, one of the partners is the Haida Nation rather than a small energy co-operative. The First Nation has (in principle, since it has yet to be

---

9 Steve Rison, interview by the author, October 2009. Rison's subsequent comments are also from this interview.

built) a much stronger share in the project than does the co-operative in the Bear Mountain wind farm. Like the PEC, the Haida Nation is interested in both diversifying its power resources and promoting local economic development. While the NaiKun project did not receive an electricity purchase agreement from BC Hydro in 2010, they did succeed in getting provincial and federal environmental assessment approvals in 2009 and 2011, respectively. At the time of writing, the project is still awaiting BC Hydro's next Clean Power Call Request for Proposals to move forward with the project.

In terms of sustainability and social economy, there are both significant benefits and serious drawbacks to the proposed NaiKun development. Haida Gwaii is the largest geographical portion of British Columbia that is not connected to the electrical grid, meaning that the island's power comes primarily from diesel generation. (Epcor runs a small microhydro facility.) The project proponent, Vancouver-based NaiKun Energy, had originally planned the project to connect to the BC transmission system (bypassing Haida Gwaii) to sell wind-generated power to BC Hydro and to California. However, local opposition, based largely on the potential impacts of such a large offshore development on local wildlife and fisheries, has led to a reformulation of the project, with the Haida Nation as a development partner. The project has not yet been approved, nor has all local opposition been eliminated (more on that below).

The most recent proposal for the partnership structure involves two companies, one for generation and one for operation. The Haida Nation would own 50 percent of the operating company, have no liability, constitute 50 percent of the board, receive 50 percent of the revenues, and increase local employment without any up-front financial investments. The proposed structure for the generation company is that the Haida would have the option to buy in up to 40 percent, Calgary-based Enmax would be a potential partner up to 50 percent, and NaiKun would own the other 10 percent. This level of First Nations involvement in such a large wind farm is unprecedented in Canada.[10] However, in December 2011, members of the Haida Nation voted overwhelmingly (73 percent) against investing the required $265 million in the generation project (NaiKun Wind Energy Group 2011).

The reasons for this local opposition are myriad and complex. Opposition was particularly strong in Old Masset, as compared to Skidegate. Some nearby First Nations (including the Gitxaala) view new renewable-power developments as part of a resource-based "green grab" and associate such projects with the

---

10 In Ontario, there is a number of either fully or partially owned First Nations wind-development projects, but none of this size.

encroachment of oil and gas interests, including the highly controversial Enbridge pipeline. Accordingly, "renewable energy development is understood as yet another development endeavor in the region, rather than as a distinctly different renewable energy project" (Rodman 2013, 5). Another issue underlying local opposition was the fact that the NaiKun project was not originally developed by and for the community. Engagement with the Haida Nation and neighbouring affected groups began only after the business decisions had been made by investors and energy developers in large urban centres (Krupa, Galbraith, and Burch 2013). Given the problematic history of industry–First Nations partnerships in Canada, the intent, clarity, and sequencing of project phases needs to be carefully considered for proposed projects to be successful. According to Joel Krupa and colleagues (2013, 14), "the adoption of a transmission link to address the 'diesel problem' came too late in the process and the proposal was not perceived as genuine. Indeed, the transmission link was never fully guaranteed to be part of the project, and mistrust had been generated and was never fully addressed." The authors point out that without deeper and much earlier collaborative planning, these energy projects may actually lead to deeper divisions within communities.

Despite different levels of support among communities, one researcher pointed out that the discussions and debates generated by the project seem to have stimulated local knowledge and awareness of energy issues. This is especially important since replacing diesel generators can have a significant environmental impact.[11] One such initiative involves the development of a new organization, the Haida Power Authority, which was set up to review energy permitting and to develop a local process for issuing investigative use permits. The NaiKun project has also led to deeper engagement with strategic land-use planning and to an ongoing discussion over diesel generation in Haida Gwaii. Despite these gains, challenges abound and "easy wins" are elusive.

Electricity: REAs, Spark Energy, and Weather Dance

The electricity sector in Alberta is structured very differently from that in British Columbia, providing both opportunities and challenges for social economy actors. While in BC the system is structured around a vertically integrated (generation, transmission, and distribution) public utility, BC Hydro, the Alberta electricity system is characterized by private utilities trading power at market rates. Extensive deregulation and political aversion to public ownership has made Alberta's power

---

11 Lindsay Galbraith, pers. Communication with author, June 2011.

system unique in Canada. A lack of public provision has led, for example, to the development of extensive networks of distribution co-operatives in the province, notably in electricity and natural gas. These co-operatives emerged because the distribution of these goods to sparsely populated areas was not lucrative for private companies, and the Province was unwilling to engage in public service provision. As a result, social economy actors in Alberta's electricity sector may have a role to play in sustainability insofar as they have institutional links, infrastructure, policy experience, and, in some cases, the desire to move toward new green developments.

Alberta has the largest network of electricity distribution co-operatives in Canada and the largest network of natural gas distribution co-operatives in the world. There were approximately fifty co-operative rural electrification associations (REAs) in the province in 2010. These fall under two types: self-operating associations and associations that own the lines but contract their maintenance and operation to either ATCO or FortisAlberta, the two main investor-owned utilities in Alberta. Members of an REA work together on a volunteer board to oversee the co-operative's distribution lines. These lines electrified rural Alberta at a time when the province's farmers were lagging far behind their counterparts in other parts of the country (Dolphin and Dolphin 1993). REAs often work in close partnership, via long-term contracts, with ATCO and Fortis. A co-operative's assets consist of the distribution lines, which are worth millions of dollars. In recent years, REA co-ops have experienced pressure to demutualize (change their legal form to that of a joint stock company) as a result of pressure from larger private utilities to buy the lines, the increased complexities of operating in a restructured power market, and a membership based in aging and shrinking rural communities.[12] Without active local member involvement and effective public education about the co-op model, it seems likely that these organizations will shrink in terms of membership and assets. The primary driver of these pressures is rural devitalization, wherein human and financial resources move away from rural communities and into cities. In this context, the long-term benefits of investment in infrastructure is outweighed by an attractive influx of immediate cash.

The self-operating co-operatives, currently involved only in distribution, could conceivably move into generation at some point, but one major barrier to this is finding the initial capital. Indeed, community-based power generation in Alberta does not seem likely without the creation of supportive government policies, as is

---

12 Interviews by author with REA directors and Alberta Rural Utilities Branch employee, 2009.

happening in Ontario and Québec. However, there are other ways in which already established REAs could contribute to building a more sustainable power grid in Alberta. In 2013, the largest REA, Central Alberta Rural Electrification Association (CAREA) merged with South Alta REA into EQUS, the largest member owned (co-operative) utility in Canada with 11,500 members stretching from Barrhead to the US Border (EQUS 2013). Prior to the merger, CAREA initiated a green-tags initiative that allowed member-owners, for a supplementary fee, to purchase renewable electricity in the form of renewable energy credits. For twenty dollars a month, members can purchase 1 MW of renewable energy that is "physically metered and verified in Alberta" (CAREA 2010). EQUS continues to provide members with basic information on REC purchases as well as information on micro-generation (EQUS 2015). Members thus encourage wind development in the province by paying more for a green power source than the market price for conventional power. This creates a market for green power that increases the financial viability of renewable energy projects.

Another recent community-based power initiative is Alberta's Spark Energy Co-operative. Started in 2010, this co-operative, which is not part of an REA, is a power retailer in Alberta's electricity marketplace. According to the organization's website, members buy shares and purchase their power through the co-op, which then uses the funds to buy wind, solar, and biomass electricity from the Alberta power pool. Renewable-energy certificate systems like this are plentiful in Alberta. There is no reason why other social economy groups or co-operatives with a retail arm could not join in this market. The self-operating co-operatives in the province have the added organizational advantage of recirculating profits back to members. Unlike other power retailers, the co-operative is not incentivized to increase power consumed, only to provide for the power needs of its membership (whatever those may be) in an effective way. As a result, co-operative power retailers are less likely to oppose demand-side management initiatives.

Social economy partnerships in the electricity sector also occur between indigenous communities, municipal utilities and private corporations. Projects on Piikani Nation land in southern Alberta, illustrate a variety of possible partnership projects. The Piikani Nation owns Piikani Resource Development Ltd (PRDL). PRDL projects as of 2015 include a partnership with EPCOR on a Weather Dancer wind turbine, a 25% interest in the Oldman River Hydro-electric plant (with ATCO), a small solar energy project PRDL buildings. It also negotiated an option for a 51% equity share in a recent AltaLink transmission line running through Piikani land (PRDL 2015).

The first of these energy projects was the Weather Dancer turbine, 900 kW turbine project near Pincher Creek installed in 2001. It was the first Canadian project to generate renewable electricity on First Nations land. The Piikani Nation is situated in an extremely turbine-dense part of the province. As one participant at a community-power forum held in Red Deer in 2010 put it, "When you're driving through our reserve, all we see are those big 240 kV towers. You used to be able to see the mountains, and now there is only wind turbines." Piikani Indian Utilities Corporation partnered with EPCOR in the 1990s, when windfarms in Canada were in their infancy. EPCOR had already developed wind farms in British Columbia and Ontario. The wind resource is strong, so many other wind parks are projected to develop in the area over the coming years.

However, the Weather Dancer project also illustrates some of the contentiousness within communities over the nature and scale of development. Like the NaiKun wind farm proposed in British Columbia, the Weather Dancer turbine project on Piikani land was controversial. Some community members did not feel adequately consulted, drawing a distinction between the participation of powerful and/or confident members of a community versus wide-ranging buy-in and participation.[13] At the Community Renewables forum in Red Deer in 2010, attendees from the Piikani Nation emphasized the importance of avoiding the creation of a tiered system within the community. The project partner, EPCOR (the generation arm of which is now private Capital Power Corporation), has increased its ownership share in the turbine, and in 2010, technical issues with its operation reduced project income.[14] In November 2014 the Weather Dancer turbine began generating power again, after a $400,000 investment to refurbish the machine (Stoesser 2014).

A number of other changes have taken place, with accompanying challenges, in the thirteen years since the turbine was installed, the most prominent being the long-standing legal disputes between different organizations in the First Nation that are involved in developing energy projects. In 2012 and 2013, the Piikani Investment and Piikani Energy corporations were declared insolvent (Ruling ABQB 719; Grant Thornton Alger 2014). At issue were a number of loans made in the development of the Oldman River Dam from Piikani Investment out of a larger trust for the community. The current PDCL is the result of the restructuring and reorganization following these issues with the earlier investment arrangements.

---

13 Personal communication with former local project developer July 2010.

14 The City of Edmonton used to own generating assets through EPCOR Energy Services but divested these assets to a private company, Capital Power, in 2009. EPCOR is the major shareholder in Capital Power, but the creation of a separate company, with a distinct CEO and Board, creates barriers to direct control by the city (and to public control).

The Weather Dancer project is a noteworthy example of social economy power. In Alberta, a number of First Nations own their own electricity distribution networks (through REAs); this community ownership provides an opportunity on which to build, as well as local institutional capacity in electricity distribution. In addition, First Nations developments are exempt from some of the regulatory hurdles that face other communities, since they fall under federal jurisdiction. Given the long history of Aboriginal communities being patronized rather than involved as active participants in energy project decision-making, these locally led projects are important. Both the Weather Dancer experience and the Piikani's ownership of their REA have led to a body of experience in developing, negotiating, and assessing projects. A number of resources are specifically available to First Nations that may provide a supportive framework for this type of development (Canada 2004; Windfall Ecology Centre, n.d.). But the Weather Dancer project also highlights some of the important challenges related to financial success, consultation, and community buy-in. Moreover, initial successes—for example, constructing a project and bringing it to the point of generation—are but one part of a much longer organizational journey that brings with it a range of new challenges and conflicts.

Pembina Institute

Mike Gismondi, Celia Lee, and Kailey Cannon

Pembina Institute was established by a group of locals in 1985 after a deadly sour gas accident that left two dead in northern Alberta. The Institute's initial focus was improving safety standards in the oil and gas industry, but as the dangers—both environmental and social— of unabated use of fossil fuels became more clear, the organization directed its efforts toward promoting "sustainable energy solutions through innovative research, education, consulting and advocacy" (Pembina Institute 2009). Its commitment to catalyzing and enabling the transition to a post-carbon economy makes Pembina stand out as an excellent example of a social economy actor that has integrated an environmental component in a way that enhances the Institute's original mission of increasing health and safety in the oil industry.

Today Pembina describes itself as Canada's "go to source" of energy expertise. The Institute has offices in Alberta, British Columbia, Ontario, and the Northwest Territories, and employs about fifty highly skilled professionals. Its researchers publish numerous discussion papers every year. Research topics for 2014–2015 include Green Building leaders; Alberta's climate strategy; B.C. LNG as a climate change solution; the creation of an effective Canadian energy strategy, among others (see http://www.pembina.org/pubs).

Pembina Institute. 2015. http://www.pembina.org/
Pembina Institute. 2009. Sustainable Energy Solutions: Annual Report 2009. http://www.pembina.org/reports/pembina-annual-2009.pdf.

Forestry: Revelstoke Community Forest Corporation

Social economy initiatives in forestry, like those in water management and fisheries, have the potential to make a significant contribution to rural revitalization and the provision of basic services. In the forestry sector, supportive public policies and partnerships with private actors have been critical to the creation and success of new community initiatives.

In British Columbia, 56 community forests (CFs) account for 2 percent of the annual harvest (BCCFA 2015). This development is due to provincial policies in 1998 and 2003 aimed at addressing critiques of forestry management and devolving some responsibility for the sector to local groups (Ambus and Hoberg 2011). A recent report by the BC Community Forest Association points out that these groups create, on average, 50% more positions than the industry average, local accountability, and more than half are either owned by First Nations wholly or in partnership (BCCFA 2015b 3–4).

One of the earliest and largest CF is the Revelstoke Community Forest Corporation (RCFC), which is more than two decades old. Actions by the provincial government to deny the sale of cutting rights to outside firms—on the basis that the local benefits were a precondition for development—were instrumental in the creation of the RCFA (Weir and Pearce 1995). Other important policy drivers included the provincial government reducing the permitted area of a privately owned tree farm licence (TFL 23) and decreasing the cutting rights of federated co-operatives because of inadequate levels of local processing (Weir and Pearce 1995).

Since 1993, RCFC has managed 120,000 hectares of forest in British Columbia Confronted in the 1980s and 1990s with rural devitalization through sawmill closures, members of the local community mobilized in order to ensure that more of the resource was used in a way that benefited them (RCFC 2009). They began the RCFC project in partnership with three local sawmills: Downie Timber, Joe Kozek Sawmills, and Cascade Cedar. The RCFC now owns tree farm licence 56 and operates a log-sorting yard, which allows the community to benefit from the profits of timber sales and to control forest practices for local benefit, both economic and environmental. The focus of the community forest project is to ensure that timber harvested in the area is processed locally and that the tree farms are managed in a way that ensures steady and sustainable supply and maximizes tourism and recreational use. According to the mayor of Revelstoke:

> Prior to RCFC, we were a net exporter of raw logs and the vast majority of processing was done in other communities. We have seen a complete turnaround in that regard in that a major percentage of our logs are processed locally or traded for logs to be processed locally. This has been accomplished partly because of the creation of RCFC but also through more localised ownership of Downie Sawmill, one of our industry partners. (RCFC 2009)

The community forest association has had successes such as keeping local logging and processing going and using wood waste to power municipal buildings, but there have also been challenges. The RCFC experienced losses from 2004–2009, mainly because of extremely poor conditions in the BC forestry sector. According to the 2008–9 annual report, these losses netted out at just $181,000 (RCFC 2009, 4). This was due to a number of factors, which included the crash of US housing markets, the mountain pine beetle infestation, and the focus on exports of raw logs (rather than local processing), these figures are consistent with overall sectoral trends. By 2011–2012, however, the tides have turned slightly and the RCFC made a profit of $75,000 (RCFC 2013, 3). During these years the RCFC also provided a loan to expand the Revelstoke Community Energy Corporation (district heating system) in 2010, which is owned by the city and Downie sawmills. This recirculation of assets and support for local initiatives is one of the clear assets of community-owned resource management.

In 2015 proposals by the province and BC Timber Sales to expand timber harvesting around Revelstoke have raised local opposition, due to conflicts with recreational use of nearby Mount Macpherson. While no solution has been found at the time of writing, one suggestion considered was to have the RCFC take over the area. This is likely due to the focused goal of the RCFC on facilitating both economic development and recreational use in the region. (Cooper 2015, RCFC 2015b)

The enthusiasm for social economy projects such as those described above is due to a variety of factors. Some initiatives were undertaken because state and corporate actors were not moving quickly enough toward renewable energy development or were failing to develop useful (but currently unprofitable) resources, as in the case of the community forests. The REAs were created not because of a desire for renewables but out of a need for basic service provision of rural electricity. And the impetus for most of the wind energy projects came from public policies that opened the power sector to private actors, prompting communities to try to secure some small share.

Examining resource projects that participate in the social economy provides important insights regarding both the sectors in which they operate and their contribution to eco-social sustainability. Four contributions stand out from those projects described in this chapter. First, it is important to obtain local control of resources so that their development can be used to meet local needs. While local ownership by no means guarantees sustainability, connections between resource owners/managers and stakeholders in affected communities can enhance the mechanisms for sustainable management (Ostrom 1990). Second, social economy actors play an important role in "modelling the possible" by using and promoting new technologies, management methods, and/or institutional forms. Third, social economy initiatives in energy and resource management can play a key role in combatting NIMBYism by engaging community members and giving them a stake in resource projects. Finally, these initiatives, whether successful or not, contribute to developing more informed, aware, and mobilized constituencies. I move now to a discussion of each of these four key insights.

Local Control of Resources

In nearly all the social economy projects described in this chapter, local employment and access to the resource were key goals, and securing both of these was a major contribution of the organizations involved. A critical first step was obtaining the rights to access and develop the resource by, for example, acquiring investigative use permits for wind farms or licences for tree farms. Economic and social benefits for the local community, including employment, meant that those paying the costs in terms of local taxes and land and resource use had an interest in seeing a project succeed.

The local spinoffs of resource development varied according to form of owner-ship. In co-operative models, profits were used either to distribute surplus back to members or to reinvest in other projects undertaken by the co-operative, creating a pool of capital in the community that was very useful for a variety of local develop-ment purposes. One US study that compared the economic multiplier from local (not necessarily co-operative) versus non-local ownership of wind-power genera-tion found a significant difference between the two, with significantly more dollars staying in the local community and the state in the case of local ownership (see table 5.1). So not only does a social economy approach to resource development enhance local employment and rural development directly (as with the case of the REAs in Alberta), but the benefits of such development filters through other parts of the community; such bonuses include revenue from municipal taxes, an increase in service industries and, in the case of forestry, opportunities for value-added processing.

Table 5.1 Where the dollars go: A comparison of different project-ownership structures

	Large wind projects owned by out-of-state companies	Small wind projects owned by local community members
$ stay in community	12,200	65,900
$ stay in state	5,100	100,300
$ leave the state	148,000	21,300

NOTE: Analysis reflects figures per 1 MW annual generating capacity.
SOURCE: Galluzzo (2005), table 2.

Furthermore, not only the presence but the degree of community ownership matters, particularly for the environmental outcome of the project. In the Bear Mountain project, for example, PEC's control over the use and management of the resource evaporated after the initial stage of negotiating the transfer of the inves-tigative use permit: the private developer now controls the resource (electricity) and its management, leaving little, if any, room for changing patterns of resource use down the road.

Modelling the Possible

Resource projects in British Columbia and Alberta that are rooted in the social economy demonstrate the sheer range and variety of economic sectors in which local actors can participate and the different structures that such projects can use, whether co-operative, non-profit, or municipally led. Working alternative models such as these demonstrate that "another world is possible," the mantra of the World Social Forum. In these two provinces alone, social economy and community actors are managing their own local forests, water, and electric utilities, with projects ranging from the very small (biodiesel distribution) to the very large and technologically complex (rural electric utilities powering thousands of homes). They also range from distribution through to generation processing and retailing of everything from conventional oil to solar panels, wood waste, and biodiesel. Having an assortment of institutional, technological, and resource-based models to draw from can strengthen sustainable transitions in several ways. Such models offer a starting point from which to strengthen subsequent developments and identify best practices and key challenges. Another contribution is in negotiating proposals for change with more conventional actors: governments and corporations. Being able to point to other jurisdictions where innovative social economy projects have achieved success strengthens the case for viable and desirable alternatives.

The real question, of course, is whether social economy projects in the resource sector are actually much different, in terms of social and environmental sustainability, from a typical shareholder-owned development. The answer is complex and depends on the type of project, the social economy actors involved, the arrangement of control between project partners, and the degree of support from public policy. There is certainly evidence from research on electricity distribution co-operatives in Alberta that these actors are less likely to focus on increasing sales for profitability because their goal is to meet member needs rather than create them (MacArthur 2016). In the case of wind generation, while the projects built by communities may look similar in terms of the technology used, they tend to be smaller, have more local siting input, and involve a greater circulation of profits than other firms (BCCFA 2015b, Galuzzo 2005). More study is needed to understand how wind-power projects in British Columbia and Alberta compare to similar projects in other regions.

In many social economy projects, whether local or not, the profit motive is either absent or not central to the organizational mandate. While conventional corporate actors are sometimes small and local, the different treatment of profit makes social economy initiatives structurally distinct. Moreover, as illustrated by most of the cases discussed in this chapter, a single project, even an unprofitable or unsuccessful one, can spur new ideas and initiatives.

Combatting NIMBYism

Social economy resource management can also play a role in deepening sustainability through combating NIMBYism, the not-in-my-backyard attitude frequently used to disguise opposition as qualified acceptance. Public backlash against environmental reform is one problematic consequence of divorcing environmental sustainability policies from the economic realities of a given population.

Gordon Walker and colleagues (2007) argue that the initial "dash for wind" that occurred in the UK caused a significant local backlash. Despite general public support for renewables, lack of substantive involvement of the local community in such projects can lead to project opposition. Similar challenges have occurred in British Columbia, where carbon tax, which is seen by many environmentalists as a vital element in greening the power sector, is extremely unpopular. In Chetwynd, vigorous community opposition delayed the proposed Dokie wind farm, owned by Plutonic Power and General Electric Financial Services, although it was eventually completed November 2010. By comparison, the local approval processes for the Bear Mountain project, in which the Peace Energy Co-operative partnered with Aeolus and AltaGas, were much smoother. Steve Rison, a former PEC director, attributes the difference to direct community involvement rather than ad-hoc consultation.

Some nuance around treatment of the role of community in overcoming NIMBYism is clearly required, given the NaiKun and Piikani examples discussed in this chapter. Barry, Ellis and Robinson (2008) explore the role of community opposition in the lack of wide-scale renewable energy development with particular attention to the rhetorical constructions surrounding the concept of NIMBYism. They found that while an element of climate change denial existed in some local opposition movements, community opposition was largely based on a strong suspicion of the mechanisms through which renewable sources are being developed. Some opponents, for example, were concerned that utility companies are making money at the community's, and the public's, expense. Others had little trust in government, regulatory processes, and wind farm developers: "Those presenting the anti-wind energy position are keen not to be regarded as motivated by self-interest, but are skeptical of 'non-local forces' (state and business) coming in and trying to pull the wool over their eyes with what they see as 'PR stunts' portrayed as consultations" (82). These arguments, based on a case of opposition to a proposed offshore wind farm in Northern Ireland, suggest that overcoming opposition to wind development is not just a matter of providing more information to a misguided or misinformed populace but of ensuring deeper and more democratic engagement with the local community regarding new project development.

Building Capacity and Growing a Movement

The fourth potential contribution of social economy actors to sustainability is in aiding in the development of local capacity and movements. Through the process of initiating and running a project, and sometimes even through failing to achieve project goals, local social economy actors in resource sectors have developed expertise and deepened awareness of key issues facing British Columbians and Albertans. In the Haida Nation's NaiKun project, this means engagement with electricity permitting and sustainable resource planning; in the Bear Mountain case, the PEC now has a continuous revenue stream as well as experience in project development and in provincial policy related to the power sector. This experience and expertise is being shared through the development of networks. Links with provincial agencies have resulted from community groups starting to take control—to differing degrees—of local resources, and umbrella groups have formed, such as the BC Community Forest Association, through which different forest-based actors across the province are sharing best practices and tools to help each other survive in difficult times in that sector. This kind of networking is invaluable.

These diverse forms of capacity development have implications for long-term socio-economic change. Community-based resource management has succeeded in jurisdictions through both bottom-up and top-down processes. In places like Denmark, Germany, and Ontario, community mobilization has played a key role in creating policy changes and in developing networks and constituencies to move forward once financing is in place. This contribution from community groups is critical, not only for policy change but also for demonstrating the feasibility of community projects and engaging the broader (sometimes skeptical) public. This educational and mobilizing role can be undertaken by non-profit co-ops, community associations, or successful for-profit projects.

Public policy supports have been crucial to the success of social economy projects in British Columbia and Alberta, either through funding supports or through regulatory changes that allow actors access to key sectors. Certainly, policy supports have created enabling financial conditions and a stable framework for the development of wind projects. These policy innovations have included, for example, grant programs for community development and feed-in tariffs targeted at local and community actors (providing a set rate for power with profitability built in); in some cases, such supports have given community actors the first access to resource development projects. These policies are crucial because the introduction of expensive new technologies, together with the deep pockets of other private sector competitors, makes resource sectors prohibitively costly for social economy actors.

BARRIERS TO SCALING UP

Despite the real potential that social economy initiatives have for developing community capacity, overcoming NIMBYism, and providing alternative organizational forms, the challenges to scaling up are substantial. What follows is a discussion of some of the key challenges facing energy and resource projects in facilitating a transition to strong sustainability and strong social economy.

Public Austerity and Economic Policy

At the heart of the challenges to a deep and sustainable social economy lies our current system of economic governance and the public policies and institutions that support it. Economic policy in Canada, particularly in resource sectors, is directed toward extraction for sale in continental and global markets rather than toward local sufficiency. This means that local social economy initiatives are swimming against a very powerful tide. Indeed, at the same time as fossil fuel extraction and processing is playing a large role in western Canadian provincial economies, the federal government is cutting funding to environmental initiatives: cuts of $1.6 billion, according to one estimate, including 1,211 jobs lost and $222 million cut from Environment Canada (Council of Canadians 2011). These cuts to environmental management are part of a broad program of neoliberal austerity sweeping across both developed and developing nations. As public agencies shrink, communities are likely to face increasing challenges, without correspondingly devolved funds, power, or technical assistance.

The shift to marketization (rather than public ownership)—popular with provincial governments in British Columbia and Alberta, as well as with the current federal government in Ottawa—does not provide a level playing field for community-based actors. Social economy actors face more difficulty with respect to financing and institutional capacity in dealing with complex regulatory bureaucracies, and they are far less likely to be able to survive long contract negotiations and delays. The bigger the project and the more complex the industry (e.g., electricity), the greater the challenges, presenting immense barriers to scaling up the social economy in the resource sectors. While part of the promise of social economy initiatives is in developing alternatives despite the activities of governments or large for-profit corporations, these larger trends toward marketization and government austerity mean that competition over control and use of forestry, fisheries, and energy resources will be fierce. The increase of community forest associations has shown that when an industry is in decline and cannot sustain high rates of profit, opportunities open up for social economy actors to act as a stopgap for rural decline. If and when this profitability crunch turns around, so do the fortunes of the local forestry groups, which come under pressure to sell out. That is why REAs in Alberta are currently under intense pressure to sell their infrastructure to private firms: the power sector is, once you get in, intensely profitable (MacArthur 2016). Hence, profitability has a contradictory effect: it strengthens the social economy potential while at the same time increasing pressures for demutualization, for skilled workers to be cherry-picked by competitors, and for complacency and member disengagement.

Financing and Partnerships

Social economy actors also face formidable barriers to getting projects initiated, from site access, to regulatory approval, to the most pernicious challenge in the post-2008 economy—financing. Without prior project development experience, or deep pockets, or lots of time and energy, or all of the above, securing loans can present an insurmountable hurdle. Social economy actors rarely have any of these advantages, working, as they do, with member financing, government grants, and a significant amount of "sweat equity." This means that partnering on a project with a larger entity, either a municipality (as was the case with Canada's first urban co-operative wind turbine, WindShare, in Toronto) or a private developer (as with Bear Mountain or NaiKun). Depending on actor partnerships, however, may significantly water down the strength of the social economy and sustainability benefits of the project, both in terms of control and the local multiplier.

But partnership also has clear benefits: most significantly, it helps a community group manage risk, raise capital, and learn from the institutional expertise of its partner. Linking with an established organization makes for a much more appealing proposal for creditors. One benefit of the municipal partnership route is that the project can be scaled up beyond what the local community could accomplish on its own, while public control is retained. The community groups that partner in large projects secure a number of benefits, one being a share in a fairly lucrative revenue stream. However, the specific shape and form of agreements and the prevalence of models in which partnerships are necessary rather than optional are problematic for scaling up the social economy to the capacity needed for a deep transition to sustainability. The power of the community actor in the negotiations over the shape of the partnership is crucial and depends on factors such as the level of community cohesion, local control over land use (e.g., whether the land is provincially leased, municipal, or private), and the level of local awareness about the potential value of the resource. In short, a mobilized, aware community with control of the land has an excellent negotiating position for extracting maximum project control and local benefit.

Greenwashing the Social Economy

A final set of challenges relates to the disingenuous use of both social economy and sustainability projects as legitimating tools for initiatives that contribute to strengthening neither. Such projects can actually hamper movement toward stronger versions of social economy and sustainability insofar as the legitimacy of the concepts is eroded by their misuse. It is politically useful and profitable today to frame an initiative as green in order to garner public support. Likewise, involving and consulting community groups lends an air of legitimacy to a project. The result of false framing and ineffective community consultation leads to a system that is neither equitable nor environmental. Walker et al. (2007, 78) caution that "perhaps the critical judgment here is the extent to which the 'shallow' use of the term community, to include essentially technical projects with minimal local collective involvement or benefit, is corrosive of deeper principles of socialized, locally-led and owned distributed generation." They also point out that based on UK evidence, some of these projects "have done little to pursue or realize any form of participation, empowerment or wider civic outcome" (77).

The development of renewable electricity can come with corresponding negative environmental impacts when power is developed for international trade rather than for efficient use and reduced demand. Social economy developers thus need to be cognizant of these larger issues. In the case of BC's run-of-river power development, communities were enabled, as independent power producers, to build generation at the same time as Bill 30 withdrew planning power for development sites from local and "community" levels (WCEL 2009). Furthermore, a challenge that social scientists and philosophers have been wrestling with for centuries plagues new "green" projects: the definition of community. Do five local landowners who wish to begin a project constitute "community"?

Future research on social economy potential needs to examine the practices of both community ownership and broader development oversight in energy and resource management. Ultimately, contemporary forms of greenwash that generate temporary affluence in particular communities as part of a new business opportunity but do not address root causes of instability, environmental degradation, and exploitation at the broader level are problematic.

CONCLUSION

Governance mechanisms and institutional design matter a great deal to the acceptability of both new technologies and new resource developments. The real risks of resource developments are not solely financial; they are often human and environmental as well—and these risks are notoriously difficult to measure. The growing body of literature on sustainable institutions clearly points to the fact that local actors are far more likely to engage in voluntary demand and resource management (Ostrom 1990). Management solutions based in the social economy and local communities are gaining increasing attention as the failures of business-as-usual models become clearer. They illustrate that, in some cases, communities really can "do it themselves." Communities that are part of the project ownership structure gain additional revenue streams to conduct future projects or to inject directly back into local households. Disembedded actors have little incentive to conserve the resource they are exploiting or to reduce demand for it; indeed, they face the opposite pressure because once a resource is exhausted, they can simply relocate to another site. Therefore, when private and non-local actors are introduced as resource managers—and regulated by public entities ideologically committed to market-based and industry-led regulation—the worst of both environmental governance worlds results.

The very attributes that make social economy resource and energy projects so important—flexibility, local connections, and holism—also make them problematic. The reason is that addressing the large-scale challenges facing relatively resource-rich Canadians, as well as people around the world, will require significant collective action, not just at the local level, but also at national and global levels. Any transition toward a strong social economy and strong sustainability, therefore, requires a fundamental reorientation of our resource sectors. This includes the key actors in them and the normative principles underpinning their development. Test projects certainly will continue to hold value as innovation incubators and symbols, but without significant scale-up they are not enough. I have argued in this chapter that while there are diverse and significant cases of social economy and community-based resource management in these provinces, contemporary societal values and practices at a macro level constrain their ability to be deeply transformative.

REFERENCES

ABQB (Court of Queen's Bench of Alberta). 2012. Docket: 0901 15297 719 - Piikani Nation v Piikani Investment Corporation.

Akorede, Mudathir, Hashim Hizam, Ishak Aris, and Mohd-Sainal Kadir. 2010. "Re-emergence of Distributed Generation in Electric Power Systems." *Energy and Environment* 21 (2): 75–92.

Albo, Greg. 2006. "The Limits of Eco-localism: Scale, Strategy, Socialism." In *Coming to Terms with Nature*, edited by Colin Leys and Leo Panitch, 337–63. Halifax and Winnipeg: Fernwood.

Ambus, Lisa, and George Hoberg. 2011. "The Evolution of Devolution: A Critical Analysis of the Community Forest Agreement in British Columbia." *Society and Natural Resources* 24 (9): 933–50.

Amin, Ash. 2009. *The Social Economy: International Perspectives on Economic Solidarity*. London: Zed Books.

Barnosky, Anthony D., Elizabeth A. Hadly, Jordi Bascompte, Eric L. Berlow, James H. Brown, Mikael Fortelius, Wayne M. Getz et al. 2012. "Approaching a State Shift in Earth's Biosphere." *Nature* 486 (7 June): 52–58.

Barry, John, Geraint Ellis, and Clive Robinson. 2008. "Cool Rationalities and Hot Air: A Rhetorical Approach to Understanding Debates on Renewable Energy." *Global Environmental Politics* 8 (2): 67–98.

BCCFA (BC Community Forest Association). 2015. Status of Community Forest in BC. http://bccfa.ca/index.php/about-community-forestry/status

BCCFA 2015b. "Community Forest Indicators 2014: Measuring the Benefit of Community Forestry". http://bccfa.ca/pdf/BCCFA%20Report%202014%20Jan%20 31%20for%20Web.pdf

BC Hydro 2014. "Information Sheet: About Site C". https://www.sitecproject.com/ sites/default/files/info-sheet-about-site-c-january-2015.pdf

Canada. 2004. *Sharing the Story: Aboriginal and Northern Energy Experiences—Energy Efficiency and Renewable Energy*. Ottawa: Indian and Northern Affairs, Public Works and Government Services, and Natural Resources.

———. 2010. *National Inventory Report, 1990–2008: Greenhouse Gas Sources and Sinks in Canada*. Part 1. Ottawa: Environment Canada, Greenhouse Gas Division. http:// publications.gc.ca/collections/collection_2010/ec/En81-4-2008-1-eng.pdf.

———. 2012a. *National Inventory Report, 1990–2010: Greenhouse Gas Sources and Sinks in Canada*. Part 1. Ottawa: Environment Canada, Greenhouse Gas Division. http://

unfccc.int/national_reports/annex_i_ghg_inventories/national_inventories_ submissions/items/6598.php.

———. 2012b. *Modernizing the Regulatory System for Project Reviews.* 4 June 2012. http://actionplan.gc.ca/en/blog/modernizing-regulatory-system-project-reviews.

———. 2013. *National Inventory Report, 1990–2011: Greenhouse Gas Sources and Sinks in Canada.* Part 1. Ottawa: Environment Canada, Greenhouse Gas Division. http:// unfccc.int/national_reports/annex_i_ghg_inventories/national_inventories_ submissions/items/7383.php.

———. 2015. *National Inventory Report, 1990–2013: Greenhouse Gas Sources and Sinks in Canada.* Part 1. Ottawa: Environment Canada, Greenhouse Gas Division. http:// unfccc.int/national_reports/annex_i_ghg_inventories/national_inventories_ submissions/items/8812.php

———. 2015b. *National Inventory Report, 1990–2010: Greenhouse Gas Sources and Sinks in Canada.* Part 3. Ottawa: Environment Canada, Greenhouse Gas Division. http:// unfccc.int/national_reports/annex_i_ghg_inventories/national_inventories_ submissions/items/8812.php

CAREA (Central Alberta Rural Electrification Association). 2010. *CAREA at a Glance.* Innisfail, AB: CAREA.

Carson, Tim, and Lisa Hardy. 2009. *Strengthening Economies in Rural Alberta (REAP Project).* Edmonton: Alberta Association of Agricultural Societies.

Cohen, Marjorie Griffin. 2007. "Imperialist Regulation: U.S. Electricity Market Designs and Their Problems for Canada and Mexico." In *Whose Canada? Continental Integration, Fortress North America, and the Corporate Agenda*, edited by Ricardo Grinspun, Yasmine Shamsie, and Maude Barlow, 439–58. Montréal and Kingston: McGill-Queen's University Press.

Council of Canadians. 2011. "Prominent Scientists, Environmentalists Decry Cuts to Public Sector and Their Effect on Canada's Freshwater Heritage." Media release, Council of Canadians, 5 July. http://www.canadians.org/media/water/2011/04-Jul-11.html.

Dolphin, Frank, and John Dolphin. 1993. *Country Power: The Electrical Revolution in Rural Alberta.* Edmonton: Plains.

EQUS. 2013. "The Evolution of EQUS." Member Newsletter, January. http://www.equs. ca/resources/newsletter/January%202013EQUSNewsletter.pdf

———. 2015. "Green Energy." http://www.equs.ca/green-energy.html

Galluzzo, Teresa Welsh. 2005. *Small Packages, Big Benefits: Economic Advantages of Local Wind Projects.* Mount Vernon, IA: Iowa Policy Project.

Gattinger, Monica, and Geoffrey Hale. 2010. *Borders and Bridges: Canada's Policy Relations in North America.* Don Mills, ON: Oxford University Press.

Grant Thornton Alger. 2014. "Piikani Investment Corporation." Grant Thornton. www. grantthornton.ca/services/reorg/bankruptcy_and_insolvency/Piikani.

Hill, Chris. 2002. *Anti-capitalism: The Social Economy Alternative*. London: Spokesman.

Hoffman, Steven M., and Angela High-Pippert. 2009. "Community Energy: A Social Architecture for an Alternative Energy Future." *Bulletin of Science, Technology, and Society* 25 (5): 387–401.

Homer-Dixon, Thomas. 2009. *Carbon Shift: How the Twin Crises of Oil Depletion and Climate Change Will Define the Future*. New York: Random House.

Innis, Harold A. 1967. "The Importance of Staple Products." In *Approaches to Canadian Economic History*, edited by W. T. Easterbrook and M. H. Watkins, 16–19. Toronto: McClelland and Stewart.

——. 1995. *Staples, Markets, and Cultural Change: Selected Essays*. Edited by Daniel Drache. Montréal and Kingston: McGill-Queen's University Press.

Johnson, Genevieve Fuji. 2008. *Deliberative Democracy for the Future: The Case of Nuclear Waste Management in Canada*. Toronto: University of Toronto Press.

——. 2011. "The Limits of Deliberative Democracy and Empowerment: Elite Motivation in Three Canadian Cases." *Canadian Journal of Political Science* 44 (1): 137–59.

Krupa, Joel, Lindsay Galbraith, and Sarah Burch. 2013. "Participatory and Multi-level Governance: Applications to Aboriginal Renewable Energy Projects." *Local Environment: The International Journal of Justice and Sustainability* 20 (1): 1–21.

Laville, Jean-Louis, Benoît Lévesque, and Marguerite Mendell. 2007. "The Social Economy: Diverse Approaches and Practices in Europe and Canada." In *The Social Economy: Building Inclusive Economies*, edited by Antonella Noya and Emma Clarence, 155–88. Paris: OECD.

Loring, Joyce McLaren. 2007. "Wind Energy Planning in England, Wales, and Denmark: Factors Influencing Project Success." *Energy Policy* 35: 2648–60.

MacArthur, Julie L. 2016. *Empowering Electricity? Co-operatives, Private Power, and Sustainable Renewable Electricity in Canada*. Forthcoming. Vancouver: UBC Press.

Mackintosh, W. A. 1967. "Economic Factors in Canadian History." In *Approaches to Canadian Economic History*, edited by W. T. Easterbrook and M. H. Watkins, 1–15. Toronto: McClelland and Stewart.

MacPherson, Ian. 2009. *A Century of Co-operation*. Ottawa: Canadian Co-operative Association.

McCarthy, James. 2005. "Devolution in the Woods: Community Forestry as Hybrid Neoliberalism." *Environment and Planning* 37 (6): 995–1014.

McMurtry, J. J., ed. 2010. *Living Economics: Canadian Perspectives on the Social Economy, Co-operatives, and Community Economic Development*. Toronto: Emond Montgomery.

NaiKun Wind Energy Group. 2011. "Haida Decline Opportunity to Invest in NK Wind Farm." News release, 12 December. http://www.naikun.ca/news_media/news.php?id=132.

National Energy Board. 2011. *Canadian Energy Overview 2010*. Ottawa: National
  Energy Board. http://publications.gc.ca/collections/collection_2011/one-neb/NE4-
  2-9-2011-eng.pdf.

Nikiforuk, Andrew. 2008. *Tar Sands: Dirty Oil and the Future of a Continent*.
  Vancouver: Douglas and McIntyre.

Ostrom, Elinor. 1990. *Governing the Commons: The Evolution of Insitutions for
  Collective Action*. Cambridge: Cambridge University Press.

Ostrom, Elinor, Larry Schroeder, and Susan Wynne. 1994. *Institutional Incentives
  and Sustainable Development: Infrastructure Policies in Perspective*. Boulder, CO:
  Westview Press.

Paehlke, Robert. 2008. *Some Like It Cold: The Politics of Climate Change*. Toronto:
  Between the Lines.

PEC (Peace Energy Co-operative). 2012. "About Us." Peace Energy Co-operative. http://
  www.peaceenergy.ca/about-us.

———. 2014. "Peace Energy – A Renewable Energy Cooperative"
  http://peaceenergy.ca/wp-content/uploads/2014/09/
  ExecutiveSummaryIncludingBearMountainWindo210.pdf

RCFC (Revelstoke Community Forest Corporation). 2009. *Annual Report*, 2008–09.
  Revelstoke: RCFC. http://rcfc.bc.ca/wordpress/wp-content/uploads/2012/07/RCFC-
  ANNUAL-REPORT-2009.pdf.

Rifkin, Jeremy. 2002. *The Hydrogen Economy*. New York: J. P. Tarcher/Putnam.

Restakis, John. 2010. *Humanizing the Economy: Co-operatives in the Age of Capital*.
  Gabriola Island: New Society Publishers.

Rodman, Laura. 2013. "Spinning Wind into Power: Energy and Industry in Gitxaala
  Nation, British Columbia." Master's thesis, Resource Management and
  Environmental Studies, University of British Columbia.

Sheer, Herman. 2007. *Energy Autonomy*. London: Earthscan.

Soots, Lena, and Mike Gismondi. 2009. *Sustainability, the Social Economy and the
  Eco-social Crisis: Travelling Concepts and Bridging Fields*. BALTA. Retrieved from
  http://auspace.athabascau.ca/handle/2149/1801

Stoesser, John. 2014. "Piikani's Giant Wind Turbine Spins Again", *Pincher Creek Echo*.
  *http://www.pinchercreekecho.com/2014/11/25/piikanis-giant-wind-turbine-weather-
  dancer-spins-again*.

Uluorta, Hasmet. 2008. *The Social Economy: Working Alternatives in a Globalizing Era*.
  London and New York: Routledge.

Walker, Gordon. 2008. "What Are the Barriers and Incentives for Community-Owned
  Means of Energy Production and Use?" *Energy Policy* 36 (12): 4401–5.

Walker, Gordon, Sue Hunter, Patrick Devine-Wright, Bob Evans, and Helen Fay. 2007.
  "Harnessing Community Energies: Explaining and Evaluating Community-Based
  Localism in Renewable Energy Policy in the U.K." *Global Environmental Politics* 7
  (2): 64–82.

WCEL (West Coast Environmental Law). 2009. Independent Power Producer Projects in British Columbia. Vancouver: WCEL.

Weir, Doug, and Cindy Pearce. 1995. "Revelstoke Community Forest Corporation." *Making Waves* 6 (4): 13.

Windfall Ecology Centre. N.d. "Ontario First Nations and Renewable Energy: Context, Opportunities, and Case Studies." Toronto: Ontario Sustainable Energy Association. http://www.turtleisland.org/resources/renewenergy.pdf.

Wuttunee, Wanda. 2010. "Aboriginal Perspectives on the Social Economy." In *Living Economics: Canadian Perspectives on the Social Economy*, Co-operatives, and Community Economic Development, edited by J. J. McMurtry, 179–215. Toronto: Emond Montgomery.

6

Evolving Conceptions of the Social Economy

The Arts, Culture, and Tourism in Alert Bay

Kelly Vodden, Lillian Hunt, and Randy Bell

The Kwakwa̲ka̲'wakw are peoples of northern Vancouver Island and the south-central coast of British Columbia—a place where territory, culture, and livelihoods are intimately intertwined. In this chapter, we draw from the example of the 'Na̲mgis First Nation, focusing in particular on their efforts to steward and protect these central aspects of their lives and on their partnerships with others who share their home of Alert Bay on Cormorant Island. Since the late 1800s, Cormorant Island has served as a centre of administration, services, and social gathering for not only the 'Na̲mgis but also other Kwakwa̲ka̲'wakw First Nations.[1] Many Aboriginal people from outlying villages have moved to the community, while still maintaining connections to their own traditional territories. Offices of 'Na̲mgis and Kwikwasut'inuxw Haxwa'mis First Nation and the Whe-La-La-U Area Council are located in Alert Bay, as well as the U'mista Cultural Centre, which serves all Kwakwa̲ka̲'wakw peoples. In many ways, the community of Alert Bay therefore extends beyond Cormorant Island to the North Island/Kwakwa̲ka̲'wakw region as a whole.

Directly adjacent to Cormorant Island, on Vancouver Island, the Nimpkish River empties into Broughton Strait. The 'Na̲mgis are the people of the Nimpkish

---

1 Although the term *Kwakiutl* is often used to describe this cultural group, the term *Kwakwa̲ka̲'wakw* is more appropriately used to refer to the group as a whole. Kwakiutl is the name of a specific nation within the Kwak'wala-speaking peoples. For more information, see "The Kwak'wala Speaking Tribes," U'mista Cultural Society, http://www.umista.ca/kwakwakawakw/index.php.

River (Gwa'ni). According to the legend of the river's origin, Gwa'ni was placed there by the Creator to support "many kinds of salmon . . . food for your descendants for as long as the days shall dawn on the world" (Speck 1987, 67). It was these salmon runs that gave birth to the community of Alert Bay.

In this chapter, we describe the development efforts of the 'Namgis and Kwakwaka'wakw peoples through two alternative economic lenses: the social economy and sustainable community development (SCD). Through our analysis of development in Alert Bay, we conclude that there are two major concerns with how the social economy is generally conceptualized: first, there is a lack of recognition of the fundamental role of lands, resources, and ecology in social and cultural well-being, and second, not enough emphasis is placed on the role that governments at various levels play in community development. The social economy might therefore be appropriately viewed as subsumed under the more holistic and inclusive SCD approach.

SUSTAINABILITY, SOCIAL ECONOMY, AND COMMUNITY DEVELOPMENT:
ABORIGINAL PERSPECTIVES

The Canadian Social Economy Research Partnerships defines the social economy as follows:

> The Social Economy consists of association-based economic initiatives founded on values of:
>
> * Service to members of community rather than generating profits;
> * Autonomous management (not government or market controlled);
> * Democratic decision making;
> * Primacy of persons and work over capital;
> * Based on principles of participation, empowerment. (CSERP 2009, 2)

CSERP envisions the social economy as a continuum from totally voluntary organizations on one end to activities that blend the private sector with social enterprise on the other. The common thread is an acknowledgement of the utility of economic activities as a tool for achieving social benefits.

Given this definition, the social economy is subject to the same critique as community economic development (CED), which became popular in the late 1980s and is sometimes described as the predecessor of the social economy (Decter and Kowall 1989; ECC 1990). Focused on social and economic dimensions of development, the social economy and CED tend to have human-centred objectives such as social justice and self-reliance (Shea 1994; Bryant 1999). In contrast, sustainable community development (SCD) is an approach to development that explicitly combines the principles of both sustainable development and CED: the SCD approach strives for the health of both ecosystems and communities and recognizes their many complex interconnections. SCD, then, emphasizes the realities of the natural world in general (e.g., the limitations on human use of the environment as a source of resources and as a waste disposal site) and the local social, cultural, ecological, and economic realities, which are brought into the SCD process through meaningful public participation.

Many Aboriginal communities are determined to participate in economic development that is consistent with their culture and traditions. Studies of successful Aboriginal economic development point to projects that seek ways of keeping culture and traditions alive. Gaining control of land and resources and of how these resources are managed and developed has also been shown to be critical to achieving self-sufficiency, self-determination, and sustainability (ACOA 2003; Cornell and Kalt 1992). Aboriginal enterprises often adopt a collective approach, employing structures such as co-operatives, non-government organizations, and joint ventures, all of which are consistent with a social economy framework. These enterprises may also be supported and in some cases fully owned by First Nations governments (Vodden, Miller, and McBride 2001).

Throughout rural Canada, communities have turned to tourism as one strategy for adapting to declining primary-sector economies, "especially in areas that have unique natural and cultural amenities" (Koster 2010, i). The same is true of Aboriginal communities (Johnson 2010). The 1990s saw a rapid proliferation of Aboriginal tourism as an extension of a long tradition of tourists' interest in the "exotic Other" (Notzke 2004), but with the important difference that Aboriginal peoples have increasingly assumed control of these tourism developments.

This chapter presents a case study of the efforts of the 'Namgis First Nation to capitalize on opportunities in tourism as a response to political and economic restructuring and to draw on the arts and culture as a long-term strategy for resilience in the face of repeated and long-standing threats to livelihoods and cultural security. In particular, we explore the role that social economy and SCD approaches have played in the struggles of the 'Namgis First Nation and the community of Alert Bay to ensure cultural and economic survival based largely on the resources of the surrounding land and sea.

Cormorant Island is occupied by the municipality of the Village of Alert Bay; a small unincorporated area; three reserves belonging to the 'Namgis First Nation; and the Whe-La-La-U Area Council, a twelve-acre parcel of land set aside by the Department of Indian and Northern Affairs as a home for people from surrounding Kwakwaka'wakw First Nations. The municipality, 'Namgis Nation, and Whe-La-La-U all have elected councils. Aboriginal rights and title and ongoing treaty negotiations apply directly only to First Nations but impact the island community as a whole. Despite this complex governance environment, most community leaders and residents identify themselves as members of one community—Alert Bay.

Alert Bay lies within the Mount Waddington Regional District, the boundaries of which closely align with those of the territory of the Kwakwaka'wakw; the Regional District includes the northern third of Vancouver Island, the adjacent mainland, and the islands in between. The total population of the region, as of the 2006 Census, was 11,370 people, 26 percent of which were Aboriginal people (GSGislason and Associates 2011). Alert Bay is a community of approximately 1,000 residents, roughly two-thirds of whom identify themselves as Aboriginal. Alert Bay's island-wide population has remained relatively stable over time, with recent declines in the municipal population and growth on reserve, according to census figures (Statistics Canada 2012).

Located within the Pacific maritime ecozone, the region is one of world's most productive ecosystems—it is a land of mountainous topography; warm, wet climatic conditions; and lush temperate rainforests (Gilkeson et al. 2006). Ancient forests, fjords and inlets, and rivers fed by rainfall and mountain glaciers support all six species of Pacific salmon, along with many other fish species, wild game, high concentrations of bald eagles, waterfowl, orcas, porpoises, and dolphins (Prescott-Allen 2005). The economically valuable and culturally significant western red cedar and Pacific salmon are especially important to the livelihoods and way of life of the 'Namgis.

These rich resources also drew European settlers to the area. The village began when a salmon and herring saltery opened on the island in the 1860s, followed by a cannery in 1881 (Lyons 1969). The 'Namgis people became the labour force and were convinced to move from their homes on the Nimpkish (Gwa'ni) River to a village next to the saltery (Speck 1987). In 1871, British Columbia joined the Dominion of Canada, placing "public lands" under the control of the provincial government and ignoring the pre-existing rights and the social and legal systems of the

Kwakwa̲ka̲'wakw peoples (Weinstein 1991). 'Na̲mgis access to the Nimpkish River and its salmon runs was restricted. The 'Na̲mgis people were assigned three small reserves in the lower Nimpkish Valley, two on Cormorant Island, and 130 acres on small islands to be used as halibut fishing stations. 'Na̲mgis reserve lands totalled less than 600 acres (of a 500,000 acre territory). Requests for additional lands to protect traditional village sites and resource-harvesting rights were rejected, and new fishing, canning and logging industries began.

Despite having retained relatively high levels of natural capital, ecosystems in the region are threatened. Habitat protection is either lacking or inadequate, and sharp declines in fish populations and timber reserves have reduced sources of provisioning and cultural services. While the region may be considered pristine on a national or global scale, the decrease in natural resources relative to historic levels and the vulnerability of the area to intensive resource developments makes conservation concerns significant (Prescott-Allen 2005). The forests of the Nimpkish valley have been logged extensively for more than a century; most of the area's old growth has been harvested. The Nimpkish River was once one of BC's top four sockeye producers, but salmon returns continue to decline, despite significant investments in enhancement, restoration, and conservation. Reasons for fisheries declines are complex but include overfishing, habitat degradation, and changing ocean conditions (Vodden 2006).

Like much of rural British Columbia, the Mount Waddington Regional District experienced significant restructuring of its economy throughout the 1990s and early 2000s because of poor market conditions, reductions to annual allowable cuts of timber supply, and changes in the fisheries. Policy changes in the mid-1990s sought to reduce the size of the salmon fleet in a time of already depleted resources; this was coupled with other policies favouring centralization, intense competition, and fishing pressure. Aboriginal coastal communities, already experiencing lower than average levels of economic well-being, were disproportionately impacted by the fisheries declines of the 1990s (Vodden 1999). Alert Bay was deemed a fishing-dependent community in "crisis" (Von Specht 1996); it was one of the communities on the BC coast most impacted by fisheries restructuring (Gislason, Lam, and Mohan 1996). A provincially commissioned study reported a loss of sixty-three jobs, representing 11 percent of total community employment and 28 percent of employment in the salmon industry (Gislason, Lam, and Mohan 1996). Prior to 1996, the community relied on the salmon industry for 39 percent of community employment, with sixty vessels employing approximately 222 people (Gislason, Lam, and Mohan 1996). By 2004, fishing employment had fallen to less than 50 individuals (Penfold, Salter, and Carley 2004). In addition, Alert Bay had joined the dozens of coastal communities whose fish-processing plants no longer operate. It is estimated that at least 79 percent of jobs lost in Alert Bay belonged to Aboriginal people (Vodden 1999).

Despite the rise of world commodity prices and the decline of unemployment rates in the early 2000s, some researchers suggested that the problems evident during the late 1990s remained, including resource dependency and resulting vulnerability (e.g., Young and Matthews 2007; Markey et al. 2005). New sectors such as tourism, resource management, silviculture, watershed restoration, botanical forest products, aquaculture, and, most recently, mining, along with employment by First Nations governments, have been unable to fully compensate for declines in traditional sectors, although they have provided work for some in Alert Bay and elsewhere in the region who have been displaced and they have helped supplement declining fishing incomes (Ommer 2007; Synergy Management Group 2003). Many new jobs have been filled by Aboriginal peoples, which is significant given historic economic discrepancies (Vodden 2006).

Geographic isolation and kinship ties contribute to a sense of interdependence among communities in the region. The sense of community belonging is strong in the region compared to the rest of British Columbia; however, performance on numerous health indicators is low (BC Stats 2012). Strength of and pride in culture are important factors in health and well-being in the community of Alert Bay, contributing to self-esteem, mental health, and a spirit of helping one another—and increasingly, to economic activities (Vodden 1999). It is critical, therefore, to recognize that cultural well-being and ways of life are threatened in the region, in large part because of ecosystem decline and vulnerability (Rumsey et al. 2003).

SUSTAINING CULTURE, ECOSYSTEMS, AND PEOPLE IN THE 'NAMGIS TERRITORY

In the face of these ongoing challenges, the 'Namgis First Nation has been involved in a variety of efforts to protect and sustain their culture and the ecosystems and peoples that are inseparable from it. These efforts include integration of culture in education; language revitalization; the recording and protection of heritage resources and archaeological sites; ecosystem-based forestry management; and fisheries stewardship and restoration, particularly with respect to salmon. Wismer and Pell (1981) cite the Nimpkish Integrated Development Approach (NIDA) as an exemplar Canadian community economic development (CED) program.

Implemented in the 1970s, NIDA's integrated, long-term, coordinated approach was considered to be "unique and innovative" for its time. The five-year plan for educational, cultural, social, and economic development included goals and objectives approved by the entire community. Outcomes included an on-reserve school (the T'lisalagi'lakw School), the U'mista Cultural Centre, and the 'Namgis Salmon Enhancement Program. Many of the individuals who received training and experience during the NIDA years remain in positions of community leadership today. The plan provided a foundation for community development activity that has continued for more than three decades.

The treaty process represents a major effort by the 'Namgis to sustain many generations to come. The Nimpkish (now 'Namgis) Band Council formed a Land Claims Committee and, in 1974, declared sovereignty over the Nimpkish Valley as the "rightful owner and custodian of the watershed and its resources" (Weinstein 1991, 10). In 1997, the 'Namgis First Nation began treaty negotiations. They are now in the fourth stage of the treaty process, with the first draft agreement-in-principle (AIP) rejected in March 2013. As part of this process, the 'Namgis have negotiated or are pursuing interim measures in forestry, parks and protected areas, governance, cultural resource management, fisheries, and other areas (Cranmer 2004).

In addition to provincial and federally driven land-use planning exercises, the 'Namgis First Nation has been conducting its own extensive land, resource, and economic planning. The 'Namgis treaty team has completed a bioregional atlas describing the physical, biological, and cultural "identity" of 'Namgis traditional territory in a series of more than sixty digital maps. Land use plans are being developed at multiple scales (territorial, watershed, community, and special areas). Each of these plans describes goals, objectives, and action plans that are linked to a range of land use zones (NFN 2006). The Nimpkish Resource Management Board, with leadership from the 'Namgis First Nation and together with other partners, also developed the Nimpkish Watershed Salmon Recovery Plan in 2003.

After a provincial government clawback of 20 percent of major licensed tenures in 2004/2005, new annual allowable cut allocations were made for First Nations. A Forest and Range Agreement was signed between the 'Namgis First Nation and the Government of British Columbia in March 2005 that provided access to timber and $3.8 million in revenue sharing over five years (British Columbia 2006). The 'Namgis are working with the present tree farm licence holder to log and sell the timber, and they have used land-use planning efforts to guide harvesting.

Other current economic development projects include Orca Sand and Gravel and small-scale power production. The 'Namgis are partners with Vancouver-based

Polaris Minerals Corporation in Orca Sand and Gravel Ltd., a sand and gravel extraction operation and associated ship-loading facility. The quarry is expected to generate over $1 million per year in revenue for the 'Namgis and up to twenty-five new jobs. Currently, over half of the quarry's employees are Aboriginal people. The venture is also contributing to a foundation dedicated to supporting the social, cultural, and environmental interests of the 'Namgis and local communities. The 'Namgis are involved not only as owners and employees but also as participants in award-winning environmental monitoring and management of the project.

Several small-scale run-of-river hydroelectric projects have been proposed within 'Namgis territories. Following the model of Orca Sand and Gravel, the 'Namgis First Nation has partnered with Brookfield Renewable Energy to develop Kwagis Power LP. Care was taken to ensure that environmental concerns, particularly impacts on fish and fish habitats, could be eliminated or minimized to acceptable levels (NFN 2006). Negotiations and scoping of available opportunities is ongoing. Most recently, the 'Namgis's closed-containment project (KUTERRA LP) was launched to demonstrate the viability of producing Atlantic salmon in a land-based, closed-containment aquaculture system rather than the ocean-based aquaculture operations that have put the wild salmon fishery at risk (NFN 2012). Sales began successfully from the facility in 2014.

THE ARTS AND CULTURE: KEY ELEMENTS OF DEVELOPMENT IN ALERT BAY

The community of Alert Bay is world-renowned for Kwakwaka'wakw song, dance, and carving, activities that are considered art by some but are thought of as much more than art by those for whom these practices represent an essential part of their identity and their long history of resistance to assimilation. William Wasden Jr., member of 'Namgis First Nation and singing teacher explains "the songs are cultural property . . . specifically to families. And that's pretty sacred and important to people. And the masks, masks go along with the songs" (quoted in Bell, Raven, and McCuaig 2008, 40). For the Kwakwaka'wakw, the dances and songs, and the masks and regalia associated with them, also represent life teachings. Lillian Hunt (2011) explains, for example, that the "laughter dance" reminds us that we have to make each other laugh because laughter is important for well-being.

These stories, songs, and dances can be viewed as a cultural heritage, with particular families and villages having rights to certain ancestral images, crests, songs, and creation stories. In its traditional use, an object such as a mask "has little to no meaning or value if it is separated from the other elements of its whole being," such as "particular songs, dances, land use, or rights, names, and families associated with it" (Bell, Raven, and McCuaig 2008, 39).

In traditional times, chiefs held potlatches for the purposes of distributing surplus wealth and carrying out ceremonies associated with important events such as the naming of children, memorials, marriages, the raising of totem poles, and the transfer of rights and privileges. Catherine Bell, Heather Raven, and Heather McCuaig (2008, 46) explain: "Potlatches were the foundation of Kwakwaka'wakw economic, political, social, spiritual, and legal systems and the means for transferring cultural knowledge to future generations. They also promoted values such as humility, generosity, responsibility, and respect. Potlatches were the 'essence of Kwakwaka'wakw culture.'" Artists were commissioned to make regalia, masks, and gifts for these ceremonies, as well as totem poles and other carvings to indicate rank and acknowledge special occasions (Hawthorn 1979; Hunt and Neary 2000). Wasden explains: "In the olden days, artists were hired and paid with blankets and things of value at the time because the artwork was really valued and the artists were very highly respected" (quoted in Neufeld 2009, 108). Peter Mcnair, Alan Hoover, and Kevin Neary (1984) suggest that the Kwakwaka'wakw people are one of few First Nations groups of the Pacific Northwest who resolutely and continuously maintained their ceremonial and artistic traditions despite the efforts of others to destroy them. The Government· of Canada banned potlatches in British Columbia in 1884. In 1921, forty-five Kwakwaka'wakw were charged, twenty were jailed, and goods were seized when a large potlatch was held by Chief Dan Cranmer of Alert Bay (Sewid 1969). Legal prohibition, coupled with the Depression, caused the near collapse of the potlatch in the decades to follow. The disappearance of the potlatch would have been devastating, for "to destroy it was virtually to destroy the culture itself" (BC Indian Arts Society 1982).

After the Second World War and a period of international criticism of the Canadian state, treatment of Aboriginal peoples by the federal and provincial governments began to change. The potlatch prohibition was lifted in 1951. By 1960, Aboriginal people were recognized as full citizens of Canada; they were granted the right to vote and to organize for land claims. Kwakwaka'wakw potlatches were once again publicly practiced, and the Alert Bay Big House, referred to as Gukwdzi, was built in 1965 for holding potlatches and other cultural events. The Big House is described as "the cultural and spiritual center" of the 'Namgis and other Kwakwaka'wakw people (Wiwchar 2000). To the dismay of community members, an arsonist destroyed the Big House in 1997. A tribute to the community's resilience, a new Big House (christened I'tusto, "to rise again") was built in

1998–99 after an extensive fundraising effort. The potlatch remains an important institution in the community. As young men inherit chieftainships or other significant privileges and young adults name their children, new songs and dances continue to be created for ceremonial purposes, contributing to cultural maintenance and rebuilding.

The U'mista Cultural Society was formed in 1974, and the U'mista Cultural Centre opened six years later. The mandate of the non-profit society is to provide protection for the cultural values and property of the Kwakwaka'wakw peoples. The cultural centre and museum was created to house the regalia that had been confiscated during the potlatch ban and returned by the National Museum of Man (now the Canadian Museum of Civilization), the Royal Ontario Museum and the Smithsonian Institute's National Museum of the American Indian. The society has continued to work to reclaim confiscated artifacts and historical items, including those sold to collectors by Indian Agents. The returned pieces of potlatch regalia are extremely important for young artists, who, since the first items were returned in 1979, have studied how they were created, learning about their First Nation's culture and teachings in the process. The histories, dances, and songs associated with these items are infused with cultural significance. Thus, the repatriation of potlatch items and the information associated with them provides a "basis for rebuilding and strengthening" Kwakwaka'wakw culture (Bell, Raven, and McCuaig 2008, 62).

The U'mista Cultural Society and Cultural Centre act as a repository for language, heritage, and cultural resources and as a central location for culturally related development activities. The society offers culture and language education programs for all ages in its waterfront location next to the former St. Michael's residential school building which was torn down in February 2015, where people's language was once taken away, and has been involved in developing legislation for the protection of Aboriginal languages. The society conducts research as a method of retaining traditional knowledge and assisting members to gather information about their family histories. In 1991, for example, U'mista initiated the recording of traditional songs, along with related legends and histories, which were then entered into an audio database and catalogued according to family (Bell, Raven, and McCuaig 2005). This resource is now available to all Kwakwaka'wakw people, including future generations.

Since the mid-1990s, the U'mista Cultural Society, through its gift shop, website, and wholesale activities, has also served as a worldwide marketing and distribution centre for local artists. In 2009, fifty to sixty practicing artists were selling their work in Alert Bay (Neufeld 2009), roughly double the estimated twenty-five artists who earned a significant portion of their incomes from artistic activities in the late 1990s (Vodden 1999). The art produced includes not only carvings, totem poles, and masks, but also the work of Kwakwaka'wakw singers, drummers, and writers, as well as items traditionally considered "craft," such as blankets and baskets and other cedar-bark weaving (Neufeld 2009). The 'Namgis First Nation has developed a cedar strategy to ensure that cedar resources needed for cultural purposes are protected from forestry activities—just one example of their ongoing resource management and stewardship activities (Vodden 2006). Red cedar, "the tree of life" to the 'Namgis, is still used today to create ceremonial regalia, cedar canoes, artwork, jewellery, and more.

Other organizations, such as the T'sasala and Gwa'wina dance groups, also play important roles in the cultural well-being and artistic life of the Kwakwaka'wakw people, as do the individuals who commit themselves to learning, practicing, and sharing their language and culture. Artists play essential roles in the community as teachers and holders of the culture. They also contribute to the local economy, selling their work locally in shops and galleries, in markets in Vancouver and Victoria, and to international collectors. They are capitalizing on what Neufeld (2009, 90) describes as a "resurgence of Northwest Coast art as a form of cultural expression and economic development." For some, their creation of art for the community and their ceremonial responsibilities are paramount, with artistic income seen as a way to facilitate these cultural activities. Others are more business focused. These multiple roles are not always easy to balance as contemporary artists struggle with questions such as what is appropriate to sell and what is not, what is authentic, and how to respond to the varying expectations of the market and the community (Bell, Raven, and McCuaig 2005; Neufeld 2009).

First Nations governments, such as the 'Namgis First Nation, and non-government organizations, such as U'mista, both play a role in supporting these individuals, but artists and community leaders argue that more could be done. The language and culture of the Kwak'waka'wakw remain threatened despite strong leadership over many generations. Language is considered key to long-term cultural survival (Anonby 1997). Yet a study done by the U'mista Cultural Society demonstrated that less than 9 percent of Kwakwaka'wakw people speak their language fluently. Lack of funding has been identified as the single most important barrier to language retention programs, along with the need for further curriculum development, more Kwak'wala teachers, and more support from community leaders and parents (UCS 1997). With respect to the arts, the biggest challenges have been the high cost and legal barriers to protecting and repatriating heritage resources. Residents argue that these costs are properly borne by the government agencies and institutions responsible for the loss of cultural items and by private parties who have benefited from this process (Bell and Napoleon 2008).

Greater support for the mentoring and training of young artists may be useful in strengthening this culturally and economically important element of the community. While senior artists have traditionally taken on the role of mentoring and training young people, "a structured program would only enhance that and could offer more room for artists, but it's not the number one priority in the community" (Randy Bell, pers. comm., 16 August 2004, quoted in Neufeld 2009, 109).

ECO-CULTURAL TOURISM AS A DEVELOPMENT STRATEGY

As jobs are lost in the traditional resource sectors, the community of Alert Bay increasingly looks to tourism—particularly tourism focused on education, culture, and ecology. Cormorant Island is a launching point and service centre for many people who come to the surrounding area by boat to visit the numerous archaeological sites, abandoned villages, totem poles, and other cultural sites and to participate in outdoor activities such as whale watching, sea kayaking, sport fishing, nature tours, and diving. The highest growth in tourism markets is occurring in the areas of wilderness and cultural experiences, and these are tourism demands that Alert Bay is well positioned to meet. Visits to the Alert Bay Tourism Information Centre rose from 1,526 in 1986 to over 12,000 in 2006. In the words of 'Namgis artist Bruce Malidi Alfred, "People come here from all over the world to study the language, the art, the potlatch. This is the Mecca" (quoted in Neufeld 2009, 96).

Until recently, however, few First Nations firms were providing tourism services. Today, Aboriginal tourism products and services are being offered to visitors, along with culturally related attractions that include the U'mista Cultural Centre, the T'sasala and Gwa'wina dance groups, totem poles, culturally modified trees, a traditional-style Big House, and tours in traditional cedar canoes. Residents are involved in whale watching, fishing, and nature tours; accommodation (hostel, hotels, and B&Bs); and food services businesses. Several of these tourism-related businesses have been launched by First Nations operators, and the Aboriginal tourism industry is expected to expand in the future as new products are developed and residents receive training and experience. The work of world-renowned Kwakwaka'wakw artists and carvers attracts visitors, and in turn, tourism helps artists to build relationships that can lead to on-site sales and private commissions.

The 'Namgis Nation's ecotourism and cultural development strategy includes the reopening of ancient trade routes, joint management of protected areas, and resort development and land-based whale watching. The 'Namgis have developed a campground and trails and have acquired additional park facilities: two recreation sites, including camping facilities, were turned over to the 'Namgis First Nation by the ministry of Forests in 2003, and in May 2006, the 'Namgis First Nation signed an agreement with the Province to co-manage six provincial and marine parks and four ecological reserves within their traditional territory. One of these is the world-renowned Robson Bight Ecological Reserve (an orca rubbing-beach sanctuary). Three neighbouring nations (Mamalilikulla, 'Namgis, and Tlowitsis), through the Yukusam Heritage Society and in co-operation with the Province, agreed in 2003 to co-manage Hanson Island (Yukusam) and its significant cultural and ecological resources. In 2010, representatives of the 'Namgis First Nation and the ministry of Tourism, Culture, and the Arts signed a memorandum of understanding to work together for future development of the Mount Cain Ski Area as a regional ski resort.

Training Aboriginal people in outdoor guiding and entrepreneurship has been an important aspect of the 'Namgis tourism strategy. Speaking of tourism development, Harry Alfred, a 'Namgis land use planner, says, "What is clear is that we need to gain experience step-by-step. And as we do so, not only do we benefit from an expanded presence in our territory, but we are able to create new employment opportunities too" (2003, 4).

The U'mista Cultural Centre is a focal point for Alert Bay tourism. The centre, itself a tourism destination, provides instructions for proper protocol when visiting cultural sites and has sponsored training programs in tourism, marketing, and entrepreneurship. In 1996–97, U'mista facilitated the re-creation of a Kwakwaka'wakw village for a permanent display in the Netherlands; the crafting and construction of the village employed eight Alert Bay residents In the summer of 1998, six Alert Bay youth were employed to share their culture with thousands of park visitors for five weeks (Speck 1999). The exhibit continues to promote the community in Europe.

In 2003, U'mista entered into a partnership with the local Nimmo Bay Wilderness Resort to incorporate a cultural component into the resort's high-end tourism product: resort guests were offered the opportunity to visit the cultural centre, hear stories, participate in dance presentations, and visit First Nations territories (UCS 2003, 19). This is the type of collaboration encouraged by the 'Wi'la'mola Accord, whose purpose is "nurturing cultural renaissance and economic revival through tourism business joint ventures with experienced, ethical local operators" (UCS 2006). 'Wi'la'mola means "we are all travelling together." As the business arm of the U'mista Cultural Society, the 'Wi'la'mola Program pursues opportunities to create economic benefits while nurturing and stewarding the cultural heritage of the Kwakwa̲ka̲'wakw through education of both visitors and local residents. It does so by combining "the cultural expertise of the Kwakwa̲ka̲'wakw people and the successful experience of business operators" to produce "high-quality cultural tourism products" (Thomson 2010, 9).

The Village of Alert Bay operates a campground and invested significant resources in the late 1990s in waterfront beautification. The precedent-setting Alert Bay Accord was signed by the 'Na̲mgis First Nation and Village of Alert Bay in 1999 in recognition that the two governments "have historically worked together to promote a better standard of living for all the residents of Cormorant Island." The two jurisdictions resolved to coordinate their efforts to revitalize the economy (e.g., through tourism and infrastructure development), to obtain community and government support for these efforts and to "preserve and enhance the unique environment, heritage and other qualities of Alert Bay which are important to the community and the well-being of its inhabitants." The regional government of Cormorant Island and various organizations have collaborated to enhance infrastructure on the island that serves residents and visitors alike. Both the Village of Alert Bay and the U'mista Cultural Centre received significant funding from a federal adjustment program initiated in the late 1990s for waterfront and infrastructure improvement. The Village and the 'Na̲mgis have also undertaken joint funding of island-wide services such as a new hospital, sewage treatment facilities, and a waste management system. Recently, the 'Na̲mgis Nation embarked upon a partnership with the Village and the regional school district to launch the Cormorant Island Community Learning Centre. While some underlying tensions do exist, the community is seen as a model of co-operation between Aboriginal and non-Aboriginal communities.

Despite these successes, enthusiasm is tempered by the reality that, to date, First Nations-owned tourism companies (and several non-Aboriginal companies as well) have struggled to achieve business success. This is also true for Aboriginal tourism in Canada more generally. Notzke (2004, 32) suggests that to date, Aboriginal tourism development in Canada has fallen "far short of its potential." Reasons include a lack of training and the rush to enter the industry necessitated by the need to survive in a changing economy. Reluctance on the part of the former fisheries workforce to accept tourism as a new economic base has further slowed progress. The transition from a primary sector to a service-based economy is a slow and difficult one—for both individuals and communities.

The market realities are also difficult. Although demand for wilderness and cultural experiences is among the segments with the highest growth in BC tourism, the Mount Waddington region attracts only 2 percent of total visitors to Vancouver Island. The vulnerability of the tourism-based economy is highlighted by such circumstances as the increasing value of the Canadian dollar, the events of 9/11, and the sinking of the BC Ferries vessel *Queen of the North* in 2006, which disrupted ferry service on the Inside Passage route, a major tourist draw in this region (Penfold, Salter, and Carley 2004). After peaking in 2006, visitation numbers in Alert Bay began to drop in the late 2000s. Economic conditions and the discretionary nature of tourist activity are important factors (British Columbia 2012).

Finally, the Alert Bay community recognizes that tourism activities are not intrinsically sustainable and involve dangers such as cultural exploitation and ecological disturbance. As a result, care has been taken to ensure that tourism development is conducted in an ecologically and culturally sensitive manner, that it makes positive contributions to the community, and that it provides economic and social benefits such as opportunities for youth employment and engagement (Vodden 2002). Tourism development in Alert Bay remains a work in progress; it proceeds under significant constraints but also with great potential for the future, and the community's enthusiasm to get involved is increasing.

REFLECTIONS ON THE CONVERGENCE OF THE SOCIAL ECONOMY AND SCD

A key strategy used by Alert Bay organizations is the formation of partnerships and alliances with others in pursuing common or complementary goals. As described above, alliances have been formed with local, regional, provincial, and federal governments; environmental groups and industry; private foundations; academic institutions; and other entities. These partnerships, some of which are financial, have been established to protect areas of social, cultural, and economic significance; restore and more responsibly manage resources and habitats; and build stronger local economies and communities. For U'mista, as government cutbacks create growing financial challenges, foundation and private donations together with volunteer efforts have become increasingly important. The 'Namgis Nation has been a key partner in and supporter of U'mista. Both organizations have also entered into partnerships with private firms to begin joint ventures such as Orca Sand and Gravel and the 'Wi'la'mola-initiated Nimmo Bay project in an attempt to reduce reliance on government funding and foster corporate social and environmental responsibility. The 'Namgis have also collaborated with both the forestry industry and provincial and federal government agencies to restore and protect fisheries resources. Ecotrust Canada has provided technical and financial assistance for community initiatives, and partnerships have been formed with postsecondary institutions to launch a range of research and education programs. Perhaps the most significant collaboration in recent years has been between the Village of Alert Bay and 'Namgis First Nation, as described above.

This strong collaborative ethos, together with engagement of an active civil society in community and economic development and an insistence on corporate social responsibility, is well aligned with a social economy perspective. Service clubs have raised money for infrastructure projects such as a boat launch and playground; associations have hosted well-attended annual community events and are engaged in cultural development, treaty, health, and other issues; and citizens participate in land use and resource management planning, volunteer for community services, and contribute on an ongoing basis to trail and community beautification projects. All of these efforts have played a role in tourism and cultural development.

Several authors argue that activities related to subsistence and the informal economy—the part of the economy that is not taxed, monitored by government, or included in formal economic measurements—form a critical part of Aboriginal social economies (e.g., Bennett, Lemelin, Johnston and Łutsël K'e Dene First Nation 2010; Natcher 2009; Southcott and Walker 2009). The importance of the informal economy is evident in Alert Bay. Although many residents and community leaders suggest that mutual aid has declined, food is still distributed among friends and relatives within large extended families. Duties such as wood cutting, fishing, hunting, and gathering are also shared. Households often include a mix of those employed full-time in the cash economy and those who contribute in other ways. This mixed economy helps to enable seasonal industries such as tourism (Vodden 2006).

All of these characteristics together—the collaborative approach, the civil engagement, and the informal economy—have provided Alert Bay with a vibrant social economy. While the unique circumstances of this region may not be directly replicable in other communities seeking to employ a social economy approach in their development efforts, there are lessons to be learned from the case of Alert Bay that might be applicable to other regions. Partnerships and alliances could be built and nurtured, for example, and mixed economies, which remain important in many rural communities across the country, could be encouraged and supported.

The social economy—economic development that focuses on people and social benefits rather than on profit for its own sake—has captured imaginations across Canada and beyond and has resonance with development approaches focused on culture and community, such as those being used in Alert Bay. Yet the Alert Bay and 'Namgis First Nation examples highlight two major concerns with the social economy as it is generally defined and practiced. The first is a critical weakness in the social economy literature and in many social economy initiatives: the lack of attention to ecological sustainability despite the importance of ecosystems to socio-economic well-being. While a focus on social rather than purely economic impacts is an important advance over conventional economic development approaches, the social sphere is intimately connected with culture *and* environment—they are all parts of the interconnected whole of social-ecological systems. Alert Bay leaders and organizations have adapted to the changes that threaten their community's survival by putting into place a proactive, community-driven, comprehensive approach to tourism and territorial development that incorporates planning, training and education, infrastructure development, cultural research, and protocols that ensure cultural *and* environmental responsibility and stewardship. This approach is accompanied by continued efforts to increase local control over lands and resources. We suggest that it is more appropriate to conceptualize the 'Namgis responses to restructuring as sustainable community development (SCD) than as a social economy approach to development. Christopher Bryant (1999, 84) argues that community economic development has evolved from a "war on poverty" to an integrated approach that includes environmental values—which might now more appropriately be referred to as sustainable community development. The same shift is needed in the social economy: both practice and literature need to incorporate and converge with issues of sustainability. To some extent, this integrated approach is already present, but surely the primary importance of ecological integrity to sustainable development demands explicit recognition of the need for a movement toward ecological sustainability and environmental responsibility, along with social and economic change. As suggested by the United Nations in the report on the Conference on Environment and Development (UN General Assembly 1992, Principle 22), "Indigenous people and their communities and other local communities have a vital role in environmental management and development."

A second issue highlighted by the Alert Bay story concerns defining the social economy as being necessarily driven by non-governmental organizations and individuals from outside both the private sector and government—sometimes referred to as the "third sector" (Johnson 2010). In the case of Alert Bay, however,

First Nations and municipal governments, as well as private firms, have been key players in economic development broadly and in cultural and ecotourism activities more specifically.

Historically, a relatively small proportion of natural resource benefits have flowed to First Nations and local communities, in part because rights to forest harvesting in the Mount Waddington region are held primarily by large multinational companies. Opportunities for such benefits, including access to land for tourism development and to forest resources critical to artistic endeavours, have begun to increase. These benefits are expected to increase as relationships between First Nations governments and forest companies improve—in large part due to assertion of Aboriginal rights and title and the pursuit of treaties led by 'Namgis First Nation and other Kwakwaka'wakw governments.

Despite the worthwhile efforts described above, the community of Alert Bay is struggling to reshape itself after over two decades of upheaval in the fishery, an industry that created and has supported the community of Alert Bay since its inception. The community and the region as a whole have experienced significant ecological, economic, and social restructuring in recent decades. Yet they are no strangers to change and adaptation, having survived through the eras of Kwakwaka'wakw–European trade and European settlement and colonization, as well as through cyclical depressions and boom years. The arts have been an element of each of these eras while tourism has taken on a prominent role in the most recent period of adaptation. Both municipal and First Nations governments have been key players in the growing importance of tourism. Thus, social economy definitions that exclude government also exclude First Nations as critical participants in development within their territories and are thus inadequate as a way of explaining the development process underway in Alert Bay.

The experiences of the community of Alert Bay illustrate the need for greater integration of SCD and social economy perspectives. One possibility is to view the social economy as subsumed under the broader SCD approach, since the social economy does not—as of yet—fully incorporate the importance of cultural and ecological dimensions of development or the roles that municipal and First Nations (as well as Inuit and Métis) governments, as well as the private sector, can and do play as social economy actors.

REFERENCES

ACOA (Atlantic Canada Opportunities Agency). 2003. *Aboriginal Economic Development in Atlantic Canada: Lessons Learned and Best Practices:*

Understanding Conditions for Successful Economic Development in Aboriginal Communities. Moncton, NB: Atlantic Canada Opportunities Agency, Université de Moncton.

Alfred, Harry. 2003. "Managing Our Territory." *Treaty Update*, October. Alert Bay: 'Namgis First Nation.

Anonby, Stan J. 1997. "Reversing the Language Shift: Can Kwak'wala Be Revived?" Master's thesis, University of North Dakota.

Bell, Catherine, and Val Napoleon. 2008. "Introduction, Methodology, and Thematic Overview." In *First Nations Cultural Heritage and Law: Case Studies, Voices, and Perspectives*, edited by Catherine Bell and Val Napolean, 1–32. Vancouver: University of British Columbia Press.

Bell, Catherine, Heather Raven, and Heather McCuaig. 2008. "Recovering from Colonization: Perspectives of Community Members on Protection and Repatriation of Kwakwaka'wakw Cultural Heritage." In *First Nations Cultural Heritage and Law: Case Studies, Voices, and Perspectives*, edited by Catherine Bell and Val Napolean, 33–91. Vancouver: University of British Columbia Press. http://www.ubcpress.ca/ books/pdf/chapters/2008/FirstNationsCulturalHeritage.pdf

Bennett, Nathan, Raynard Lemelin, Margaret Johnston and Łutsël K'e Dene First Nation. 2010. "Using the Social Economy in Tourism: A Study of National Park Creation and Community Development in the Northwest Territories, Canada." *Journal of Rural and Community Development* 5 (1–2): 200–20.

BC Indian Arts Society. 1982. *Mungo Martin: Man of Two Cultures.* Sidney, BC: Gray's Publishing.

BC Stats. 2006. "First Nation and Tribal Councils in the Treaty Process—'Namgis First Nation." http://www.gov.bc.ca/arr/negotiation/first_nations_in_the_process/. Accessed Oct. 5, 2012.

——. 2012 "Local Health Area 85 - Vancouver Island North 2012 Socio-Economic Profile." http://www.bcstats.gov.bc.ca/StatisticsBySubject/SocialStatistics/ SocioEconomicProfilesIndices/Profiles.aspx.

——. 2012. "Visitor Centre Network Statistics Program Year over Year Report 2012— Alert Bay." Victoria: BC Tourism.

Bryant, Christopher R. 1999. "Community Change in Context." In *Communities, Development and Sustainability Across Canada*, edited by John T. Pierce and Ann Dale, 69–89. Vancouver: University of British Columbia Press.

Cornell, Stephen, and Joseph P. Kalt, eds. 1992. *What Tribes Can Do: Strategies and Institutions in American Indian Economic Development.* Los Angeles: American Indian Studies Center, University of California, Los Angeles.

Cranmer, B. 2004. "Chief Bill Cranmer." *'Namgis Treaty News*, November. Alert Bay: 'Namgis First Nation.

CSERP (Canadian Social Economy Research Partnerships). 2009. *The Social Economy in Canada.* Pamphlet. Victoria, BC: CSERP.

Decter, Michael, and Jeffrey Kowall. 1989. "Yukon 2000: Comprehensive Planning for Diversification." Economic Council of Canada Local Development Paper No. 13. Ottawa: Economic Council of Canada.

ECC (Economic Council of Canada). 1990. *From the Bottom Up: The Community Economic Development Approach*. Ottawa: Economic Council of Canada.

Gilkeson, Linda, Lynne Bonner, Robin Brown, Kelly Francis, Duncan Johannesen, Rosaline Canessa, Jackie Alder et al. 2006. *Alive and Inseparable: British Columbia's Coastal Environment, 2006*. Victoria: BC Ministry of Environment.

Gislason, Gordon, Edna Lam, and Marilyn Mohan. 1996. *Fishing for Answers: Coastal Communities and the BC Salmon Fishery*. Victoria, BC: Job Protection Commission.

GS Gislason and Associates. 2011. *The Marine Economy and the Regional District of Mt. Waddington in BC*. Sointula, BC: Living Oceans Society; Port McNeill, BC: Regional District of Mount Waddington.

Hawthorn, Audrey. 1979. *Kwakiutl Art*. Seattle: University of Washington Press.

Hunt, Lillian. 2011. "Sustaining Culture and Livelihoods Through Ecotourism." Presentation to Culture, Place, and Identity at the Heart of Regional Development Conference, St. John's, NL. October 13–15, 2011.

Hunt, Richard, and Kevin Neary. 2000. *Richard Hunt: Through My Father's Eyes*. Victoria, BC: Art Gallery of Greater Victoria.

Johnson, Peter A. 2010. "Realizing Rural Community Based Tourism Development: Prospects for Social-Economy Enterprises." *Journal of Rural and Community Development* 5 (1–2): 150–62.

Koster, Rhonda. 2010. "Introduction: Rural Tourism and Recreation in Canada." *Journal of Rural and Community Development* 5 (1): i–ii.

Lyons, Cicely. 1969. *Salmon, Our Heritage*. Vancouver: BC Packers.

Markey, Sean, John Pierce, Kelly Vodden, and Mark Roseland. 2005. *Second Growth: Community Economic Development in Rural British Columbia*. Vancouver: University of British Columbia Press.

McNair, Peter, Alan Hoover, and Kevin Neary. 1984. *The Legacy: Tradition and Innovation in Northwest Coast Indian Art*. Victoria: British Columbia Provincial Museum.

Natcher, David. 2009. "Subsistence and the Social Economy of Canada's Aboriginal North." *Northern Review* 30: 69–84.

Neufeld, Margaret R. M. 2009. "Connecting to the Art Market from Home: An Exploration of First Nations Artists in Alert Bay, British Columbia." *American Indian Culture and Research Journal* 33 (1): 89–117.

NFN ('Namgis First Nation). 2005. *'Namgis Treaty News*, December.

———. 2006. http://www.namgis.bc.ca/treaty/pages/planning.htm.

———. 2012. "KUTTERA Land-Based Closed Containment Salmon Farm." 'Namgis First Nation. http://www.namgis.bc.ca/CCP/Pages/default.aspx.

Notzke, Claudia. 2004. "Indigenous Tourism Development in Southern Alberta, Canada: Tentative Engagement." *Journal of Sustainable Tourism* 12 (1): 29–54.

Ommer, Rosemary E. 2007. *Coasts Under Stress: Restructuring and Social-Ecological Health.* With the Coasts Under Stress Research Project team. Montréal and Kingston: McGill-Queen's University Press.

Penfold, George, B. Salter, and D. Carley. 2004. *A Regional Economic Development Strategy for the Regional District of Mount Waddington.* Port McNeill, BC: Regional District of Mount Waddington.

Prescott-Allen, Robert. 2005. *Coast Information Team: Review Report.* Victoria, BC: Coast Information Team.

Rumsey, Chuck, Jeff Ardron, Kristine Ciruna, Tim Curtis, Frank Doyle, Zach Ferdana, Tony Hamilton et al. 2003. *An Ecosystem Spatial Analysis for Haida Gwaii, Central Coast, and North Coast British Columbia.* Victoria, BC: Coast Information Team.

Sewid, James. 1969. *Guests Never Leave Hungry: The Autobiography of James Sewid, a Kwakiutl Indian.* Edited by J. Spradley. New Haven: Yale University Press.

Shea, Cynthia Pollock. 1994. *Employment and Sustainable Development: Opportunities for Canada.* Winnipeg, MB: International Institute for Sustainable Development.

Southcott, C., and V. Walker. 2009. "A Portrait of the Social Economy in Northern Canada." *Northern Review* 30 (Spring): 13–36.

Speck, Dara Culhane. 1987. *An Error in Judgement.* Vancouver: Talonbooks.

Speck, Lori, ed. 1999. "Time-Line of Historical Events: Beyond 2000—What Does the Future Hold?" *U'mista News*, Fall/Winter 1999. Alert Bay, BC: U'mista Cultural Society.

Statistics Canada. 2012. Alert Bay, British Columbia (Code 5943008) and Mount Waddington, British Columbia (Code 5943) (table). Census Profile. 2011 Census. Statistics Canada Catalogue no.98-316-XWE. Ottawa. Released October 24, 2012. http://www12.statcan.gc.ca/census-recensement/2011/dp-pd/prof/index.cfm?Lang=E.

Synergy Management Group. 2003. "Proprietary Economic Modelling and Impact Analysis for the Mt. Waddington Region." Pilot project report produced for Province of British Columbia. Victoria, BC: Ministry of Sustainable Resource Management.

Thomson, Sandra. 2010. *Lessons from the Land and Sea: A Best Practices Guide to Cultural Ecotourism for Coastal First Nations of British Columbia.* Vancouver: Rainforest Solutions Project.

UCS (U'mista Cultural Society). 1997. *Annual Report.* Alert Bay, BC: U'mista Cultural Society.

——. 2003. *U'mista Cultural Society Newsletter*, Summer.

——. 2006. "'Wi'la'mola Program." U'mista Cultural Society. http://www.umista.ca/wilomola/index.php.

UN General Assembly. 1992. "The Rio Declaration on Environment and Development." New York: UN General Assembly. http://www.un.org/documents/ga/conf151/ aconf15126-1annex1.htm.

Vodden, Kelly. 1999. "Nanwakola: Co-management and Sustainable Community Economic Development in a BC Fishing Village." Master's thesis, Simon Fraser University.

———. 2002. "Sustainable Community Development in a Coastal Context: The Case of Alert Bay, British Columbia." *Canadian Journal of Aboriginal Economic Development* 3 (1).

———. 2006. "Adapting to Uncertain Futures: Alert Bay Community Background Report." Burnaby, BC: Simon Fraser University. http://http-server.carleton. ca/~mbrklac/Background%20Reports/Alert%20Bay%20Background%20Report. pdf

Vodden, Kelly, Anne Miller and John McBride. 2001. *Assessing the Business Information Needs of Aboriginal Entrepreneurs in British Columbia: Literature Review.* Prepared for Western Economic Diversification Canada and BC Ministry of Small Business, Tourism, and Culture. Burnaby, BC: Simon Fraser University, Community Economic Development Centre.

Von Specht, F. 1996. "Alert Bay—A Fishing Village in Crisis." *Awa'k'wis.* Port Hardy, BC: Kwakiutl District Council.

Weinstein, Martin. 1991. *Nimpkish Valley: A History of Resource Management on Vancouver Island—Lands of the Nimpkish Indian People, from Aboriginal Times to the 1980s.* Alert Bay, BC: Nimpkish Band Council.

Wismer, Susan, and David Pell. 1981. *Community Profit: Community-Based Economic Development in Canada.* Toronto: Is Five Press.

Wiwchar, David. 2000. "They Will Dance Again." *Raven's Eye*, June.

Young, Nathan, and Ralph Matthews. 2007. "The Economic Spaces of Community and Industry in Rural British Columbia: The Political Reconstitution of a Rural Economy." *Area* 39 (2): 176–85.

7 Non-Profit and Co-operative Organizations and the Provision of Social Housing

George Penfold, Lauren Rethoret, and Terri MacDonald

Social housing, also known as affordable or accessible housing, encompasses a wide range of housing arrangements, from emergency shelters that address the needs of the poor and homeless through to both market rental units and market sale units that people living on a limited income can afford to access. Table 7.1 provides a brief overview of this continuum (Curran and Wake, 2008, 3). The social economy plays a significant role in the delivery of almost all the non-market housing services included on this continuum. Otherwise put, it is the main delivery mechanism for housing aimed at the most disadvantaged. That role naturally declines as the market economy and the private sector assume responsibility for the provision of housing. Furthermore, problems such as poverty and homelessness are frequently accompanied by issues beyond basic shelter requirements: for example, the need for addictions and mental health services or for income or rental supplements for the working poor. The social economy often has a significant role to play in the delivery of these services as well.

Table 7.1 The affordable housing continuum

Housing type	Provider	Delivery
Emergency shelter Transition housing Social housing	Government or other subsidy	Social economy and partners

Housing type	Provider	Delivery
Affordable rental (rent subsidies) Affordable ownership (limited resale values)	Non-market housing	Social economy, private sector, and partners
Affordable rental Affordable ownership	Market housing	Private sector and partners

SOURCE: Data from Curran and Wake (2008), tables 1 and 2.

A flexible mandate is one of the potential advantages that the social economy brings to the social housing sector. Without the bureaucratic delineations that limit the integration of the various silos of the public sector, or the drive of the private sector to achieve economies of scale by limiting the breadth of their product or service offerings, actors in the social economy are better able to tailor their mandates to address complex social problems like those at the heart of homelessness and poverty. For example, as Nancy Neamtan (2005) points out, many organizations in the social economy aim to employ marginalized citizens to carry out their work. The influence of these organizations therefore extends beyond their primary objective (e.g., to provide social housing) to other social challenges, such as dependence on income-supplement programs. An integrated approach to service delivery not only improves the effectiveness of social programs, but it may also increase the sustainability of non-profit organizations attempting to diversify their funding sources or volunteer base (Marason Management 2004).

Station Pointe Greens
Juanita Marois

Currently in the research and design stage, Station Pointe Greens will be a landmark sustainable high-rise housing development in northeast Edmonton. The ambitious plans include achieving net-zero status (zero net energy consumption and zero carbon emissions) while remaining affordable. The development will consist of ten townhouses and mid- and high-rise apartments. While the overall development will consist of approximately 220 units for both purchase and lease, the creation of distinct but attached buildings, each with its own co-operative community association (seniors, artists, etc.), will create smaller and friendlier "neighbourhoods." The objective is to create an urban village that is mixed in terms of income, size, household configuration, housing tenure, and age of residents.

Coupled with the residential component will be over fourteen thousand square feet of commercial and retail space, as well as a day care centre located within the community centre. The design plan allows easy pedestrian access to the open urban spaces beyond its walls, the adjacent Belvedere LRT station and bus terminal, and the centrally located community centre, accessible by both residents of the complex and the surrounding community. Parking for the residential and commercial facilities will be located in an underground parkade.

The Communitas Group, the developer of the Station Pointe Greens project, has cultivated the development of 59 housing projects that provide housing to 2,070 households ... with their individual capital costs ranging from a low of $300,000 to a high of $20 million. Throughout this time, Communitas has collaborated with a range of housing clients, including continuing housing cooperatives, home ownership cooperatives, mixed tenure cooperatives, community based land trusts, cohousing groups, non-profit companies and societies developing special purpose housing and private developers. Projects have ranged in size from 3 units to 118 units. (The Communitas Group 2015)

The Communitas Group. 2015. http://www.communitas.ca/.
Station Pointe Greens. 2015. http://stationpointegreens.ca/.

SUPPLY AND DEMAND OF AFFORDABLE HOUSING

Housing affordability is driven by issues related to both demand and supply. On the supply side, the housing market focus has, in the last several decades, been on the "boomer" generation. As that demographic group accumulated wealth and moved into the higher-end market, price increases in both land and housing followed close behind. These rising costs, however, have been disproportionate to increases in personal and household income across the broader population. In addition, various attempts by provinces to control rent increases and manage the relationship between landlords and tenants have not successfully addressed the problem of the growing gap between the real costs of constructing rental housing and the ability of tenants to keep up with rising rents. That gap has generally resulted in a rate of construction of rental units that is too low to adequately meet the demand for affordable housing (Hulchanski 1997).

On the demand side, the size of the population in need of affordable housing options is increasing. According to the Canada Mortgage and Housing Corporation (CMHC), for rent or mortgage payments to be affordable, the cost of housing that is acceptable in terms of condition and size should be less than 30 percent of before-tax household income (Luffman 2006, 16). In British Columbia, between 2000 and 2010, average residential property values increased 133 percent, from $216,989 to $505,178 (BC Stats 2014), while average household incomes increased only 34 percent, from $57,593 to $77,378 (Statistics Canada 2011). The number of households spending more than 30 percent of their income on shelter increased 22 percent, from 425,960 to 519,470 (Statistics Canada 2011). In 2011, approximately 30 percent of households in the province were rental households, and 45.3 percent of these were spending more than 30 percent of their income on shelter costs (Statistics Canada 2011).

A number of other factors have also affected the demand for social housing, including a growing population and an increasing proportion of the overall population in low-income brackets; proportionately more renters than owners; an increasing number of single-person, single-income households; a growing number of seniors; and a rising number of homeless people as a result of various economic, social, and psychological problems. One of the significant factors that impacted homelessness in Canada was the closure of psychiatric hospitals and mental health institutions in the 1970s and 1980s (Sealy and Whitehead 2004). The continuing implications of those closures, along with overall increases in total population and structural changes in the economy means that the number of homeless continues to rise: for example, in Metro Vancouver in 2008, the number of homeless people had increased by 22 percent from the previous count in 2005, and by 137 percent from 2002 (Klein and Copas 2010). In the province as a whole, according to a 2008 study by Simon Fraser University's Centre for Applied Research in Mental Health and Addictions, the estimated number of individuals with severe addictions and/or mental illness (SAMI) across BC who are inadequately housed and inadequately supported ranges from approximately 17,500 to 35,500, and that between 8,000 and 15,500 individuals with SAMI are absolutely homeless (Patterson et al. 2008, 33, 43).

Until the mid-1990s, the Canadian federal government provided leadership and support for housing for those less able to compete in the housing market. Because of fiscal constraints, that role was downloaded to provinces, many of which subsequently either downloaded the responsibility to municipalities or regions or abandoned it altogether (Schuk 2009.) In British Columbia, some responsibility for social housing has been maintained at the provincial level through BC Housing. The Province of B.C. offers various subsidy programs for clients in need, and supplies housing providers within the social economy with some assistance in the areas of research and capacity-building support, and mortgage assistance. But the Province still relies heavily on the social economy for the provision of shelter: for example, BC Housing's programs in 2012–13 involved partnerships with some eight hundred housing providers—mostly non-profit societies and housing co-operatives (BC Housing 2013). As of 2010, over 60 percent of subsidized housing units were provided by organizations operating within the social economy, including all emergency shelter programs in the province except those in the City of Vancouver (BC Housing 2010).

More than 98,000 households in about two hundred communities throughout British Columbia were assisted through subsidized housing in 2012–13 (BC Housing 2013, 2). The types of support ranged from emergency shelters and housing for the homeless (11,000 households), to transitional housing and assisted living (18,900 households), to independent social housing (41,000 households), to rent assistance in the private market (27,300 households) (BC Housing 2013, 9). In total, government-assisted housing accounts for about 6 percent of the total housing stock in BC, but this statistic varies across the province. Rates are lower in the North and Interior (4.5% and 4.8%, respectively) and higher on Vancouver Island and in the Lower Mainland (5.4% and 6.7%, respectively,) (BC Housing 2013, 12).

Most of the non-profit housing organizations in the province are members of the BC Non-Profit Housing Association (BCNPHA), and the majority of these organizations are funded at least partially through ongoing operational subsidies from the provincial government (BCNPHA 2009). In addition, there are approximately 261 non-profit housing co-operatives throughout the province, providing more than 14,572 units (CHF BC.) Of that inventory, 2,844 units operate under the Federal Co-operative Housing Program, which requires that a minimum of 30 percent of all units in a housing co-op receive rent supplement. Since 1993, new housing co-operatives have had to establish themselves within the private market because in that year, public funding for start-up cooperative housing was terminated. This end to subsidies has significantly limited the ability of co-op housing to address affordability needs. The existing co-operative and non-profit organizations simply cannot meet the affordable housing needs in British Columbia; in 2008, BC Housing had over 13,400 applicants on its waitlist (Klein and Copas 2010), and in 2010, there was an average of 3.1 units for every ten low-income seniors (BCNPHA 2010). The BCNPHA (2011, 4) estimates that there are 614 non-profit housing societies that employ 22,115 people across British Columbia and provide over 50,000 housing units. Within that inventory, the overall emphasis is on seniors' housing and support services (BCNPHA 2010).

The distribution of social housing needs does appear, however, to vary with the regional context. For example, a 2008 inventory of social housing organizations in the Kootenay Columbia region of British Columbia found that of the 103 non-profit housing organizations in the region, 52 percent of the organizations focused on seniors, 22.3 percent on low-income earners, 11 percent on disabled adults, 3 percent on people with mental health issues, 8 percent on transitional housing, and 4 percent on emergency shelters (BC Real Estate Foundation 2008). The total number of units oriented toward seniors represented 79 percent of all social housing units in that region, well above the average reported by the BCNPHA, but this is understandable considering that the Kootenay Development Region has the oldest median age (47.1 years) of any development region in British Columbia (Statistics Canada 2014).

In comparison, a recent research report and survey of social housing providers in the Fraser Valley Regional District found a total of 182 providers serving approximately 28,000 people and employing approximately 12,700 people; these were divided into five groups with the following distribution: group 1 serves the elderly (23%) and persons with disabilities (32%); group 2 serves poor (low-income) families (9%), low-income individuals (5%), women (4%), and children and youth (2%); group 3 provides services related to rehab and recovery (7%), parole/incarceration (5%), and abuse (4%); group 4 serves the homeless (5%); and group 5 serves Aboriginal clients (4%) (Van Wyk and Van Wyk 2011a, 19). This study also found that housing was the exclusive mandate of only 12 percent of existing non-profit housing providers. The remainder offer their clients a variety of services beyond housing, including services related to health (30%); basic needs provision (18%); health services and care (17%); accompaniment for daily tasks (12%); counselling (6%); and referrals, legal, and outreach (5%) (Van Wyk and

Van Wyk 2011a, 18). Even with that supply and those services, an estimated 345 persons were homeless in 2011 (Van Wyk and Van Wyk, 2011b, 16).

Another striking difference between the social housing sectors in the Kootenay Columbia and Fraser Valley regions is the scale of housing service provision by social economy players. In 2004, the Fraser Valley Regional District represented 65 percent of total units in the BCNPHA inventory but 47 percent of total societies, whereas the Kootenay Columbia Region had only 15 percent of total units and 27 percent of total societies (Marason Management 2004, 9). Those differences reflect the different scale of communities, needs, and capacities within the two regions. Furthermore, almost two-thirds of all societies in the non-profit housing sector manage only a single building, 30 percent manage two to five buildings, and only 8 percent manage six or more developments (11). Hence, the sector consists mostly of relatively small enterprises.

The scale of social housing provision appears to be directly related to management capacity and financial sustainability. A study of the financial state of the non-profit housing stock by the BCNPHA (Wenmann 2009) examined four characteristics: urban/rural geography, portfolio size, operating agreement program, and the "segment" to which a society was assigned according to the BCNPHA's segmentation framework—which was based on the society's primary mandate and size and the tenant group served.

> Of the four characteristics examined, the one most strongly related to financial strength is portfolio size. Buildings operated by societies with larger portfolios are most likely to be characterized as "positive" (47%) compared with buildings operated by both medium (44%) and small societies (18%). The evident strength of buildings within large and medium sized portfolios reflects the fact that more of these buildings have both capital plans and replacement reserve investment strategies in place. In addition, 78% of buildings managed by large societies cover their expenses with their subsidy and rental income compared with 75% of buildings managed by medium sized societies and 66% of buildings managed by small societies.
>
> ... Urban buildings are more likely than rural buildings to be characterized as "positive" using the financial strength index largely because fewer rural buildings (27%) have a capital plan compared with their urban counterparts (56%). Fewer of the older federally administered programs can be characterized as "positive" compared with buildings operating within newer bilateral or provincially administered programs. ... Large societies with housing as their primary mandate are one of two segments most likely

to be characterized as "positive". The segment that groups societies offering health or supportive services to tenants who are most at risk is the other segment faring well according to the financial strength index, possibly because this segment has been a recent priority in terms of provincial funding and programming. (Wennman 2009, 5)

In summary, the social economy is a crucial component of the delivery of support programs related to government housing and of addressing the local and regional affordable-housing needs of communities and regions throughout British Columbia. The regional variations in social housing supply and demand discussed above point to an important advantage of the social economy in delivering social housing services, at least as compared to provincial or federal governments. The decentralized nature of the social economy allows organizations to draw on local knowledge to implement strategies that reflect the specific needs of a community's population. In fact, governments, as they have progressively transitioned away from direct service provision, have explicitly sought out partnerships with social economy actors under the assumption that organizations with closer community ties could provide a higher quality of service. This approach has been seen by some as an effective use of the strengths of both the public and non-profit sectors (Quarter and Mook, 2010, 15) and criticized by others as simply an effort by governments to save money or as an unfortunate expansion of the political realm into civil society where "the staff of non-profit agencies are the new street-level bureaucrats" (Smith and Lipsky, 1993, 13).

Community Car Shares I
Kailey Cannon

In light of increasing costs associated with car ownership and concern about the environmental impact of vehicle use, carsharing has emerged as a worldwide alternative transportation movement. Western Canada is no exception, and various non-profit co-operative organizations dedicated to carsharing are currently operating in major centres such as Calgary, Vancouver, and Victoria. Western Canada is also home to two of the few carshares in North America operating in a rural region: the Kootenay Carshare Co-op, servicing the communities of Nelson, Fernie, Kaslo, Kimberley, and Revelstoke, and the GO2 Carshare Cooperative, servicing residents of Smithers and the Bulkley Valley. Some carshares are entirely volunteer run (Calgary Carshare), while others have from six (Kootenay Carshare) to 28 (Vancouver's Modo) paid employees. Most carshares have a board of directors that meet monthly and vote on strategic decisions. Directors are elected annually by members at annual general meetings. Modo, one of the largest carshares in Canada, has approximately 10889 users who are owner/operators and a fleet of 351 vehicles (as of March 2015). Modo's fleet includes cars, trucks, mini-vans and hybrids. Modo now operates in Richmond and Surrey, and just opened with 24 vehicles in Victoria, BC after merging with Victoria Car Share (http://www.modo.coop/blog/report-from-the-board/).

FACTORS IMPACTING THE FUTURE ROLE OF THE SOCIAL ECONOMY

One of the major challenges of non-profit and co-operative organizations in responding to housing needs is access to financial support. The most significant changes in that regard came with the decisions by the federal government to stop financial support for co-operative housing in 1993 and then, in 1996, to download the responsibility for affordable housing to provinces. The end result of progressive cuts in federal transfer payments for social housing was a failure by senior levels of government to provide adequate funding to social assistance programs related to housing (Hulchanski 2005).

How, then, are social economy actors addressing the financial challenges they face in the delivery of affordable housing? New housing co-operatives are now generally market oriented, but co-operatives that were established before 1993 have assets that were acquired with public support and have equity that could be leveraged to free up capital to help build additional affordable housing. However, Carol Murray and Rebecca Pearson (2008) note that leveraging those assets to build additional affordable co-op housing is unlikely to happen because of the significant financial barriers to building new co-operative housing in the current Canadian housing market. In their discussions with co-op housing experts, it became evident that the main barrier to building new affordable co-op housing is not access to financing but the high costs of building new housing. Specifically, even if remortgaging fully amortized housing co-op assets would make some funds available to lend at market interest rates, this would do nothing to decrease the costs of land, labour, and building materials, the main cost drivers of new housing construction. Building new housing is so expensive that without significant subsidy, the cost to access that housing would be unaffordable. Murray and Pearson (2008, 2) list additional challenges facing co-ops:

> The end of their mortgage also spells the end of their operating agreement with Canada Mortgage and Housing Corporation (which has served as a sort of housing co-op "constitution" thus far) and the end of the associated government subsidy for low-income members. Many co-ops are also dealing with deferred maintenance issues, and/or required repairs. . . . As a result of these factors, re-mortgaging may be necessary for subsidy and/or maintenance purposes, leaving little or no room for additional leveraging.

If subsidy-linked remortgaging is not available or is not taken up as a refinancing option, the social housing component of co-operative housing could be reduced. The co-op housing sector has the added challenge of building and maintaining a significant capital asset at a cost that will still allow residents to live affordably.

The most common current vehicle for affordable housing delivery and management is a non-profit corporation or society. The results of a survey of 135 non-profit housing societies undertaken by the BCNPHA generated several key findings relating to the financial stability of these societies (Marason Management 2004). First, few of them share operational services and processes with other societies, although a large number would be willing, under favourable financial circumstances, to consider sharing employed staff, contracted services, and administrative systems. Second, the societies' limited use of volunteers focuses primarily on the delivery of tenant services and board participation. Finding suitable board members and individuals who could assist with operations is a common problem. Many groups would like to increase the level of volunteerism but face barriers such as locating appropriate volunteers and having limited time and staff resources to train and manage them. These challenges are linked to general trends in volunteerism that include organizations' concerns around liability and changing expectations among potential volunteers that can be difficult for non-profit entities to meet. These include taking on shorter-term or flexible commitments; volunteering only as a group or as a family; and wanting to use professional skills or to do something that is not in the volunteer's skillset, which often necessitates training (Volunteer Canada 2013). These expectations do not often align with the need for a long-term volunteer commitment as a board member or as the manager of a housing development from inception through to operation. A third finding of the study was that there are growing concerns, especially given uncertainty about future funding, regarding the ability of social housing organizations to maintain current maintenance and operation standards. The sector is faced with rising costs in energy, labour, and materials, and as buildings age and systems deteriorate, this challenge will only increase.

Threats to the long-term financial sustainability of non-profit housing entities also seem to revolve around organizational governance and human resources. Only 40 percent of the responding groups in the Marason study produce an annual plan (2004, 26). Societies appear to need guidance in identifying which operational adjustments would benefit them the most and in developing effective implementation strategies for those adjustments. Human resource challenges are common to both the social and market economies: an aging workforce, the need for skills development, and particularly in the social economy, the struggle to offer competitive wages and benefits.

Community Car Shares II
Kailey Cannon

Carshares seek to provide a low-cost alternative to car ownership, reduce the number of vehicles on the road, and cut carbon emissions by encouraging sustainable transportation practices. Advocates of the service suggest each car share eliminates 9-13 cars from the road (Modo 2015). Carshares vary from place to place, but the general idea is that people pay a monthly and/or yearly membership fee and, in some cases, a fully refundable damage deposit and are then able to book vehicles for as little as $5.00/hour and $0.25/km. Rates are generally based on distance and time, and include the cost of insurance and gas. Carshares provide an affordable alternative to car ownership, which is, of course, no small investment. Using a carshare rather than owning a car can free up a significant portion of disposable income—approximately $10446 per year (TravelSmart 2015). These savings could be put toward public transit passes, rent or better housing, or household costs, an indication that linking affordable housing and smart transportation could facilitate the collaboration of social economy and sustainability actors in constructing a policy framework to enable social and environmental sustainability.

A number of car cooperatives have a partnership with Scrap-It, the BC branch of the nation-wide Retire Your Ride program, which promotes voluntary early retirement of vehicles by offering a number of sustainability-inspired incentives. Measures are taken to ensure that all "retired rides" are recycled in an ethical manner. In addition to giving recyclers the option of transit passes, a $400 rebate for a new bike, or a credit towards an electric vehicle, participants can receive a credit on membership with a number of car cooperatives (British Columbia Scrap-it Program 2015).

British Columbia Scrap-it Program. 2015. https://scrapit.ca/apply/incentive-choices/.
Calgary Carshare Cooperative. 2015. http://calgarycarshare.ca.
Canadian Carsharing Association. 2015. http://www.carsharing.org.
Car2Go Vancouver. 2015. https://www.car2go.com/en/vancouver/.
GO2 Car Share Cooperative. 2015. Smithers BC Car Share Coop. www.onesky.ca/go2carshare.
Kootenay GO2 Car Share Co-op. 2015. http://www.carsharecoop.ca.
Modo. Vancouver and Victoria Car Share. 2015. http://www.modo.coop.
TravelSmart. 2015. "Cost of Owning a Car." http://www.travelsmart.ca/en/GVRD/Driving/Cost-of-Owning-a-Car.aspx.
Victoria Car Share Co-op. 2015. http://victoriacarshare.ca.

The most significant difficulties facing the social housing sector of the social economy are financial. Societies are willing to consider a wide range of alternatives in their efforts to cope with decreases in subsidies, increases in overall operating costs, and the search for capital for new development. Indeed, the variety of governance and funding options available to non-profit housing providers is another potential strength of the social economy approach to providing social housing. The flexibility to adopt novel approaches to decision making or to access unconventional financial supports allows social economy organizations to be opportunistic, to respond to socio-economic trends, and to experiment with unconventional approaches to service delivery. This concept of experimentation is further developed by Jack Quarter, Laurie Mook, and Ann Armstrong (2009), who assert that the social economy can be viewed as a laboratory where the feasibility of innovative ideas is tested before those ideas are adopted by interests in the private sector. As summarized by Marie Bouchard (2011, 47), "The social economy plays an important role in solving new social problems with pioneering solutions, especially in the field of public services."

As part of BALTA's research on social housing (Svedova, Penfold, and Buczkowska 2009), a literature review was conducted to identify tools and strategies currently in use, primarily in North America and Europe, that could aid in strengthening the environmental and economic sustainability of social housing through improved collaboration among the public, private, and social economy sectors. The following points summarize the key strategies identified, as well as some of the most prominent discussion points found in the associated literature. No particular strategy or approach stood out as being more effective than others; rather, the relative strength of these approaches depends on a particular organization's circumstances and the specific skills of the individuals undertaking the initiative.

Contributions from Senior Levels of Government

Although the role of senior levels of government (federal and provincial) in providing financial support has declined over the past twenty years, it has not been eliminated, with the exception of support for new co-operative housing in Canada. Where senior government programs are available (e.g., CMHC's Affordable Housing Initiative and BC Housing's Community Partnership Initiatives), they are a key piece of the financial support puzzle. Without adequate government support, the role of the social economy in social housing provision becomes severely limited. However Van Wyk notes that: "current federal policy, which could be described as inadequate, ad hoc, and piecemeal; the availability of federal resources is also subject to time limits. This approach does not facilitate investing comprehensively, strategically, and over the long term to provide affordable housing." (2011b, 49)

    With this in mind, the organizations at the lowest risk of financial disruption due to changes in government funding programs may be those that provide services that have traditionally been thought of as the public domain. For this reason, social housing organizations with an expanded mandate that includes sectors like education or health may be better able to dependably access government funding sources.

Contributions from Foundations and Trusts

And important part of financial sustainability is direct contributions from individuals or businesses or contributions (sometimes including government funds) aggregated and distributed through community, regional, or province-wide trusts and foundations. In the latter case, funds are usually acquired through a competitive application process and are most relevant to capital projects (e.g., Real Estate Foundation BC, Vancity Community Foundation, Columbia Basin Trust). A recent example from British Columbia is the 2012 partnership between the Government of Canada, the Province of BC and the Columbia Basin Trust. This partnership resulted in a contribution of $10 million over three years to support affordable housing for low- to moderate-income households in the Columbia Basin region. To date, eight societies across the region are working in partnership with BC Housing to develop new affordable rental housing (BC Housing 2012).

Contributions from Volunteers and Residents

The use of volunteer labour can take many forms, including sweat equity (e.g., Habitat for Humanity, Self-Help Homeownership Opportunity Program [SHOP— USA]) or maintenance activities to reduce operational costs (e.g., co-op housing). This approach can be used to offset costs in situations where adequate volunteer skills and support are available. Some data suggest that rates of volunteerism may be higher in British Columbia than in other provinces, especially among smaller organizations (Restakis 2006). Given that smaller organizations characterize the social housing sector, these data suggest that social housing organizations in BC have access to a sizable pool of volunteer labour. As discussed above, however, reliance on volunteers presents several challenges for organizations with limited management capacity. It is also important to note that the contributions of volunteers more often than not cannot replace the work of paid staff; these two roles should be thought of as complementary (Handy, Mook, and Quarter 2008).

Collaboration to Achieve Common Goals

Many local social housing organizations are members of umbrella associations that offer leadership and support to their members in various forms, including research, training and capacity development, and professional support and advice. The BC Non-Profit Housing Association and the Co-operative Housing Federation of BC are two such organizations: both are active in advocacy, training, capacity development, research, and bulk purchasing. Many authors have found that the capacity of organizations to achieve their objectives is higher among those exhibiting strong partnerships, a benefit that can be attributed to the enhanced amount and diversity of human, social, and financial capital made available through these relationships (e.g., Loza 2004; Sanyal 2006).

Land Acquisition, Building, and Development Approaches

In developing new social housing projects, organizations have found various ways of reducing costs by acquiring land at below-market costs. Examples include surplus government lands, brownfield lands, foreclosure properties, and redevelopment properties. Properties can also be rezoned to higher density: some organizations have used rezoning to develop a portion of the property for market sales and then use the profits to subsidize housing projects on the rest of the property. Partnering with a land trust or municipality to get access to land at a nominal rental rate is also a useful strategy.

Affordable Housing and Community Land Trusts
Juanita Marois and Mike Gismondi

Community land trusts develop affordable housing by separating the two cost elements: the market price of the land and the price of the house itself. By removing the land from the market and placing it in a CLT, "the unearned equity resulting from escalating land values is taken out of the equation, to the benefit of low- and moderate-income households and the broader community. . . . By allowing for individuals to own equity in the housing itself (but not in the land), the incentive to maintain and enhance the quality of the housing is retained" (Lewis and Conaty 2012, 87).

A good North American example is the Irvine Community Land Trust (ICLT). In 2005, the average house price in Irvine, California, was $700,000. At the time, the City was facing the closure of a military base. City Council established a housing task force to address the looming affordable housing challenge. CLTs became the task force's core strategy, and the ICLT was created to pursue the City's goal of having 10 percent of the housing stock in Irvine permanently affordable by 2025. The ICLT is supported by affordable housing policies, including a zoning bylaw requiring all new developments to have an affordable housing component, with the option of paying a capital sum in lieu of doing the development on their own. The ICLT then uses this capital to develop and manage both rental and ownership units through ground leases and resale formulas.

The most recent development of the ICLT is the Doria Apartments, with 134 rental units for households earning various income levels—30, 45, and 60 percent of the area median income. Built by a non-profit developer, the complex incorporates a number of community elements, including Energy Star appliances, a tutoring lab and after-school care, a computer lab, and recreational facilities (U.S. Office of Policy Development and Research 2014). "Irvine is a wonderful city, anchored by a major university and home to 13,000 businesses and more than 100 national headquarters," said Mayor Beth Krom in an interview. "Our long-term success requires housing for the people who work in our city. It's that simple" (Jacobus and Brown 2007).

U.S. Office of Policy Development and Research. 2014. "Doria Apartments Adds to Irvine's Housing Spectrum." *The Edge*, 6 October. U.S. Department of Housing and Urban Development. http://www.huduser.org/portal/pdredge/pdr_edge_inpractice_100614.html.

Jacobus, Rick, and Michael Brown. 2007. "City Hall Steps In." *NHI Shelterforce Online* 149 (Spring). http://www.nhi.org/online/issues/149/cityhall.html.

Lewis, Mike, and Pat Conaty. 2012. *The Resilience Imperative: Cooperative Transitions to a Steady-State Economy*. Gabriola Island, BC: New Society Press.

Green Construction and Energy Retrofits

Savings can be realized by utilizing financing or capital cost offset programs for energy efficiency or other green initiatives in new or existing developments. This strategy is especially relevant in the current context, given the prominence of emissions reduction and energy security on the political agenda. Since most of the social housing stock in British Columbia is old and in need of repair, significant opportunity exists to implement such cost-saving measures in building construction and maintenance. Of course, social housing organizations face challenges in implementing green building strategies, including inadequate capital reserves to finance projects and a shortage of capacity to assess retrofit options for their suitability to individual developments (Tsenkova and Youssef 2011).

The Light House Sustainable Building Centre
Celia Lee and Mike Gismondi

The Light House sustainable building centre was founded in 2005. According to the centre's website, it is "dedicated to advancing green building and the sustainable infrastructure and economic systems into which green buildings are intrinsically integrated" (www.sustainable buildingcentre.com). The centre benefited early on from its networking with other social enterprises and from its partnership with the Simon Fraser University Centre for Sustainability. Light House's website describes the centre as "a not-for-profit company dedicated to advancing green building and the sustainable infrastructure and economic systems into which green buildings are intrinsically integrated" and outlines its mission as follows:

1. To be an information point of service on green building practices, policies, and projects as well as green building professionals.
2. To develop and deliver timely and relevant education, training and outreach that will foster a deeper awareness of and commitment to sustainable building practices.
3. To support and advance public sector programs and initiatives through research, development and implementation of tools and resources applicable to and optimized for construction and real estate industries.
4. To advocate for and catalyze the sustainable building sector.

Its educational programs, research, white papers, promotion of best construction practices, and effective networking and advocacy of sustainable building at all three levels of government and among industry players has helped fuel demand for its fee-based services. Light House has established itself as "a nationally recognized clearinghouse . . . for information on green building policy and practices" (The Light House Building Centre 2015). In July 2014, Light House joined the U.S. Department of Energy's Better Buildings Residential Network.

The scale of Light House's impact is both vertical and horizontal. It has been strategic in catalyzing changes at the municipal government level and at the level of provincial building codes, as well as advocating at national and international forums on building sustainability indicators and life-cycle analysis. At the same time, their work with contractors and construction trades is unique, and aims at changing construction management practices and greening the everyday unsustainable building practices widely accepted by construction trades.

The Light House Building Centre. 2015. http://www.sustainablebuildingcentre. com/.

Social Enterprise

Some non-profits use social enterprise to generate revenue to support social housing projects. These enterprise activities can also be linked to employment support and skills development for the residents (e.g., Habitat for Humanity and ReStore, Fernwood Neighborhood Resource Group and the Cornerstone Cafe, Atira Women's Resource Society, and Atira Property Management). However, Van Wyk (2011b) cautions against the expectation that social enterprise strategies can lead to financial independence among social housing providers. These organizations are primarily serving clients with little or no material resources—their ability to generate a profit that can be recycled to cover the expense of operation and growth may therefore be limited. Ray Hudson (2009) also describes tensions that arise when social economy organizations are driven to compete in the mainstream economy, especially when the nature of their enterprising activities is in conflict with the original mandate of the organization.

Vertical and Horizontal Partnerships and Alliances

The nature of the relationship between the social economy and the public and private sectors is dynamic, and no sector can be fully understood independently from another (Quarter, Mook, and Armstrong 2009; Restakis 2006). Partnerships with the private sector and with non-market actors such as municipalities and trusts are an emerging strategy among social economy organizations. Those alliances can range from long-term relationships in which goods and services are exchanged for promotion or fulfillment of ethical plans or policies to partnerships that involve the private sector in development activities directly. For example, in support of Habitat for Humanity, Sleep Country acts as a broker for donated mattresses, and Whirlpool Corporation has donated labour, appliances, and cash. In Red Deer, Alberta, Convent Park, a ninety-five-unit affordable housing development, is the fifth joint venture between P&S Investments, a private development company, and the Canadian Mental Health Association. Anita Van Wyk and Ron Van Wyk (2011a, 26) emphasize the value of cross-sectoral partnerships: "Collaboration involving the social economy, the public sector, and the private sector facilitates community participation, brings about service integration, and bolsters social support, all of which contributes to housing affordability and thus increases housing stability."

While the development of adequate and sustainable social housing in Canada faces major hurdles, the need for such housing is growing, especially with respect to housing for seniors, rent-subsidized housing for low-income earners, transitional housing, and housing for the homeless. Given the current political and economic climate, with continuing fiscal constraints both federally and provincially, it is unlikely that federal or provincial governments will increase their funding of or direct participation in social housing initiatives. Increasingly, the responsibility is shifting to communities and social economy organizations to address social housing needs.

In the BC context, the social economy deals with a number of ongoing challenges related to the increasing demand for social services, such as human resource management, sourcing and effective training and use of volunteers, and organizational development and planning. Additional obstacles faced by social economy housing organizations include maintaining current maintenance and operation standards as costs increase and aggregating capital or acquiring alternative capital assets for new affordable housing development. These challenges tend to be more prevalent in rural areas since social economy actors there are generally smaller in scale, have less capacity, and are more geographically isolated from each other and their umbrella organizations. Responses to these challenges are evolving, but at this point, the responses are isolated to individual cases and are not systemic.

The mandate and scope of a housing organization, and its target group of residents, significantly impact the organization's approach to financial sustainability. For example, because of specialized client needs, organizations providing supportive housing (e.g., for seniors) may have less capacity for additional revenue-generating activities and more limitations in using approaches involving volunteer resident contributions. Organizations are constrained by the legal and policy contexts of the regions in which they operate, or by the terms of their own charter. In addition, local bylaws may present obstacles by, for example, precluding a social enterprise in an area zoned for residential use. A significant barrier to land development and/or resale is the lack of financing mechanisms available to such organizations to finance their initial purchase. Traditional banks play little or no role in enabling the financing of initiatives, but credit unions are willing to work with individual organizations on solutions to their specific financing needs. In many cases, innovative approaches that have been implemented in terms of financing, infrastructure, or human resource management are the result of the initiative of one individual in the organization who championed the approach. Without such a champion, these initiatives may not occur. Undertaking innovative approaches often involves significant risk and additional work, as well as significant amounts of unpaid time, all of which has implications both for the organization and for the champion.

Partnerships with public sector actors, such as municipalities in the form of long-term leases of municipally owned land for affordable housing initiatives, are increasingly a part of innovative solutions. However, since alliances between social housing organizations and the private sector are still relatively rare, there is a general lack of experience, resources, and support in terms of managing such partnerships. More research showing how these arrangements work in different contexts could help to fill this gap. That research should include a close examination of the perspective of private sector partners and their challenges in dealing with financing, approvals, and co-management of the design and development process. It should also be noted that the opportunities for partnerships with private developers are often very limited in slow- or no-growth rural areas since few private firms are involved in large-scale development in those areas.

Many of the strategies outlined in the preceding section—such as sharing of services, volunteer management, and land trusts—require a regional-scale response. There are few operating models of regional initiatives related to these solutions in the BC context. Again, research showing how these arrangements work in other jurisdictions could help. Unfortunately, there is an inherent bias in programs and political culture toward "community-based," rather than regional, affordable housing solutions. This is a particular challenge for smaller rural communities. The umbrella organizations such as the BC Non-Profit Housing Association and the Co-operative Housing Federation do, in part, address the need for a regional response, but they could consider expanding their commitment of resources to address this issue.

A clearer portrait of social economy players in the housing field needs to be developed in Canada. The sector is very diverse in terms of scale, target clients, and range of services offered in addition to housing. According to a study conducted by Canada Mortgage and Housing Corporation (2005), organizations serving high-risk clients are more financially stable, which suggests that "crossover" solutions based on services other than housing may have some potential, but this has not been well investigated. Creating a social enterprise has the potential for a non-profit organization both to generate social impact and to provide an independent source of funding. Establishing and operating an entrepreneurial venture, however, requires tremendous commitment and capacity that not all organizations possess (Svedova, Penfold, and Buczkowska 2009).

Social Capital Partners recently evaluated the performance of five social enterprises in which they have invested (Social Capital Partners 2004–2008). In financial terms, three of the five organizations evaluated were generating a net loss, one is generating a profit of just over $35,000, and one is generating a profit of over $100,000. This latter organization, Atira Property Management Inc. (APMI), experienced rapid growth: in 2008, six years after its inception, it achieved annual sales of $1 million, but that same year, it generated a net profit of only $35,314. This profit represents only about 2 percent of the parent society's operating budget. The long-term potential of social enterprises to be an effective means to financial sustainability is not clear; however, the social impact of the enterprises evaluated was undisputed among the individuals interviewed for this study. For example, most of the 230 APMI employees were previously unemployed and lived in Vancouver's Downtown Eastside (BALTA, 2010).

In spite of the challenges outlined in this chapter, the social economy will continue to be the major delivery agent for affordable social housing in British Columbia into the foreseeable future. Societies; federal, provincial, and local levels of government; and foundations and trusts need to work together to address these challenges if non-profit and co-operative organizations are to continue to play a significant and successful role in providing housing and related services to those in need of them.

REFERENCES

BALTA. 2010. "Sustainable Management of Housing by Not-for Profit and Co-operative Organizations in Response to Decreasing Government Funded Programs." Final Report prepared for BALTA by Jana Svedova, George Penfold, and Joanna Buczkowska and Sauder School of Business. http://auspace.athabascau.ca/handle/2149/2755.

BC Housing. 2010. *Housing Matters, Annual Report 2009/10*. Burnaby. http://www.bchousing.org/resources/About%20BC%20Housing/Annual%20Reports/2010/2009-10_AR.pdf.

———. 2011. *Housing Matters, Annual Report 2010/11*. Burnaby. http://www.bchousing.org/resources/About%20BC%20Housing/Annual%20Reports/2011/2010-11_AR.pdf.

———. 2012. "New Affordable Housing Initiative for the Columbia Basin." http://www.bchousing.org/Media/NR/2012/03/20/5590_1203201427-597.

———. 2013. *Housing Matters, Annual Report 2012/13*. Burnaby. http://www.bchousing.
org/resources/About%20BC%20Housing/Annual%20Reports/2013/2012-13-
Annual-Report.pdf.

BCNPHA (BC Non-profit Housing Association). 2009. "Basics of the Non-profit
Housing Sector in BC." Vancouver: BCNPHA. http://www.bcnpha.ca/media/
Research/np%20sector%20basics.pdf.

———. 2010. "Asset Analysis Project." Vancouver: BCNPHA. http://www.bcnpha.ca/
pages/research/the-asset-analysis-project.php.

———. 2011. "Staffing in BC's Non-Profit Housing Sector." Vancouver: BCNPHA. http://
www.bcnpha.ca/media/Research/Staffing%20in%20BCs%20Non-Profit%20
Housing%20Sector.pdf.

BC Real Estate Foundation. 2008. "Kootenay Area Social Housing Stock." http://www.
cbrdi.ca/rdi-resources/kootenay-area-social-housing-stock-marchapril-2008/.

BC Stats. 2014. "British Columbia Multiple Listing Statistics." Victoria: BC Stats.
http://www.bcstats.gov.bc.ca/Files/bf9f1438-815f-410b-8211-1a90683b8ed4/
MultipleListingStatistics.pdf.

Bouchard, Marie J. 2011. "Social Innovation, an Analytical Grid for Understanding the
Social Economy: The Example of the Québec Housing Sector." *Service Business* 6
(1): 47–59.

CHF BC (Co-op Housing Federation BC). N.d. "Co-op Programs." Co-op Housing
Federation BC. http://www.chf.bc.ca/what-co-op-housing/co-op-programs.

Curran, Deborah, and Tim Wake. 2008. *Creating Market and Non-Market Affordable
Housing: A Smart Growth Toolkit for BC Municipalities*. Vancouver: Smart Growth
BC.

Handy, Femida, Laurie Mook, and Jack Quarter. 2008. "The Interchangeability of Paid
Staff and Volunteers in Nonprofit Organizations." *Nonprofit and Voluntary Sector
Quarterly* 37 (1): 76–92.

Hudson, Ray. 2009. "Life on the Edge: Navigating the Competitive Tensions Between
the 'Social' and the 'Economic' in the Social Economy and in Its Relations to the
Mainstream." *Journal of Economic Geography* 9 (4): 493–510.

Hulchanski, J. David. 1997. "The Economics of Rental Housing Supply and Rent
Decontrol in Ontario." Presentation to the Ontario Legislature Standing Committee
on General Government Hearings on Bill 96, Residential Tenancies. 26 June.
http://www.urbancentre.utoronto.ca/pdfs/researchassociates/Hulchanski_Ont-
Leg_Economic.pdf.

———. 2005. "Rethinking Canada's Affordable Housing Challenge." Toronto: Centre for
Urban and Community Studies, University of Toronto. http://www.urbancentre.
utoronto.ca/pdfs/elibrary/Hulchanski-Housing-Affd-pap.pdf.

Klein, Seth, and Lorraine Copas. 2010. "Unpacking the Housing Numbers: How
Much New Social Housing is BC Building? Key Findings." Vancouver/Burnaby:
Canadian Centre for Policy Alternatives, BC Office/Social Planning and Research

Council of BC. http://www.policyalternatives.ca/sites/default/files/uploads/
publications/2010/09/CCPA-BC-SPARC-Unpacking-Housing-Numbers.pdf.

Loza, Jehan. 2004. "Business-Community Partnerships: The Case for Community
Organization Capacity Building." *Journal of Business Ethics* 53: 297–311.

Luffman, Jacqueline. 2006. "Measuring Housing Affordability." *Perspectives on Labour
and Income* 7 (11): 16–25.

Marason Management. 2004. *Sustaining the Non-profit Housing Sector in British
Columbia.* In partnership with the BC Non-profit Housing Association; submitted
to CMHC. http://www.bcnpha.ca/media/documents/SustainNP.pdf.

Murray, Carol, and Rebecca Pearson. 2008. "Innovative Uses of Co-operative Housing
Assets: A BALTA Research Project." Port Alberni, BC: BC-Alberta Social Economy
Research Alliance.

Neamtan, Nancy. 2005. "The Social Economy: Finding a Way Between the Market and
the State." *Policy Options* (July–August): 71–76.

Patterson, Michelle, Julian M. Somers, Karen McIntosh, Alan Shiell, and Charles
James Frankish. 2008. *Housing and Support for Adults with Severe Addictions and/
or Mental Illness in British Columbia.* Vancouver: Centre for Applied Research
in Mental Health and Addiction, Simon Fraser University. http://www.sfu.ca/
content/dam/sfu/carmha/resources/hsami/Housing-SAMI-BC-FINAL-PD.pdf.

Quarter, Jack, and Laurie Mook. 2010. "An Interactive View of the Social Economy."
Canadian Journal of Nonprofit and Social Economy Research (Fall): 8–22.

Quarter, Jack, Laurie Mook, and Ann Armstrong. 2009. *Understanding the Social
Economy: A Canadian Perspective.* Toronto: University of Toronto Press.

Restakis, John. 2006. "Defining the Social Economy: The BC Context." Paper
prepared for the BC Social Economy Roundtable, January. http://www.msvu.ca/
socialeconomyatlantic/pdfs/DefiningSocialEconomy_FnlJan1906.pdf.

Sanyal, Paromita. 2006. "Capacity Building Through Partnership: Intermediary
Nongovernmental Organizations as Local and Global Actors." *Non-profit and
Voluntary Sector Quarterly* 35 (1): 66–82.

Schuk, Carla. 2009. *Overcoming Challenges in Centralized and Decentralized Housing
Models: Ontario and British Columbia Compared.* CPRN Research Report,
December. Ottawa: Canadian Policy Research Networks and Social Housing
Services Corporation. http://www.cprn.org/documents/51971_EN.pdf.

Sealy, Patricia, and Paul C. Whitehead. 2004. "Forty Years of Deinstitutionalization of
Psychiatric Services in Canada: An Empirical Assessment." *Canadian Journal of
Psychiatry* 49 (4): 249–57.

Smith, Steven, and Michael Lipsky. 1993. *Nonprofits for Hire: The Welfare State in the
Age of Contracting.* Cambridge, MA: Harvard University Press.

Social Capital Partners. 2004–2008. SROI Reports. http://www.socialcapitalpartners.
ca/index.php/portfolio/sroi-reports.

Statistics Canada. 2008 "Median age and variation of median age for economic
regions, British Columbia, July 1, 2004 and 2014." http://www.statcan.gc.ca/
pub/91-214-x/2015000/tbl/tbl210-eng.htm.

———. 2011. "NHS Profile 2011." National Household Survey. Ottawa: Statistics Canada.
http://www12.statcan.gc.ca/nhs-enm/2011/dp-pd/prof/index.cfm?Lang=E.

Svedova, Jana, George Penfold, and Joanna Buczkowska. 2009. "Approaches to
Financially Sustainable Provision of Affordable Housing by Not-for-Profit
Organizations and Co-operatives: Perspectives from Canada, the USA, and
Europe." Centre for Sustainability and Social Innovation, Sauder School of
Business, UBC http://auspace.athabascau.ca/handle/2149/2757

Tsenkova, Sasha, and Karim Youssef. 2011. "Green and Affordable Housing in
Canada: Investment Strategies of Social Housing Organisations." Presentation by
University of British Columbia, on behalf of BC-Alberta Social Economy Research
Alliance. Paper presented at the 23rd annual conference of the European Network
for Housing Research, 5–8 July, Toulouse. http://www.enhr2011.com/sites/default/
files/Paper-SashaTsenkova-W11.pdf.

Van Wyk , Anita, and Ron van Wyk. 2011a. "Affordable Housing and the Social
Economy in the Fraser Valley Regional District." Port Alberni, BC: BC-
Alberta Social Economy Research Alliance. http://auspace.athabascau.ca/
bitstream/2149/3177/1/BALTA%20A6%20-%20Fraser%20Valley%20Affordable%20
Housing.pdf.

Van Wyk , Anita, and Ron van Wyk. 2011b. *Homeless in the Fraser Valley: Report
on the 2011 Fraser Valley Regional District Homelessness Survey*. Chilliwack,
BC: Fraser Valley Regional District. http://www.fvrd.bc.ca/InsidetheFVRD/
RegionalPlanning/Documents/Housing/Final%20FVRD%20Homeless%20Report.
pdf.

Volunteer Canada. 2013. *Building the Bridge for Volunteer Engagement*. Ottawa:
Volunteer Canada. https://volunteer.ca/content/building-bridge-ii-full-report.

Wenmann, Christine. 2009. *The Financial State of British Columbia's Non-profit
Housing Stock: Current and Emerging Opportunities*. Vancouver: BC Non-
profit Housing Association. http://www.bcnpha.ca/media/Research/The%20
Financial%20State%20of%20British%20Columbiarsquos%20Non-profit%20
Housing%20Stock%20Sept%202009.pdf.

8

Land Tenure Innovations for Sustainable Communities

Marena Brinkhurst and Mark Roseland

Communities everywhere, including those in urban landscapes, are underpinned by layers of formal and informal property rights and land tenure arrangements. Land tenure arrangements exert surprising influences on land use and development in industrialized nations, influences that become particularly apparent when the interests of private-property owners conflict with those of the wider community. Given that community land-use planning involves identifying and supporting both individual and community-development goals, it must often contend with conflict between individual and collective interests. Increasingly, collective interests in environmental and social sustainability are facing opposition from private interests. At the local level, those advocating for the public interest often find themselves in a contest with the owners of private property.

Our research focuses on the role that land tenure innovations and new forms of ownership could play in resolving conflict between private interests and community sustainability. In this chapter, after reviewing several models of land tenure innovation, we consider the possibility that local governments could support these innovations and assess the effectiveness and feasibility of this option in the context of sustainable planning in Canadian communities. On the basis of this assessment, we turn our attention to land readjustment, voluntary easements, and community land trusts. A number of land tenure innovations and alternative land ownership arrangements have the potential to be useful to local governments and planners, but much uncertainty exists regarding the use of such tools. While this review examines already recognized alternative tenure arrangements, it encourages further investigation of other, less familiar forms of shared tenure, as well as the question of how local governments, or perhaps other actors, can use and support these as tools for sustainable community development.

BACKGROUND AND RATIONALE

A vast literature exists concerning the nature of private land ownership, its advantages and weaknesses, and its protection or reform. A comprehensive review is not within our scope, but for clarity and justification, we define the key terms and explain the need for examining the role of land ownership arrangements in planning for sustainable communities. Land tenure refers to the arrangement of the "rights and obligations of the holder" (Bruce 1998, 1). There are many forms of land tenure that can be contained within any given land tenure system, ranging from private control to leasehold, shared common land, or state-controlled lands. Different land tenure arrangements are often illustrated as a "bundle of rights" because specific rights over land can be combined to create different degrees of control. For example, an individual may have the right to use or access a piece of land but lack the right to manage it or sell it. Lai (2006, 74) explains private property ownership as a bundle of rights that includes (1) an exclusive right to use the resource; (2) an exclusive right to derive any income from the resource; and (3) the exclusive right to alienate, combine, and divide the first and second rights. To this may also be added the exclusive and effective right to manage the use of the resource (Schlager and Ostrom 1992).

As James Karp (1993, 741) observes, the existence of private property limits the government's "ability to promote the public good," and for this reason, the institution produces "an unrelenting tension . . . between the protection of an individual's private property and the fostering of community rights." Public agencies or governments are typically involved in land tenure systems through protecting property rights and also through land-use management responsibilities. Land management by public agencies can take many forms; however, in urban communities, and for the purpose of this chapter, the role of the public agency is considered to be through planning, specifically through regulation of land use and development. Arno Segeren and colleagues (2007, 10) classify government approaches to planning as either "passive"—that is, based on rules that restrict and regulate individual actions—or "(pro-)active," in the sense that government is "actively involved in working with the land owner to change the land use." This active involvement can entail: encouragement of certain actions or investments; provision of information or financial help to land owners; coordination the actions of land owners; or construction of public infrastructure that influences how land owners decide to use their land (Segeren et al. 2007, 10). Planning in Canada is the jurisdiction of provincial and local governments, which generally use largely passive planning methods (Grant 2008, 339).

In contemporary North American communities, planning is increasingly focused on promoting development that is proactively sustainable in terms of economics, society, and the environment (Roseland 2012). Within the growing literature on sustainable development and community planning, attention is turning to the institutional factors that shape the challenges to and supports for sustainable development, including the design of land tenure systems (Godschalk 2004; Staley 2006a; Williamson et al. 2009). Land tenure systems have always passively shaped land-use planning, but there is renewed interest in how to use that influence more actively in order to encourage the development of sustainable urban communities (Ho 2006, Ingerson 1997; Staley 2006a, 2006b). Many researchers and planners now stress that patterns of land ownership and the structure of property rights should be integral to any community planning strategy (Buitelaar and Needham 2007) and that there is great potential for innovations in land tenure that would support sustainability goals (Heisler 2009; Lai 2006; Roseland 2006).

DOES PRIVATE LAND OWNERSHIP WEAKEN PLANNING FOR SUSTAINABLE COMMUNITIES?

Private land ownership is accompanied by many community benefits, such as the creation of incentives for private land management and protection of land values, participation in land-management processes, and innovative resource use (Gilbert, Sandberg, and Wekerle 2009; Lai 2006). In fact, many researchers argue that private property systems can support sustainability goals, sometimes more effectively than government initiatives (Buitelaar and Needham 2007; Karp 1993). In addition, in the context of North America, private property interests are well entrenched and protected by law, which means that any planning initiative must respect individuals' property rights (Grant 2008, 339). While these factors should not be discounted or overlooked, many researchers also argue that private land ownership, as currently understood and legally defined, frequently results in obstacles to community sustainability (Blomley 2008; Daniels 2009; Godschalk 2004; Lee and Webster 2006; Staley 2006a).

These barriers can include: resistance from land owners against environmental regulations or sustainability initiatives, such as building high-density urban centers around public transit infrastructure (Godschalk 2004, 10); competition between local governments "to expand their property tax bases, often at the expense of environmental quality and social cohesion" (Daniels 2009, 190–191); private control over lands critical for achieving sustainable development goals (Roseland 2006, 10–11); or the enclosure of the urban commons or shared/unclaimed property, which are often used by economically disadvantaged residents of a city (Blomley 2008, 322, 326; Lee and Webster 2006, 29). A variety of tools are used to address many of these challenges, such as changes in tax policy (Löhr 2010, 75–77) or provision of public parks and infrastructure. However, government-led sustainability initiatives may appear to be at odds with interests of private property owners and can face stiff opposition if imposed. This leads us to ask, are there other mechanisms that might be more effective?

USING MARKET MECHANISMS TO ADDRESS MARKET FAILURES

Local governments have found that some market mechanisms can be used to guide, reward, monitor, and penalize private sector involvement in planning decisions and development projects. Roseland (2006) suggests that new approaches are needed to orient these influences toward sustainable community development:

> In order to achieve specific land-use planning goals, there is a need for more flexible economic evaluation processes and a broader range of market-based approaches than currently exist. These new approaches need to be responsive not only to the market but also to proactive community participation, since local social structures are powerful forces in the determination of urban processes.
>
> Community economic development and social economy approaches are two means of working toward sustainable development at the community level: that is, sustainable community development (SCD). To fulfill the potential contributions of SCD initiatives to community planning, the private sector must engage with proposals and initiatives that advance sustainability. In most cases, however, we are missing a market actor to function in this capacity.

SCD requires that we go beyond the notion that land is a mere commodity. Even in conventional economic terms, land is a peculiar commodity in that its supply cannot increase, no matter how high the price. Roseland (2006) explains the implications of this for SCD:

As demand for land grows, the wealth of landowners tends to grow regardless of how well or how badly they use the land. In his 1879 classic, *Progress and Poverty*, Henry George proposed a solution to this dilemma: taxing the value of land produced by anything other than private efforts. Such a land-value tax would keep private landowners from unfairly capturing the benefits of natural resources, desirable locations, and public services. George also believed that this tax would force landowners either to put their land to its "highest and best" use themselves or to make it accessible to someone who would. While such comprehensive public approaches are essential, it is clear that other complementary and nimble approaches must be developed and employed as well. The market works well enough (beautifully, some would say) for private purposes, but when we are talking about the common good, its failings become readily apparent. While the land market generally functions well for individual property owners, it responds to price signals that reflect conventional understandings of "highest and best" use. Therefore, if left solely to its own devices, the market will substitute financial capital for other forms of capital, resulting in such actions as converting agricultural land to shopping centres (depleting natural capital) or developing on sacred sites (depleting cultural capital). Its more egregious failings will be rectified by protected area designations, parks, agricultural land reserves, and so on. However . . . there are more subtle market failures that have a huge impact on community sustainability—for example, by influencing the amount of private (automobile) versus public transportation or the amount of local employment and wealth creation versus economic leakage.

Roseland (2006) further argues that while,

> sustainability requires comprehensive public sector engagement with regard to factors such as planning, taxation, and services, it also requires complementary private sector approaches that are more entrepreneurial. Unless they are big players worrying about reputation management, private sector actors do not generally concern themselves much with the common good, since the return on investing for the common good is rarely as high as the return on investing to maximize profit. If the market sent the right signals (e.g., through shifting to green taxes, carbon taxes, etc.), we could expect more sustainability-oriented private initiatives, and therefore, that type of policy shift is an extremely critical public agenda item. However, waiting for the day when the tax system rewards sustainable behaviour could be a very long wait, and in the meantime, we are rapidly losing

natural and other forms of capital (e.g., ecologically and culturally significant parcels of land) to unsustainable development.

We therefore need a private actor with a sustainability outlook to use
market approaches for the common good. Since the public sector does not
seem to have the necessary resources, inclination, or will to strengthen
community capital for sustainable development, we need to develop an
actor who does have those qualities. Such an actor would quietly, quickly,
and aggressively seek to control strategically significant land for sustainable
purposes using market mechanisms (e.g., ownership).

While no such actor has yet appeared on the local stage, we have some valuable
social economy models that we can learn from, as discussed below.

CAN LAND TENURE INNOVATIONS HELP ADDRESS SUSTAINABILITY CHALLENGES?

Given the negative influences that private land ownership can have on government-led efforts to plan and develop sustainable communities, attention
should be directed toward ways of addressing or overcoming these challenges.
Conventionally, discord between private and public interests is addressed through
passive planning tools such as land-use regulation, zoning, bylaws, or development controls, and occasionally through active planning tools such as offering
incentives for developments perceived to be in the public interest. However,
these tools have limitations, and their effectiveness at promoting sustainable
development is sometimes questionable (Booth and Skelton 2011; Buitelaar and
Needham 2007; Grant 2008; Hodge and Gordon 2008; Roseland 2012). In addition, as James Karp (1993, 744) explains, "piecemeal chipping away at private
property interests by state and local governments through layer upon layer of
land use regulations to protect the environment seems only to have antagonized
individuals into strong anti-government feelings." One proposed alternative to
conventional planning tools is land tenure innovation. Forms of land ownership
other than private or public property arrangements, as well as tools that modify
or regulate tenure arrangements, might offer ways to ameliorate the conflicts
between public and private interests concerning land and thus to support community sustainability.

Nelson, British Columbia: Market Failure and Community Sustainability

Mark Roseland and Marena Brinkhurst

In 2001, a 1.1-hectare parcel of lakefront property located on the central waterfront of Nelson, BC, was placed on the market by BC Buildings Corporation. Some of the proposed bids for the property included developing the land for big-box retail purposes. A group of local residents recognized the significance of this property, not only for its value as a prime development site but also for its ability to influence the design and function of future development on Nelson's waterfront as a whole. Ultimately, the group was successful in purchasing the property, and their purpose as owners was not to develop the land themselves, but to ensure its development in accordance with a long-term vision compatible with community values and Nelson's Official Community Plan (City of Nelson 2015).

City of Nelson. 2015. "Sustainable Waterfront and Downtown Master Plan." http://www.nelson.ca/EN/main/services/planning-building-services/ community-planning/current-planning-projects/sustainable-waterfront-and- downtown-master-plan.html.

In her comprehensive review of alternative land tenure models, Karen Heisler (2009, 3) defines land tenure innovations as arrangements that redefine the rights associated with land tenure" and adopt "specific practices to work within or around the traditional land tenure system." Heisler's review explores specific examples of land tenure innovations and changes to existing land ownership to explain how such strategies can be used to support environmental, social, and economic goals. The examples and strategies considered provide evidence that land tenure innovations can advance the goals of community sustainability, and yet land tenure and ownership have not been widely used as leverage points by local governments or planners. Reasons for this may include a lack of awareness of land tenure alternatives and changes, public opposition or reluctance to change property rights arrangements, limited legal or administrative feasibility, or perceived ineffectiveness, as is seen in several of the approaches reviewed.

While land tenure innovations may not yet be commonplace, they still raise important questions for local governments and planners. As Alice Ingerson (1997, 3) points out, "experiments with property rights and responsibilities raise questions that few researchers . . . have yet addressed. For example, should local and state officials help to remove regulatory barriers to group ownership of land, or support new criteria for mortgage financing of group-owned land?" Following Ingerson, our work conducts a preliminary evaluation of various land tenure and sustainability strategies, their feasibility and effectiveness, and potential roles for local government within the context of Canadian communities.

MODIFICATIONS TO URBAN LAND TENURE: EXAMPLES AND PRECEDENTS

Analysis of academic and community-produced research yields a wide range of examples of policies, planning tools, and grassroots initiatives that modify urban land tenure, ranging from coercive to voluntary and from large-scale to site-specific. In this section, strategies and examples deemed relevant to the context of Canadian communities are synthesized into three categories, following the classifications proposed by Segeren et al. (2007) and Gerber et al. (2009).

Changing the Distribution of Private Property and/or the Provision of Land

The first three approaches that we explore—land swaps, land banking, and land readjustments—involve a local government facilitating or forcing changes to the distribution of private land holdings. Note that land expropriation and forcible land redistribution are not included, since neither is considered relevant to this chapter given their limited use in the context of contemporary Canadian communities, except for major infrastructure projects (Gerber et al. 2009).

Public-private land swaps. In a land swap (or land exchange), a local government trades a parcel of public land for a privately owned parcel in order to further an economic, social, or environmental goal. The use of a land swap to reach a community sustainability goal is based on "the fundamental belief . . . that government ownership will provide greater protection for environmentally sensitive lands" (Hanna et al. 2007, 344) and will be more effective at advancing social, economic, or environmental goals than the private land market.

Kevin Hanna and colleagues (2007) provide an example of a successful land swap used to further sustainable planning goals. In the rapid-growth setting of the Greater Toronto Area (GTA), efforts to protect the environmentally sensitive Oak

Ridges Moraine included a land exchange. Property owners negatively affected by the area's conservation plan, which included "development firms and speculators," were compensated by exchanging their land in the moraine area for parcels of provincial land in another area on the edge of the GTA (Hanna et al. 2007, 344). In a similar case, the City of Saint John, New Brunswick, developed a policy to exchange city-owned lands for privately owned parcels within the city's two watersheds, with the intention of providing better protection for environmentally sensitive and ecologically valuable watershed lands through municipal ownership (Chilibeck 2009).

Land swaps have also been used by cities seeking to secure strategic locations for municipal infrastructure or facilities. For example, the City of Snellville, Georgia, negotiated a land swap in 2000 in order to secure a privately owned abandoned supermarket so as to renovate it into a municipal complex. The goal of this land swap was to "revitalize vacant retail space" and the city centre, while also addressing concerns that the abandoned big-box store was decreasing the value of neighbouring properties (Ippolitto 2000). While land swaps are currently used by municipalities in North America, they are not always feasible: the local government may lack suitable lands to exchange, the area sought may be extremely valuable and therefore difficult to acquire, or there may be pronounced public opposition.

Public land banking. As described by Heisler (2009, 34), land banking is "a systematic acquisition of often large pieces of land, normally land that is pre-development." Both public and private sector actors can practice land banking, but for the purpose of this chapter, only acquisition and banking of previously private lands by local governments is considered. Land banking provides a way for local governments to remove parcels of land from private ownership and "control the market speculation and development of land" in order to provide for the public interest, such as "to provide public services, control urban sprawl or provide affordable housing" (34). The local government can choose to develop these lands itself or to allow other developers to use the land while retaining ownership and ultimate control of the land (Segeren et al. 2007).

Heisler's land tenure literature review identifies a spike of research interest in public land banking in the 1970s and 1980s, followed by a sharp decline as direct government interference in land markets fell out of favour. However, Heisler urges further, contemporary research into this model because of its effectiveness at securing land, an aspect of land tenure innovation that can prove challenging for other approaches.

An example of public land banking is the City of Vancouver's Property Endowment Fund (PEF), created by City Council in 1975 to hold and administer all the City's long-term land holdings, apart from park lands and those intended for municipal purposes in the near term (Antrim 2011; City of Vancouver 2004). The PEF functions to generate revenue for the City and "support the City's public objectives" (City of Vancouver 2004). While the PEF draws opposition from private developers, it is justified on the basis that "citizens should share in the profits from any increase in land value" rather than transferring that benefit to private interests (Davis, n.d.). The PEF model has been widely admired by other municipalities, including the nearby City of Langley, which proposed the creation of a similar entity (Claxton 2011).

Land readjustment. Land readjustment (also known as land pooling, replotting, reassembly, parcellation, or repartition) is a legal instrument for facilitating the redevelopment of land that has been fragmented into many private parcels. It is frequently used internationally—the Japanese term is *kukaki seiri*, the German is *Umlegung*—but lacks extensive recognition in much of the English-speaking world (Home 2007, 459). Landowners in a targeted area who stand to benefit from redevelopment "transfer voluntarily and at existing use value the property rights over land . . . temporarily to the municipality" in order to facilitate redevelopment (Van der Krabben and Needham 2008, 661). The land parcels are temporarily pooled together and then, based on the original agreement, re-divided among the original owners following development, with the municipality retaining ownership over land that the various parties agreed could be dedicated to public use.

Land readjustment can be used to support sustainable community development in instances when existing land patterns present obstacles to projects, such as public transportation networks, or when the costs of a redevelopment cannot be fully borne by the local government. Robert Home (2007, 463) suggests several potential applications of land readjustment, including the following:

- Town expansion into peri-urban areas of fragmented ownership that lack planning or infrastructure
- Multi-level or vertical replotting of urban areas to achieve higher densities
- Regeneration sites within urban areas where land assembly may be difficult
- Antiquated subdivisions where smaller plot sizes or higher densities are sought

- Environmental protection areas (such as coastal regions or waterfronts where, for instance, a rearrangement of frontage ownerships is sought)

Joachim Thomas (2011) highlights the use of land readjustment in rural development projects to ensure that land is used efficiently and waste of land is prevented, and Ling-Hin Li and Xin Li (2007) describe the application of land readjustment to urban renewal projects in China. Land readjustment also has potential in the underdeveloped areas around railway stations: these areas are central to urban intensification and redevelopment goals, but their redevelopment is plagued by obstacles when undertaken exclusively by a private or public redeveloper (Van der Krabben and Needham 2008).

For development projects that require land assembly, land readjustment provides an alternative to purchase by a public entity (voluntary or compulsory). Instead, land readjustment facilitates redevelopment by combining and reparcelling land, and sharing financial costs and benefits of redevelopment between landowners and the development agency, which is often the local government (Home 2007). This approach has several advantages over the public purchase of lands, especially when public funds are limited or when neighbouring landowners stand to benefit substantially from public interest developments (Home 2007; Van der Krabben and Needham 2008).[1]

Legal Redefinition or Modification of the Institution of Property

Legal redefinition or modification strategies involve either legal changes to the scope, value, and/or content of private property arrangements (Gerber et al. 2009) or the legal creation of new forms of property. Of the many approaches that fall within this category, we will consider two here: transferable development rights and shared-ownership arrangements established in law. Worthy of mention, however, is the modification of the institution of property through regulatory tools that are familiar to planners, such as building standards, bylaws, zoning, and development controls (Gerber et al. 2009). All of these tools modify, restrict, or specify aspects of the bundle of rights attached to private land ownership. In this sense, local governments routinely shape and modify the institution of private property in their locale by determining what uses of land and property rights are permissible (Segeren et al. 2007). Since these tools are already well used by local governments and planners, the focus here is on two less familiar approaches.

---

1 See Home (2007) for details on the process of land readjustment using an applied example.

Transferable development rights. Transferable development rights (TDRs), also referred to as tradable or purchasable development rights, is probably one of the more familiar land tenure innovations reviewed in this chapter. While conventionally used as a tool to "shift density potential from one area to another" in terms of building envelopes and density measures, TDRs are increasingly being used as an innovative tool for agricultural land preservation and ecological planning (Hodge and Gordon 2008, 266, 345). Using TDRs involves detaching the right to develop lands within a designated "sending area" and allowing that right to be traded with other landowners within a designated "receiving area" (Curtis et al. 2008). If landowners within a receiving area desire to develop their lands beyond what is permitted by zoning or density controls, they can purchase TDRs from landowners in the sending area. The lands that have their associated TDRs sold are no longer developable; this ban on development is typically passed on to new owners through deed restrictions or easements (Hanly-Forde et al. 2014). By redirecting development away from rural or undeveloped land, TDRs can support urban intensification goals and agricultural or ecological land conservation (Hanly-Forde et al. 2014; Stoms et al. 2009).

Shared-ownership arrangements established in law. Jean-David Gerber and colleagues (2009) highlight the potential to redefine or modify the content or scope of the institution of private property by legally creating property arrangements based on shared ownership. A well-known example of this is the institution of condominium ownership. Condominium ownership, also called strata-title, is one of the "main internal governance systems adopted worldwide in the management of communal private property" (Yiu, Wong, and Yau 2006, 93). In a strata-title arrangement, residents own their individual units as private property but "common areas of a development are held by a corporate body in which each owner has a share" (93). Avi Friedman (1994) considers condominium tenure to be a tool for creating affordable and flexible housing arrangements in the Canadian context.

While condominium tenure is familiar, some researchers promote a variation of it for application to leasehold land. In certain contexts, such as Hong Kong, lands are held as leasehold rather than freehold private property (Ho 2006; Yiu, Wong, and Yau 2006). Within a leasehold context, shared tenure arrangements have developed in which "owners hold undivided shares of a whole development as co-owners together with an exclusive right to use a particular part" and the co-owners' rights and responsibilities are summarized in "a deed of mutual covenants," which is binding for all future owners (Yiu, Wong, and Yau 2006, 93).

While Hong Kong's leasehold land is embedded in the context of its state-owned land system, Eric Ho (2006, 274) argues that "the leasehold land system also serves as a means of 'planning by contract'" that can support goals of sustainable development. The leasehold model may be of interest for land tenure innovators in the Canadian context because of its combination of secure individual interests, a contract that establishes individuals' collective responsibilities, and a landowner who holds the ultimate rights to govern the use and management of the property. As Ho explains, each lease is, in effect, a development action plan situated within a wider plan (274). Lawrence Lai (2010) reaches a similar conclusion, positioning "planning by contract" as a model that integrates comprehensive planning, freedom of contract, and public participation.

Voluntary and/or Grassroots Land Tenure Innovations

Our final category of innovative urban land tenure possibilities comprises strategies that are optional for landowners and are typically supported by local government programs or non-governmental initiatives. The two strategies examined in depth here are voluntary easements and community land trusts. Within the scope of this chapter, we were unable to give detailed consideration to two additional approaches that fit within this category and that deserve mention:

- *Incentivization.* Incentives such as financial stimuli, coordination measures, or information (Segeren et al. 2007) may not have any direct impact on a landowner's property rights, but they can be very influential (Gerber et al. 2009). An example of a possible incentive for tenure innovation is a tax break for shared-ownership arrangements. Some incentives that support other approaches are the provision of information on land swap opportunities or on how to establish collective-tenure arrangements.

- *Property management.* Lai (2006) and Yiu, Wong, and Yau (2006) explore the sustainable development potential of property management. As these researchers use the term, property management encompasses various stages of property development: "planning, project appraisal, construction, estate management, and title succession" (Lai 2006). Property management is linked to tenure arrangements because in a strata-title or co-ownership arrangement, "a property owner acquires . . . a right (obligation) to participate in the management of the building" (Yiu, Wong, and Lau 2006, 93).

Voluntary easements. Easements over land, in various forms, have existed for centuries and encompass a wide range of rights of use over property that are held by someone other than the legal owner of the land. Easements are often used to ensure rights of access, in order to prevent conflicts over land use, but they are increasingly being used in land-use planning to protect lands that have ecological, agricultural, or cultural value (Molina 2007; Stoms et al. 2009). Voluntary easement is a legal tool that landowners can use to protect aspects of their land in perpetuity, thus contributing to community sustainability goals by helping to preserve ecologically or agriculturally significant lands or by preserving some strategic or communally valued aspect of a land parcel. Potential applications of property easements are wide-ranging, though there is limited literature on the use of easements outside of more conventional applications.

Community land trusts. Land trusts are most familiar in the context of environmental or agricultural land preservation by government, non-profit organizations, or citizen groups (Hilts and Mitchell 1993; Roseland 2012, 49, 159), but they can also be used in urban contexts as a land tenure innovation that removes land from private ownership and instead manages it as a community or group asset (Heisler 2009). Land trusts change how costs and benefits of land development are distributed without resorting to taxation or regulatory tools (Ingerson 1997, 1). Instead, benefits and costs are shared by a group, and priority can be placed on efforts to "foster or protect specific land uses or groups of users" rather than solely on the generation of private profit (Ingerson 1997, 3).

UniverCity: SFU Community Trust
Sean Connelly

The Simon Fraser University (SFU) Community Trust was established to develop a sixty-five-hectare parcel of land into UniverCity, a model sustainable community of about ten thousand residents with a diverse range of housing options, shops, services, and amenities on the university campus. In addition, the development would help make SFU itself more sustainable by serving as a tangible example of sustainability for students, faculty, and staff and by using revenue from the development to create an endowment fund that would support teaching and research.

The development is currently home to about 3,600 residents in LEED-certified buildings with a range of housing sizes, tenure options (strata ownership, rental, and shared-equity); a LEED Gold elementary school for 180 students; and North America's first "living building" day care that is toxic-free, was largely built with materials from within four hundred kilometres, generates more energy than it uses, and recycles or harvests from rainwater more water than it uses. Residents are also able to purchase a Community Transit Pass at approximately 20 percent of the regular cost, providing additional incentives to reduce automobile use.

Plans are in the works for a neighbourhood energy system that would link all new buildings and would be powered by excess heat from the university's data centre. The UniverCity development illustrates the kind of development that is possible by taking a proactive role in controlling the land development process. With full control of the land, the SFU Community Trust was able to set specific bylaws and density incentives to ensure that social and environmental objectives were met, resulting in a community that is diverse, ranges in income, and is less auto-dependent (Roseland 2012).

Roseland, Mark. 2012. Toward Sustainable Communities: Solutions for Citizens and their Governments. Gabriola Island: New Society Publishers.
UniverCity. 2015. http://univercity.ca/.

Karen Heisler (2009) provides an excellent overview of community land trusts (CLTs) and the various models used. While there are many types of CLTs, including co-operatives and lease-to-own arrangements, several characteristics distinguish CLTs from other land tenure approaches (CMHC 2005, 2):

- CLTs are non-profit organizations.
- They are democratically controlled by their members.
- They own the land and grant usage rights to third parties through lease agreements. Buildings are owned or leased separately
- They ensure perpetual affordability and responsibility through various constraints.

It is the shared land-ownership arrangement that sets CLTs apart from other models and provides the basis for the governance of CLTs and for their effectiveness in reducing costs and protecting land (CMHC 2005).

Community Land Trusts

Mark Roseland and Marena Brinkhurst

Community land trusts (CLTs) are locally controlled non-profit organizations that acquire, hold, and lease out land for the development of permanently affordable housing. The first CLT in North America, established in 1969 near Albany, Georgia, was an outgrowth of the civil rights movement in the American South. There are now over 240 CLTs in the United States, supported by the National Community Land Trust Network.

The Champlain Housing Trust (CHT), for example, was created in 2006 as a result of the merger of Burlington Community Land Trust and the Lake Champlain Housing Development Corporation. The CHT provides affordable housing and community facilities in the three counties surrounding Burlington, Vermont. It acquires land through purchase, donation, or bargain sale but has also received land and buildings as part of negotiated deals with private developers who must comply with local inclusionary zoning or housing replacement ordinances. If there is not already an existing residential or commercial building on the land, CHT constructs one using government grants and private donations. In the case of CHT's owner-occupied housing, an income-eligible homebuyer purchases the building and leases the underlying land from CHT for a nominal fee (e.g., $35 per month for ninety-nine years). Since the cost of the land is not included in the price of the home, the cost of the home is kept low and the homebuyer saves on mortgage costs. By leveraging government grants and subsidies and by restricting the resale price of every house and condominium in its portfolio, CHT is able to keep the cost of owning a home up to 30 percent lower than a comparable market-rate home (Fireside 2008). CHT is currently the manager and steward for 1,500 units of rental housing, several shelters and single-room occupancies for persons who were formerly homeless, and eight non-residential buildings containing neighbourhood businesses or community services.

Fireside, Daniel. 2008. "Community Land Trust Keeps Prices Affordable - for now and forever." *Yes! Magazine*, Fall 2008. http://www.yesmagazine.org/issues/purple-america/community-land-trust-keeps-prices-affordable-for-now-and-forever.

Many CLTs in the United States use models similar to those in Canada to advance local social and environmental goals, two celebrated examples being Boston's Dudley Street Neighbourhood Initiative (Ingerson 1997) and the Burlington Community Land Trust (CMHC 2015; Foldy and Walters 2004; Roseland 2012). Land trusts can be combined with affordable and/or shared housing arrangements, as has been done by the Cooperative Housing Land Trust Foundation in BC (Roseland 2012). Similarly, to provide and protect an affordable housing development, the Cashes Green redevelopment of a derelict hospital complex near Stroud, in England, used a form of shared ownership called "mutual home ownership" to combine donated public land, a community land trust, a mutual home ownership entity, and a social landlord (GLP 2011; Marsden et al. 2010; RUDI 2014) It is specifically because of the apparent advantages that CLTs have for providing affordable housing that the Canada Mortgage and Housing Corporation has expressed interest in this form of tenure innovation (CMHC 2005, 2015).

John Davis and Rick Jacobus (2008) explore ways in which local governments can, and should, support CLT initiatives. In the model they propose, the local government donates ownership or a long-term lease of government-owned land, or the funds to acquire land, to a CLT dedicated to affordable housing; the government may also be involved in helping to establish and possibly even administer the CLT (33). Davis and Jacobus demonstrate how, in the long term, this type of partnership is more cost effective than government subsidies for affordable housing, even when lost property-tax revenue (from forgone conventional development) is taken into account (7). Local governments can also support CLTs through inclusionary or preferential zoning or through regulatory measures that require private developers to contribute to the initiative (Heisler 2009, 26; Roseland 2012). As Ingerson (1997, 3) points out, in some contexts, CLTs may have to "seek special legal exemptions, or even change state property laws" if there are legal constraints on the restriction or sharing of private property rights.

Bringing the Theory and the Practice of Community Land Trusts to North America's Most Expensive City
Michael Lewis

In 2013, Vancouver was ranked as the second least affordable place to live out of 360 urban centres around the globe. The mayor of Vancouver had already announced an Affordable Housing Task Force in late 2012 as the price of an average single family home increased 33 percent to $1.6 million that year. Thirty years ago, it took 3.5 times a carpenter's annual wages to purchase a house; in 2012, it required 33 times a carpenter's annual wages.

An advocate of community land trusts (CLTs) who was well versed about the success of CLTs in preserving housing affordability in the United States, succeeded in getting a pilot of the CLT model written into the final report of the Vancouver task force. A unique public-social partnership will see the city of Vancouver lease four parcels of their land for ninety-nine years to the Community Housing Land Trust Foundation. A total of 355 units will be built. Market rentals will number 82 co-op units. The remaining units are targeted at specific low-income constituencies (families, seniors and singles, people with disabilities) and will have rental rates between 19 percent and 26 percent lower than the upper limit of low income eligibility in the region. These will be owned and managed by experienced non-profit partners Fraserview Housing Co-operative, Tikva Housing Society, Katherine Sanford Housing Society and HFBC Housing Foundation. The city approved the CLT proposal on 15 May 2013 and construction was to begin in March 2014, with the first residents moving in by November 2015 (Wong 2013).

Taking the land out of the market and putting it into the hands of the trust is the first big breakthrough for Vancouver. The second is a business model design based on multi-stakeholder solidarity; the market rentals cross-subsidize the lower-income units, thus deepening the level of affordability. Third, once all reserves built into the business model are fully funded, the surplus will be split between the city and the CLT on the condition that both parties reinvest it in affordable housing. A progressive mayor and city council created the opening, aided by some effective advocacy. The CLT designed the proposal, ably aided by the Coop Housing Federation of British Columbia, Vancity Credit Union, and a professional housing development company specializing in co-op and non-profit housing. The result is a public-social partnership actively piloting how an alternative form of land tenure and a business model motivated by community benefit and long-term viability can build affordable housing in a city where most citizens no longer thought it possible.

Mayor's Task Force on Housing Affordability. 2012. "Bold Ideas Towards an Affordable City." Vancouver: City of Vancouver. http://vancouver.ca/files/cov/Staff_report_to_Council_re_task_force_report.pdf.

Wong, Jackie. "Community Land Trust: Vancouver's Affordable
Housing Fix?" The Tyee, July 12. http://thetyee.ca/News/2013/06/12/
Vancouver-Community-Land-Trust.

AN EVALUATION OF SIX LAND TENURE INNOVATIONS

Of the seven land tenure innovations described in the above sections, we selected
for further analysis six that we believe could support sustainable community goals:

- Land banking
- Land readjustments
- Transferable development rights (TDRs)
- Shared-ownership arrangements established in law
- Voluntary easements
- Community land trusts (CLTs)

Although land swapping, the seventh innovation, is of interest, it does not sufficiently use land tenure innovation or alternative forms of ownership for the purposes of this evaluation.

The six approaches were evaluated based on their capacities in four areas:

- *The advancement of environmental sustainability goals.* The extent
  to which the option improves ecological health and integrity (such
  as biodiversity, water quality, air quality, habitat quality, or species
  population).

- *The advancement of social/cultural sustainability goals.* The extent to
  which the option improves social justice, cultural diversity and vibrancy,
  and support of individuals within communities.

- *The advancement of economic sustainability goals.* The extent to which
  the option improves local economic vitality, resiliency, opportunities, and
  innovation.

- *The alignment of public and private interests.* The extent to which the
  option reduces conflict between private and public interests.

The goal of this section is to evaluate the selected approaches against consistent criteria in order to identify which strategies might be most effective and feasible in the context of Canadian communities. The analysis is qualitative, and a summary of the strengths and weaknesses of each approach, relative to each other, is provided in table 8.1.

Table 8.1 Strengths and weaknesses of six land tenure approaches

Criterion	Approach					
	Land banking	Land readjust-ment	Trans-ferable develop-ment rights	Shared owner-ship (by law)	Volun-tary ease-ments	Commu-nity land trusts
Environmental sustainability	good	good	good	good	very good	good
Social/cultural sustainability	good	good	good	unsure	good	very good
Economic sustainability	unsure	very good	poor	good	poor	good
Effectively align interests	poor	good	very good	unsure	good	very good

CONCLUSIONS AND FUTURE DIRECTIONS

In this chapter, we have explored ways to use land tenure innovations and alternative land ownership arrangements to further goals of sustainable community development, particularly when conflicts between private and public interests concerning land present obstacles to sustainability initiatives. Based on the analysis of six very different approaches, it is clear that while a number of land tenure innovations and alternative land ownership arrangements are potentially useful to local governments and planners, much remains uncertain regarding the actual application of such tools. Limited awareness of many of these approaches presents a major barrier to their widespread adoption. Based on our review, several strategies of land tenure innovation appear to be deserving of particular attention from local governments and planners.

- *Land readjustments*: This approach was evaluated favourably for sustainability objectives, yet suffered on conventional policy criteria, primarily because of its unfamiliarity in North American contexts. As an approach used extensively around the world to facilitate co-operative reshaping of the landscape, land readjustment should be investigated further in terms of its potential application in Canada. While it does not result in a permanent alignment of public and private interests, it does appear to be successful in overcoming temporary conflicts so that private landowners and the public can both experience benefits.

- *Voluntary easements*: While easements are already a familiar feature of planning in Canadian communities, this assessment demonstrated that they may have several advantages that should be explored further. A main strength of voluntary easements is that they can permanently protect public interests once those interests can be aligned with the interests of a private landowner. Expanding the application of easements for sustainability goals—through, for example, developing a proactive role for the local government as the holder of community sustainability easements—may run counter to some conventional policy criteria (e.g., administrative feasibility or public acceptability) but perhaps not to the extent that easements would be unusable. The familiarity of easements and the ease with which they could be integrated into legal and administrative systems are strengths that could be leveraged.

- *Community land trusts*: Like land readjustments, the CLT approach scored high on objectives-based criteria but its total score was weakened by challenges of uncertainty and a lack of information on its feasibility and acceptability in Canadian contexts. Given the increasing use and success of CLTs in the United States and United Kingdom, and given their apparently strong potential to advance social, economic, and environmental sustainability objectives and to overcome public-private interest conflicts, the development and support of CLTs should be seriously considered by Canadian communities and local governments.

One limitation of this review is the exclusion from consideration of forms of shared ownership other than those that currently have formal and legal recognition.

Such voluntary property arrangements tend to be informal, bending and testing the existing rules concerning ownership, or they are on the cutting-edge of land tenure innovation and are yet to be fully recognized and legally established. Despite the potential of these land tenure arrangements, formal research on them from a planning perspective is sparse and local governments can do little to encourage them, apart from creating a legislative environment that does not unfairly penalize or restrict such arrangements. Like Karen Heisler (2009), who encourages further exploration of commonhold legislation and other tools that may enable the development of new forms of mutual property ownership and co-operative tenure, we would like to see deeper investigation of alternative, less recognized forms of shared tenure arrangements, in addition to further clarification and testing of already recognized alternative tenure arrangements.

Chapter 1 of this volume sets out a framework for exploring the social economy (SE) and sustainable community development (SCD) on a spectrum from weak to strong. Weak SE approaches are characterized as not addressing the need for societal transformation, while strong SE initiatives are focused on community-based actions that incorporate the principles of equity, redistribution, solidarity, and mutuality and that have the primary goal of meeting social needs rather than maximizing profit. For both SCD and SE, we can begin to delineate weak from strong approaches and perspectives based on the general criteria listed in table 1.3 in chapter 1. To summarize, strong approaches strive for structural change; engage in market-based activity in a way that balances economic, environmental, and social needs; focus on building capacity for self-suffiency and community-based ownership; seek to scale up and scale out; involve strong coalitions and partnerships; and challenge regulatory barriers.

Using these criteria, land readjustments fall toward the weaker end of the spectrum. They do not require or strive for structural change, nor do the individuals or organizations involved work within a network or engage in capacity building for the good of the community. Land readjustments only challenge regulatory barriers to the extent that they are relatively untried in North America, although well-known in other parts of the world. (Stein [2014] notes that seventy-four countries have NGOs dealing in some way with private land conservation). While land readjustments are market based, whether they balance economic, social, and environmental needs depends on the project for which the readjustment is done. Land readjustment does, however, have the potential to operate at scale. Voluntary easements do not strive for structural change, operate as part of a collaborative network, challenge regulatory barriers, or build capacity; they may be minimally market based, but again, whether they balance the various needs of the community depends on the project involved. Like readjustments, they can, perhaps because of their low score on the previous criteria, operate at significant scale. Community land trusts, unlike land readjustments and easements, fall at the strong end of the continuum. They require structural change, are involved in market-based activity that strives to balance various needs, operate within networks, challenge regulatory barriers, and build capacity. While they have yet to operate at scale, with the newfound interest of municipal governments in CLTs, that could change relatively quickly.

In the context of this volume, a strong/strong approach to social economy and sustainable community development requires that land tenure innovations strive for socio-ecological goals, actions and outcomes that result in scaling up, and policy change that achieves scaling out. The research and cases reviewed here suggest three emergent trends among land tenure innovations for sustainability that satisfy the criteria for a strong/strong approach to social economy and sustainable community development:

- Developing ownership arrangements that combine advantages of individual rights while expanding individuals' responsibilities to others and the wider community
- Redefining the rights and responsibilities that accompany private land ownership
- Introducing new actors to the land market to further community sustainability goals

These trends should encourage further exploration and innovation with community land tenure arrangements and governance. Opportunities for introducing new actors and entities to the land market should be of particular interest, especially given the challenges faced by local governments and planners when considering most, if not all, approaches to land tenure innovation and alternative forms of ownership. These challenges may indicate that local governments are not ideally situated to take on the role of encouraging land tenure innovation. Perhaps at this stage, exploring the full potential of tenure innovations and alternative ownership arrangements to support sustainable community development requires greater agility, flexibility, and creativity than local governments can currently supply. To echo the call of Roseland (2006), perhaps a necessary next step in sustainable community development is the emergence of new social economy actors with the capacity to use, combine, and extend the tools of land tenure to advance sustainability goals of both local governments and communities.

REFERENCES

Antrim, Sean. 2011. "Vancouver's Property Endowment Fund." *The Mainlander*, 19 February. http://themainlander.com/2011/02/19/vancouvers-property-endowment-fund/.

Blomley, Nicholas. 2008. "Enclosure, Common Right and the Property of the Poor." *Social and Legal Studies* 17 (3): 311–31.

Booth, Annie, and Norman Skelton. 2011. "Anatomy of a Failed Sustainability Initiative: Government and Community Resistance to Sustainable Landscaping in a Canadian City." *Sustainability: Science, Practice, and Policy* 7 (1): 56–68.

Bruce, John W. 1998. "Review of Tenure Terminology." *Tenure Brief* no.1 (July). Land Tenure Center, University of Wisconsin–Madison.

Buitelaar, Edwin, and Barrie Needham. 2007. "Property Rights and Private Initiatives: An Introduction." *Town Planning Review* 78 (1): 1–8.

Chilibeck, John. 2009. "Municipal Land Swap Gets Swat." *Telegraph-Journal*, 9 October.

City of Vancouver. 2004. *City Owned Properties*. http://vancouver.ca/commsvcs/planning/cityplan/Visions/rpsc/factsheets/134cityproperties.pdf.

Claxton, Matthhew, 2014. "Langley mayoral candidates sink teeth into debate," *Langley Advance*, 15 October 2014. http://www.langleyadvance.com/langley-votes/langley-mayoral-candidates-sink-teeth-into-debate-1.1426735.

CMHC (Canada Mortgage and Housing Corporation). 2005. "Critical Success Factors for Community Land Trusts in Canada." Research Highlight, Socio-economic Series 05-010.

———. 2015. "Community Land Trusts. "https://www.cmhc-schl.gc.ca/en/inpr/afhoce/afhoce/afhostcast/afhoid/fite/colatr/index.cfm.

Curtis, Jessica, Zoe Pagonis, Emma Roach, Sarah Sheppard, and Kailin Smith. 2008. *Transferable Development Rights Legislation: A Proposal for Solving Maryland's Land Use Problems*. Prepared for the Governor's Summer Internship Program, University of Maryland, Baltimore County. http://www.ibrarian.net/navon/paper/Transferable_Development_Rights_Legislation_A_Pro.pdf?paperid=13321655.

Daniels, Thomas L. 2009. "A Trail Across Time: American Environmental Planning from City Beautiful to Sustainability." *Journal of the American Planning Association* 75 (2): 178–92.

Davis, Chuck. N.d. "The Paradise Makers." The History of Metropolitan Vancouver. http://www.vancouverhistory.ca/archives_paradiseMakers.htm.

Davis, John Emmeus, and Rick Jacobus. 2008. *The City–CLT Partnership: Municipal Support for Community Land Trusts.* Cambridge, MA: Lincoln Institute of Land Policy.

Foldy, Erica, and Jonathan Walters. 2004. "The Power of Balance: Lessons from Burlington Community Land Trust." New York: NY Research Center for Leadership in Action, Leadership for a Changing World, Wagner School, New York University. http://community-wealth.org/sites/clone.community-wealth.org/files/downloads/paper-foldy-waters.pdf.

Friedman, Avi. 1994. "Narrow-Front Row Housing for Affordability and Flexibility." *Plan Canada* 34 (5): 9–16.

Gerber, Jean-David, Peter Knoepfel, Stéphane Nahrath, and Frédéric Varone. 2009. "Institutional Resource Regimes: Toward Sustainability Through the Combination of Property-Rights Theory and Policy Analysis." *Ecological Economics* 68: 798–809.

Gilbert, Liette, L. Anders Sandberg, and Gerda R. Wekerle. 2009. "Building Bioregional Citizenship: The Case of the Oak Ridges Moraine, Ontario, Canada." *Local Environment* 14 (5): 387–401.

GLP (Gloucestershire Land for People). 2011. "Cashes Green." Gloucestershire Land for People. http://www.gloucestershirelandforpeople.coop/index.php?option=com_content&task=view&id=28&Itemid=11.

Godschalk, David R. 2004. "Land Use Planning Challenges: Coping with Conflicts in Visions of Sustainable Development and Livable Communities." *Journal of the American Planning Association* 70 (1): 5–13.

Grant, Jill, ed. 2008. *A Reader in Canadian Planning: Linking Theory and Practice.* Toronto: Thomson Nelson.

Hanly-Forde, Jason, George Homsy, Katherine Lieberknecht, and Remington Stone. 2014. *Transfer of Development Rights Programs: Using the Market for Compensation and Preservation.* Cornell University, College of Architecture, Art, and Planning. http://www.mildredwarner.org/gov-restructuring/privatization/tdr.

Hanna, Kevin S., Steven M. Webber, and D. Scott Slocombe. 2007. "Integrated Ecological and Regional Planning in a Rapid-Growth Setting." *Environmental Management* 40: 339–48.

Heisler, Karen. 2009. *Alternative Land Tenure and the Social Economy: Literature Review.* Port Alberni, BC: Canadian Centre for Community Renewal on behalf of the BC-Alberta Social Economy Research Alliance.

Hilts, Stewart, and Peter Mitchell. 1993. "Bucking the Free Market Economy." *Alternatives Journal* 19 (3): 16–23.

Ho, Eric C. K. 2006. "The Leasehold System as a Land Management Measure to Attain Sustainable Development Planning by Contract: A Hong Kong Case Study." *Property Management* 24 (3): 272–92.

Hodge, Gerald, and David L. A. Gordon. 2008. *Planning Canadian Communities.* 5th ed. Toronto: Thomson Nelson.

Home, Robert. 2007. "Land Readjustment as a Method of Development Land Assembly: A Comparative Overview." *Town Planning Review* 78 (4): 459–83.

Ingerson, Alice E. 1997. "Urban Land as Common Property." *Landlines* 9 (2): 1–3.

Ippolitto, M. 2000. "Snellville May Move City Hall; Mayor Says Deal with Church to Swap Land for Strip Mall Would Allow Reshaping City Center." *The Atlanta Constitution*, 4 November.

Karp, James P. 1993. "A Private Property Duty of Stewardship: Changing Our Land Ethic." *Environmental Law* 23: 735–62.

Lai, Lawrence Wai-chung. 2006. "Private Property Rights, Culture, Property Management and Sustainable Development." *Property Management* 24 (2): 71–86.

——. 2010. "A Model of Planning by Contract: Integrating Comprehensive State Planning, Freedom of Contract, Public Participation and Fidelity." *Town Planning Review* 81 (6): 674–73.

Lee, Shin, and Chris Webster. 2006. "Enclosure of the Urban Commons." *GeoJournal* 66: 27–42.

Li, Ling-Hin, and Xin Li. 2007. "Land Readjustment: An Innovative Urban Experiment in China." *Urban Studies* 44 (1): 81–98.

Löhr, Dirk. 2010. "The Driving Forces of Land Conversion: Towards a Financial Framework for Better Land Use Policy." *Land Tenure Journal* 2010 (1): 61–89.

Marsden, Terry, Alex Franklin, Julie Newton, and Jennie Middleton. 2010. "Sustainability in Practice: Situated Learning and Knowledge for the Evolving Eco-economy." *Town Planning Review* 81 (5): 541–62.

Molina, Cristina Montiel. 2007. "Cultural Heritage, Sustainable Forest Management and Property in Inland Spain." *Forest Ecology and Management* 249: 80–90.

Roseland, Mark. 2006. "Curtain Call: In Search of a Missing Actor for Sustainable Community Development." In *Community Economic Development: Building for Social Change*, edited by Eric Shragge and Michael Toye, 206–20. Sydney: Cape Breton University Press.

——. 2012. *Toward Sustainable Communities: Solutions for Citizens and their Governments*. 4th ed. Gabriola Island, BC: New Society.

RUDI. 2014. "Government Land May Be 'Donated' to Community Landowner for Development." UrbanXtra, rudi.net. http://www.rudi.net/node/16910.

Schlager, Edella, and Elinor Ostrom. 1992. "Property-Rights Regimes and Natural Resources: A Conceptual Analysis." *Land Economics* 68 (3): 249–62.

Segeren, Arno, Femke Verwest, Barrie Needham, and Edwin Buitelaar. 2007. "(Re-) designing Markets for Land Use Decisions: Private Initiatives in a Publicly Determined Context: Lessons Drawn from Other Policy Fields." *Town Planning Review* 78 (1): 9–22.

Staley, Samuel R. 2006a. "Institutional Considerations for Sustainable Development Policy Implementation: A US Case Study." *Property Management* 24 (3): 232–50.

———. 2006b. "Sustainable Development in American Planning: A Critical Appraisal." *Town Planning Review* 77 (1): 99–126.

Stein, Peter. 2014. "The Global Emergence of Private Land Conservation." Video. Lecture to Lincoln Institute of Land Policy, Lincoln House, Cambridge, MA, 11 February. http://www.lincolninst.edu/pubs/video/4f9110cfacb145d688254528555fa 70b/The-Global-Emergence-of-Private-Land-Conservation.

Stoms, David M., Patrick A. Jantz, Frank W. Davis, and Gregory DeAngelo. 2009. "Strategic Targeting of Agricultural Conservation Easements as a Growth Management Tool." *Land Use Policy* 26: 1149–61.

Thomas, Joachim. 2011. "Uncontrolled Land Consumption Versus Resource-Saving Land Use in Germany." *Land Tenure Journal* 2011 (1): 79–99.

Van der Krabben, Erwin, and Barrie Needham. 2008. "Land Readjustment for Value Capturing: A New Planning Tool for Urban Redevelopment." *Town Planning Review* 79 (6): 651–72.

Webster, Chris. 2005. "The New Institutional Economics and the Evolution of Modern Urban Planning: Insights, Issues and Lessons." *Town Planning Review* 76 (4): 455–501.

Wehrmann, Babette. 2011. *Land Use Planning: Concept, Tools and Applications.* Deutsche Gesellschaft für Internationale Zusammenarbeit (GIZ), Agriculture, Fisheries and Food Division, Land Policy and Land Management Project, Eschborn, Germany.

Williamson, Ian, Enemark, Stig, Wallace, Jude, and Abbas Rajabifard. 2005. "Land Administration for Sustainable Development." New York: Esri Press.

Yiu, C. Y., S. K. Wong, and Y. Yau. 2006. "Property Management as Property Rights Governance: Exclusion and Internal Conflict Resolution." *Property Management* 24 (2): 87–97.

9 Sustaining Social Democracy Through Heritage-Building Conservation

Noel Keough, Mike Gismondi, and
Erin Swift-Leppäkumpu

Across Canada, many important heritage buildings have become home to social economy organizations. These buildings are used in a variety of ways, from affordable housing and artist co-ops to social and human services non-profits; from women's shelters and halfway houses to community radio stations; from youth training centres to social enterprises; from consumer co-operatives to administrative spaces for progressive social economy organizations, foundations, charities, and non-profits. Examples include the Charlotte Street Arts Centre, Fredericton; the Court Street Fire Hall/Multicultural Centre, Thunder Bay; the Robertson Building, Toronto; the Vancouver East Cultural Centre (The Cultch), Vancouver; the CN-Angus Shops, Montréal; the Fire Station for Youth at Risk, Moncton; and Hilltop House, Edmonton. Although one might not expect a relationship to exist between heritage buildings and what is broadly known as the social economy (Fairbairn 2009), the intersection of specific needs have conspired to create an association. Cash-strapped social economy organizations are frequently looking for an affordable home, while heritage-building owners (private, non-profit, or government) are often in need of tenants who are sympathetic to heritage values. But is this relationship purely a market coincidence, or have other priorities brought these diverse groups together under a heritage roof?

In her research on heritage buildings and non-profit tenancy in the United States, Vinokur-Kaplan (2001) found that donors were reluctant to give funds to non-profits for rent or for the capital costs of a new building. To compensate, non-profit organizations often collaborated with heritage-building landlords (both private and municipal or state), inhabiting and taking good care of heritage space in exchange for a longer term lease with affordable rent. Landlords benefited in at least two ways: they reduced their property taxes, and the presence of tenants protected the heritage buildings from vandalism. The moral and social capital of the social economy tenants also brought vitality to underused buildings and even improved the livability of neighbourhoods. This is a decent *quid pro quo*.

Ecological sustainability has also been taken up by heritage actors as a way to control building operation costs (Roberts 2007) and as a response to the challenges of urban sustainability (Dannenberg et al. 2011; Onyschuk et. al, 2001; Rypkema 2005). Owners and tenants now retrofit heritage buildings with efficient heating, lighting, water, and building-envelope technologies. This practical work converges with political work by activists to promote energy and material conservation via the reuse, renovation, and adaptive repurposing of existing buildings and to preserve historically compact urban form and walkability (GHPNS 2006).

This chapter explores the ecological dimensions of the sustainability of heritage buildings as well as the intangible social and cultural dimensions (Ross 2006). We argue that conservation of key built structures provides continuity between past and present political and social life. Connecting current community initiatives with physical artifacts that invoke memories of past civic or national commitments to human dignity, human rights, and social justice nourishes contemporary imaginations of social sustainability and the solidarity economy (Fennell 2009, 149; Lewis 2007).

HERITAGE BUILDINGS AND SOCIAL ECONOMY TENANTS: STORIES FROM ALBERTA

Canadian stories drawn from the province of Alberta provide examples of the common purpose and collaboration among social economy activists, heritage preservationists, and sustainability advocates. Each narrative exemplifies innovative and well-considered use or re-use of heritage architecture and the adaptation of an older building into the contemporary urban fabric in ways that align with ecological, economic, and social sustainability. Visitors to these buildings can feel the unique affinity and synergy between sustainability, heritage preservation, and the social economy. Each of these stories encourages stronger collaborative efforts toward sustainability.

The Gibson Block, Edmonton

The Gibson Block in Edmonton, Alberta, also known as the Flat Iron Building, houses the Women's Emergency Accommodation Centre (WEAC). Located on Jasper Avenue in the Boyle Street community, a transitional neighbourhood on the eastern edge of the downtown, the building was registered as a Provincial Historic Resource in 1995 (HERMIS 2013). The WEAC provides housing for up to seventy women. Constructed in 1913, the upper three floors of the Gibson Block are residential. The main floor at one time housed a café and various retail operations, including a lively neighbourhood fruit and vegetable store. The basement was home to a Turkish bath and remained a bath house until 1978. The building slowly declined, along with the original downtown core, and became "derelict, decaying and seemingly destined to be a forgotten footnote in time" (Herzog 2003). It was boarded up for ten years and was finally rescued in the autumn of 1993 by a collection of community members. Heritage planner Darryl Cariou worked with the City of Edmonton at the time:

> One day I got a call from a building inspector saying, "Darryl, I just want to give you a heads up. We're about to issue a demolition order for the building because they had a report that there were bricks falling off the cornice onto the street below." So that raised the issue to the red alert level. . . . Mayor Reimer asked her executive assistant and me to organize a public meeting in one of the meeting rooms on the main floor of City Hall. Because the meeting was coming right out of the mayor's office, there were a lot of big wigs there, movers and shakers from downtown Edmonton, bankers and lawyers, etc., and Martin Garber-Conrad was there. I presented what I knew about the building, some basic information about the history. I showed pictures of the inside so that they would know what condition it was in. I had some original floor plans, I think, so people had a sense of what was there. It was just sort of an open discussion about what to do with the building. Afterward Martin came forward and said, "I'm interested in this building." (Interview with authors, April 13, 2012)

In the 1990s, Martin Garber-Conrad—currently the CEO of the Edmonton Community Foundation, a municipal agency that provides donor-based funding to charitable programs and activities—was the director of the Edmonton City Centre Church Corporation (E4C), an ecumenical charitable organization dedicated to community service. Founded in 1970 by four inner-city churches, E4C was formed according to one of its Edmonton originators "as a voice for the voiceless, to empower the disinherited downtown" (Ivany, 2000, 5). E4C had, since its inception, managed a women's shelter in leased spaces and had, at the time the issue of the Gibson Block became public, recently secured funds for a new purpose-built shelter. Garber-Conrad offers this insight, from a community activist point of view, of the collaboration with heritage activists:

> I got the bright idea that perhaps we could do two things at once. Perhaps we could put this building to a social use and preserve its historical significance. . . . The justification I saw for compromising the social purpose with a historical or heritage purpose was that I thought it would be very exciting to get the community of people that supports arts, heritage, cultural and historical stuff also interested in homeless women, and if possible to draw resources for the project not only from the traditional housing sources, but also from the historical and cultural sources. I think we demonstrated that it's possible to do, but it certainly wasn't easy.[1]

E4C combined their recently acquired building funds with City and provincial heritage dollars to restore the Gibson Block. E4C now owns the building, and it remains the home of Edmonton's Women's Emergency Accommodation Centre.

Figure 9.1 Aerial view of the construction of the Gibson Block.

Photo: Tim Ferguson, courtesy of Eye in the Sky Aerial Photography.

---

1 "Fostering the Social Economy in Alberta," an interview with Martin Garber-Conrad by Mike Gismondi, *Aurora* (2008), http://aurora.icaap.org/index.php/aurora/article/view/80/92. Unless otherwise indicated, subsequent quotations from Garber-Conrad are drawn from this interview.

Figure 9.2 Gibson Block, 2006.
Source: City of Edmonton Archives, EA 792-191.

During an interview with a neighbourhood newsletter Garber-Conrad described how the former grandeur of the building and its link to the original downtown played a role in garnering support and collaborators:

> The building's broad appeal has brought many parts of our community together to return a vacant landmark to worthwhile service. The revitalized Gibson Block means we will be able to help more of the growing number of homeless women, who are among the neediest of our city's needy. At the same time, we all can enjoy seeing a wonderful remnant of Edmonton's past restored to its previous beauty. (Boyle McCauley News, 1994)

The improved accommodation in the women's shelter "immediately paid back all the effort, as the increased privacy and the new attitude of dignity affected the staff and clients alike" (Ivany 2000, 20). Today, that part of the city is once again at the forefront of urban renewal, including the development of a new hockey arena. As Garber-Conrad mused, having an asset provides the social economy entrepreneurs with other options: "maybe someday, it will be cost effective to let somebody buy it out and turn it into some other use."

The story of the Gibson Block points to issues of social sustainability beyond conservation—and to the role of heritage buildings as catalysts for social renewal. One caveat, though, is the problem of gentrification. While urban renewal in the

1960s took the form of demolition and modernization, today's gentrification generally includes not building demolition but the removal of undesirable elements, uses, demographic groups, and classes. A partnership between heritage preservation and social economy actors holds the potential for organizations with a social justice mission to shape urban renewal in socially just and ecologically sustainable ways that resist social exclusion.

The Alexander Taylor School, Edmonton

Named for one of the founders of the City of Edmonton, the Alexander Taylor School is on the inventory of the City of Edmonton Municipal Historic Resources. Its core tenant is the Edmonton City Centre Church Corporation (E4C), an inner-city social services agency. Construction of the school began in 1906, and it opened two years later. The Edmonton School Board closed the Alex Taylor School in 2001 to consolidate resources, since the number of children in the neighbourhood had declined.

Figure 9.3 The Alex Taylor School, Edmonton.

Originally a middle-class neighbourhood of early Edmonton, the community slipped downwards socio-economically over the years and became more multicultural, with a significant Chinese and Asian population. Today, it remains an ethnically and socio-economically mixed neighbourhood in the Boyle Street area, one of Edmonton's poorer inner-city neighbourhoods, with a range of challenges. In 2002, E4C began to run a number of school programs for children out of the building (see figure 9.3). They used their connections with the school board to negotiate in 2002 for a twenty year lease (for $1 a year) and retrofitted the building with $1 million grant from the Muttart Foundation (Herzog, 2002).

The building was repurposed into an office and community complex for non-profit organizations. It also became the new home for E4C, as well as a cluster of other social economy agencies. The building now houses the Alberta Council of Women's Shelters, the Centre for Non-Profits, a training space for Kids in the Hall Bistro, Head Start classrooms for children under four years, a garage for a community bus program, and a meeting space for community groups.

E4C consolidated its operations from four different locations into the one neighbourhood where they focus many of their services—food, housing, youth outreach, and job training for members of the inner city. As Garber-Conrad explained:

> We had been in rented high rises on Jasper Avenue in the heart of the business district for our entire life while all our work was east of the downtown in the inner city. And we began to think, "What if we moved actually into the area we served? What if we took our experience with the Gibson Block and heritage buildings and used it on this heritage school to preserve what could be preserved, but repurpose it from a school into an office and community complex?"

Garber-Conrad was also quick to note the continuities at play in taking over the building. For thirty years, the school had the same principal, Steve Ramsankar, who had turned it into a community school for the neighbourhood. As Garber-Conrad explains, E4C's proposed uses for the Alex Taylor School aligned with historical uses in other ways as well. In the 1970s, under Principal Steve Ramsankar, the school became the Chinese seniors' centre and a drop-in centre for scared and abused children. It became an early school lunch program centre. "So, at the philosophical or metaphoric level we were not in fact developing a new use for the building. . . . And in addition to everything else we actually had children back in that school."

Today, E4C has grown to a $13 million organization with many new programs. Two projects added recently are a large community garden on the playgrounds and more extensive community and school lunch and snack programs (now supplying twelve high-needs schools). Both are activities close to the hearts of activists involved in sustainability and food security issues. Unlike private owners, who often look to invest and increase the value of their capital assets in conventional ways—maintaining a heritage building façade while adding density and converting use to expensive and profitable condominiums , for example—the social economy organizations invest in their building to grow their social capital assets—for example, through a community garden or outreach programming. In other words, private owners most often seek heritage buildings to increase private assets, while social economy agents do so to increase public or social assets. Social assets, in turn, increase the moral or political capital of the organizations inhabiting the building. Over time, this increase in other types of capital can protect the heritage asset against assault by economic market forces.

The Old Y Centre, Calgary

The Young Women's Christian Association (YWCA) of Calgary was founded in 1907 to provide accommodation for unmarried women who had recently arrived in the city. Housed initially in rented property, the organization had by 1909 raised enough money to purchase land and begin construction of a permanent home, today known as the Old Y Centre (see figure 9.4). The three-storey brick and sandstone building, built in 1910 and 1911 in the Georgian Revival style, was financed in part through the YWCA's "dollar campaign," which exhorted Calgarians each to contribute a dollar toward the construction of the building.[2] As Alice Jamieson, one of the original supporters of the Calgary YWCA, recalled, "No one was asked for more than a dollar. Imagine if you can, Calgary in those days. There were no pavements or sidewalks, and the mud was everywhere. Those were the days of long skirts. Yes, we spoiled our clothes, shoes, and tempers the first day" (Calgary Public Library 1988). Suffragette Nellie McClung, one of the Famous Five who fought for the right of women to be treated as "persons" and was a resident of the community, said this about the fundraising campaign: "In many masculine minds there was a grave doubt as to their wisdom. However, in a year or so, when property values began to soar, the stout-hearted board of the YWCA was the recipient of many congratulations on their excellent judgement" (Calgary Public Library 1988).

A Calgary alderman, together with the YWCA's president, laid the cornerstone of the building, and the event included a lively public debate by two prominent citizens about the role of women in society (Calgary Public Library 1988). The main floor of the building consisted of a library, parlors, a dining room, a gymnasium, and a swimming pool. The two upper floors were devoted to bedrooms and reading rooms, which opened off of large airy corridors. Within months of its official opening in February 1911, the new facility, designed to accommodate sixty-two girls and women, was full and additional space had to be rented to meet the demand (Calgary Public Library 1988).

---

2 According to the Bank of Canada Inflation Calculator (which goes back only to 1914), $1 in 1914 would be about $21 today.

Figure 9.4 The Old Y Building, Calgary.

The Y, as it became known, helped women to find employment and offered classes in physical training, swimming, dress making, cooking, millinery, music, and Sunday bible classes. Almost immediately after opening, the association established the Traveler's Aid program, and for years, YWCA representatives met every train that arrived in Calgary. By 1915, four hundred women and girls had been taught to swim at the Y, "debunking the myth that swimming was unlady-like" (Calgary Public Library 1988).

By 1941, the mortgage had been retired, and in that same year, the Y became the first billet for the newly formed Canadian Women's Army Corps. In 1944, the residence was remodelled, and in 1954, a two-storey brick annex, which included a swimming pool and gymnasium, was officially opened. In 1971, the YWCA moved to a new facility and the old Y was taken over by the City of Calgary. The City's Social Services Committee was given responsibility for its operation. By the late 1970s, the building had deteriorated to such a state that the City seriously considered proposals to demolish it.

In 1979, the twenty or so tenants of the Old Y put a proposal to the City to form an association, the Old Y Action Groups, that would operate the building for non-profit office space. It was agreed that the society would pay an annual rent of $1 and embark on a five-year renovation plan. The Old Y was declared a Provincial

Historical Resource on 27 May 1982, the same year that the association changed its name to the Old Y Centre for Community Organizations.

The Old Y, now maintained and managed as the CommunityWise Resource Centre, offers "affordable working and meeting space while preserving, restoring and maintaining the historical aspects of the building" (Beltline Urban Society 2014). The building is home to a diverse collection of non-profits. At the time of writing, thirty-seven members of CommunityWise, which is managed by "a tenant board of directors and a small staff collective," rent space in the building, and fifty-three additional organizations are non-renting members (CWRC 2014a). Current members include the Alberta Disabled Foundation, Amnesty International, Calgary CarShare (CATCO), the Sustainable Calgary Society, the Ethiopian Community Association, Pride Calgary, and Calgary Underground Film Festival. CommunityWise focuses on strengthening the collaboration among member agencies and raising funds for the preservation and renovation of the building. Like the Alex Taylor School, the Old Y has a social justice history reflected in its current usage.

The Old Y is a hub of community activism and social service activity. It provides shelter for non-profits struggling for survival in a booming economy and facing soaring real estate markets and fierce competition for experienced workers. Commenting in 2015, the executive director of the Old Y, now called CommunityWise, said "We hear from many of our member organizations, including SMART Recovery and Calgary OutLink, that they are able to pay better staff wages and provide much needed programs and support to hundreds of clients and community members because they pay below market rent for their offices here" (Interview with authors, April 14, 2015).

The Old Y is located just south of the heart of downtown Calgary in a community known as the Beltline. Now the densest community in Calgary, with ambitions to be "Calgary's Manhattan," the Beltline has seen tremendous change over the past twenty years and has been through several boom-and-bust cycles. Galvanized by the most recent economic boom, the municipal government has turned toward more sustainable long-range planning (City of Calgary 2007). The result has been a neighbourhood renaissance. On an adjacent block to the east of the Old Y, the historic Memorial Park received a $25 million facelift.[3] Across the street from the Old Y is a new IBM office building. One block to the west, along 1st Street, three new high-rise condominium projects have sprung up, complete with upscale street-level retail shops. On the block directly to the south of the Old Y, the historic

---

3 For details on Memorial Park, the Nellie McClung residence and other historic sites in the Beltline community, see City of Calgary (1986).

Haultain Park has undergone an extensive renovation, making it a centrepiece of efforts to attract families into the inner city.

All of this holds both opportunity and threat for the building and CommunityWise. The land where the building sits is now prime real estate, and it will require significant investment to survive into the future. At the same time, the Old Y and its active social economy tenants fit well in the middle of a community that is being revitalized—they offer a living memory of the social solidarity that was at the heart of the building's construction.

The Hillhurst Cottage School, Calgary

The Hillhurst Cottage School is a two-storey wood-frame structure located in a well-treed upscale residential neighbourhood, one of the oldest in Calgary. Within walking distance of the downtown core, the streetscape is largely unchanged since the early 1900s.

Seventeen cottage schools were built in Calgary prior to 1912. Typically, cottage schools were deliberately designed to look like the residences of the period so that the schools could be converted to private residences once a larger school building was erected. The Hillhurst Cottage School is one of two remaining cottage schools in the City of Calgary and the only one of its particular design (Canada's Historic Places). Built in 1910, the Hillhurst Cottage School (see figure 9.5) functioned as a school until 1965. It was leased by the Canadian Youth Hostels Association from 1970 to 1990. The Alberta Wilderness Association (AWA) began its occupancy of the building in the early 1970s when it sublet the building from Hostelling International. In 2015, the AWA purchased the building from The City of Calgary.

The AWA, founded in 1965 by backcountry enthusiasts, is the oldest wilderness conservation group in Alberta. Most of its 3,500 to 3,600 members are Albertans, but the organization is also supported by members around the world. Following its mandate, "To defend wild Alberta through education and action," the AWA promotes the protection of wild areas of Alberta so they may be preserved in their natural state. Both paid staff and volunteers work to restore wild natural ecosystems and to enable Albertans to communicate effectively with government, industry, and citizens concerning wildland issues. The AWA educates Albertans on the value, ecologically sustainable use, and conservation of wild lands and fosters a sense of connectedness to and passion for wild places, wildlife, and natural landscapes of Alberta. The association has five full-time and three part-time staff, occasional contract staff, and over two hundred volunteers province wide (Lee 2009). The executive director of the AWA talked about the difficulty of acquiring resources, financial and otherwise, to support the organization. Given the activist nature of the AWA in its work to protect Alberta's natural heritage, ongoing government funding is hard to come by.

Figure 9.5 Hillhurst Cottage School.

During the tenure of the AWA in the building, the basement has been converted into a Wilderness Resource Centre (with one-time grants from the Province of Alberta Community Facility Enhancement Program). The Resource Centre, run with volunteer support, keeps the building alive with visitors and maintains a connection to the original educational use of the building. In 2000, the main floor was restored and is now an inviting space used for meetings and public talks. The executive director describes the AWA as "healthy" at this point in time and as an organization that prides itself in supporting other non-profit groups in Calgary by endorsing other groups' events and providing office and meeting spaces free of charge. She also contends that the AWA contributes to "*ideological* diversity" that may foster resilience in times of change (Lee 2009).

The Hillhurst neighbourhood is undergoing rapid gentrification. Old houses in good condition are being torn down and replaced by large, upscale homes.

Without heritage designation and a long-term tenant with a high profile in the community, this building would probably be privatized and replaced by a McMansion. As a result of the direct efforts of the AWA, it is now fully registered as a heritage property. AWA members consider themselves stewards of the building. The organization enjoys its location in the Sunnyside-Hillhurst area of central Calgary for the opportunities it affords to engage with other like-minded organizations in a vibrant, sustainability-oriented community (Lee, 2009).

The AWA has achieved a level of stability in part by inhabiting and championing a heritage building, thus enhancing its capacity to achieve its central mission of natural heritage conservation. In addition, the core strategy of the organization's conservation agenda—education—provides continuity with the building's historical role as a public school.

BENEFITS OF CONNECTING THE SOCIAL ECONOMY WITH HERITAGE CONSERVATION

Each of the above examples demonstrates benefits derived from collaboration among those involved in heritage conservation, the social economy, and sustainability. We focus here on three such benefits: (1) contribution to environmental sustainability, (2) recognition of non-market-based definitions of value, and (3) preservation of authenticity, place, and collective memory in the built environment.

Contribution to Environmental Sustainability

Although older buildings are often very well built, they are not all of high quality. Canadian heritage specialist Darryl Cariou is cautious about overselling the idea that preserving historic buildings necessarily contributes to a sustainable environment. Sometimes the replacement of a heritage structure with new construction makes sense in terms of energy and materials conservation. Cariou argues, however, that building quality has to do with more than energy efficiency.[4] Heritage buildings often exhibit workmanship, aesthetics, cultural value, and materials that are not found in contemporary buildings (Roberts 2007; Shipley 2007). We can learn sustainable design "tricks of an old trade" from heritage architecture (Bubelis 2009).

Weighing the demolition and construction costs for a new building against the costs of retrofitting is only one of several factors in the decision to preserve. More

---

4 Darryl Cariou, interview with Noel Keough, Calgary, April 13, 2011. Calgary.

significant considerations are lifetime operating and maintenance costs, which range from ten to twenty times the capital construction costs (Cole and Kernan 1996). If a building can be retrofitted to the operating standards of a new building, its chances of being economically viable and environmentally sustainable are much higher than those of a newly constructed building.

An Athena Institute study for Parks Canada compared demolition and construction to heritage conservation and retrofit for four heritage buildings in Vancouver, Calgary, Winnipeg, and Ottawa. In each case, the life cycle analysis found that heritage conservation resulted in the avoidance of "significant environmental impacts" (ASMI 2009, ii) through savings in energy use and GHG emissions. The report demonstrated that heritage-building conservation not only avoids building demolition and landfill impacts but also protects the embodied energy or energy investment of the existing building's materials. Conversely, reuse avoids the energy costs of extracting and processing new building materials, even allowing for renovations. As markets emerge for GHG credits, reduced GHG emissions may become part of environmental accounting protocols and accumulated credits may provide income for heritage building owners.

Beyond the energy and GHG implications of heritage conservation is the quality of heritage-building construction. Embedded in the Flat Iron, Alex Taylor, and Old Y and Hillhurst buildings is the often overlooked skill and artisanship of the original builders and labourers. To re-create in new construction the art and aesthetics of the architectural features of these heritage buildings would be very energy intensive. The Athena study shows that heritage buildings can outperform new buildings in terms of embodied life-cycle energy use and that "such embodied effects are unlikely to be overshadowed by operating energy concerns if a building has been properly renovated" (ASMI 2009, ii). The greenest building may well be the one never built, although numerous variables must be considered in the environmental cost-benefit analysis of preservation versus new construction.

In assessing the environmental sustainability of heritage conservation, urban design must also be considered. Wilson (2007) recommends measuring the transportation energy intensity of buildings, arguing that daily access to centrally located buildings creates a much lower energy footprint than similar access to new suburban construction because the latter is more auto dependent. Wilson describes eight factors that have the potential to reduce the energy intensity of a building—such as density, pedestrian connectivity, and transit availability—and recommends that these metrics be incorporated into environmental ratings for buildings. The idea of transportation energy intensity could be applied to heritage-building preservation. If, for example, the Flat Iron or Old Y building had been demolished and replaced with a vacant lot or surface parking rather than leased to non-profit and other groups, there probably would have been a net energy cost. If, however, heritage-building demolition results in a new building, then the energy cost difference is not as clear-cut.

Density bylaws are another complicating factor in the preservation-versus-demolition debate. When a land-use bylaw allows for high-rise construction, low- and medium-rise heritage buildings are often in a precarious position. The Athena Institute study supports the idea of environmental sustainability through demolition, pointing out that where there is considerable unused allowable density or air-space above an existing building, an old building can be replaced by one with many more square feet (ASMI 2009). Some urban design practitioners counter this argument with assertions that mid-rise development, as exemplified in the Flat Iron and the Old Y buildings, is more socially sustainable in that it preserves a human scale to the built environment. It maintains connection to the street, is sufficient to support densities for transit-oriented design, and is optimal for vibrant street and community life (Gehl 2011).

The Recognition of Non-Market-Based Definitions of Value

As with the economy in general, private sector investment in heritage buildings far outpaces social economy investment. The capitalist model defers to the hidden hand of the market for decision making. Yet it is widely accepted that the market mechanism is deeply flawed. There are certainly instances in which heritage building conservation makes sense in the market, but most often, the case for preservation has to be made on social, cultural, political, or ecological grounds. Many preservation tools implicitly recognize these other dimensions of value and allow owners to convert those values into financial capital via tax breaks, grants, and land and density swaps. The use of such tools is often positive for heritage-building preservation, but it can also be perverse. Some crafty capitalists have begun to acquire heritage properties in order to take advantage of heritage preservation legislation and municipal heritage programs for unsustainable development. Developers now routinely exploit heritage planning tools in ways that result in the preservation of architectural aspects of heritage buildings at the expense of social and embodied heritage. Examples include preserving heritage-building facades and constructing attached high-rise office and residential development for upwardly mobile classes; privatizing and/or converting to condominiums existing heritage apartment buildings; and increasingly, participating in density swaps, through which a developer preserves a heritage building in the urban core but transfers the associated density credits to a second project elsewhere in the city in order to be allowed to exceed the local zoning density in that neighbourhood. The swap thus conceals a sleight of hand in which sustainability gets traded away for apparent preservation. Robert Shipley and colleagues discuss the dynamics of this private development process in the province of Ontario (Shipley, Utz, and Parsons 2006). The analysis highlights how private sector actors are able to extract profit from heritage conservation either by converting social, natural, cultural, and political capital into financial capital through tax and grant incentives or by extracting higher rents from heritage properties.

This is not to say that the private sector does not play a positive role in heritage conservation. The danger is that social, natural, cultural, and political capitals are not weighed equitably in private sector calculations of heritage preservation feasibility. Randall Mason (2008) addresses this issue by making a cautious call for heritage advocates to engage economic valuation beyond the use of the term "priceless" to describe heritage buildings. David Throsby (1995) bases his argument for the inclusion of cultural capital in economic decision-making on a set of principles that bring together sustainability, economics, and culture—with heritage-building preservation being one aspect of culture. Mark Anielski (2009) has created a robust model of valuation based on the recognition of five varieties of capital assets: natural, human, social, and built, in addition to financial. Heritage conservation, social economy, and sustainability actors share a more open attitude to the consideration of multiple capital flows than do those invested in conventional economics (Wendt 2009). Willing to factor in social, natural, cultural, and political capital into decision-making about the value of heritage-building conservation, this alliance of actors recognizes not only the value of multiple capitals but also the opportunity to generate much-needed new social capital. While municipal and provincial bylaws and policies protect designated heritage buildings, they are also vulnerable to free market logic and the political process. By involving social economy and non-profits in ownership and management of heritage buildings, communities generate new social and political capital that can be mobilized in instances where capitalists armed with market logic threaten heritage conservation designations and bylaws.

In contrast to many capitalist landlords and real estate managers, social economy landlords practice within models of shared-equity building ownership and shared governance; they also use leverage tools such as land trusts to protect the integrity and affordability of buildings in perpetuity (Lewis and Conaty 2012). Such arrangements support the practice of participatory democracy and the vital political and cultural capital that such a practice creates. The buildings and their tenants/owners become a visible presence in the community and represent alternative ways of organizing that are in tune with principles of social sustainability.

The Preservation of Authenticity, Place, and Collective Memory

Authenticity. According to the conventional interpretation of authenticity, authentic individuals are people who are true to themselves. The notion of authenticity in heritage architecture is more in keeping with Charles Taylor's notion of true authenticity. Taylor (1991) situates individuals as social beings within what he calls "horizons of significance" (39)—wider contexts in which we act and live, an awareness of which is likely to lead to respect for others and the natural world. In this way, Taylor's view of authenticity connects the individual to larger political, social, or religious sources of meaning without which a person suffers what Taylor (1991) calls the "malaise of modernity."

The Declaration of San Antonio was developed out of the InterAmerican Symposium on Authenticity in the Conservation and Management of the Cultural Heritage held in Texas in 1996. It asserts that "the understanding of the authenticity of a heritage site depends on a comprehensive assessment of the significance of the site by those who are associated with it or who claim it as part of their history" (ICOMOS 1996, 42). The concern is more with the authenticity of the collective emotion (the past experiences, historical events, and community memories) than of the material fabric of the monument or building itself. Heritage, as defined by the Charter for the Preservation of Quebec's Heritage, is "a possession of the community" (Deschambault Charter 1982).

In a similar vein, Dolores Hayden has demonstrated that heritage architecture also has a role to play in illuminating political struggles that have shaped our communities. Her work emphasizes that the preservation of heritage architecture celebrates not only the conventional founders and builders of our communities but also the political, class, and ethnic and gender struggles that have shaped who we are (Hayden 1997). Social economy actors have an inherent interest in unearthing, communicating, and celebrating those layers of our history and culture. These struggles become embodied in our recollection of places in *time*, in what is valued and what is remembered of a place (Schwartz 2010)—what we might call the "memory commons."

Place. Social geographer Doreen Massey (1994, 154) urges us to imagine places as "articulated moments in networks of social relations and understandings." John Logan and Harvey Molotch (1987, 45) argue that "attributes of place are achieved through social action, rather than through the qualities inherent in a piece of land, and that places are defined through social relationships, not through nature, autonomous markets, or spatial geometry." Architects, planners, and urban designers often describe their work as place making, the assumption being that place has both an immaterial and material dimension. Architecture cannot independently create place, but it does give place material form and thus can embody cultural, social, political, and ecological processes and qualities of place. At the same time, architecture contributes to the evolution of these same processes and qualities. Architecture gathers and materializes the spirit of place, and the best architecture does this over time as buildings live and grow.

The Salmar Community Theatre
Kailey Cannon

In late 1945, several locals from the mid-sized community of Salmon Arm, BC, decided to honour the efforts of their war veterans. Seven individuals from various professional backgrounds set their sights on purchasing the local Rex Theatre with the intention of directing all profits generated by the theatre toward building a memorial ice rink. For the initial purchase, the group enlisted the help of the broader community through the sale of debentures. They bought the Rex in 1947 and ran it for two years before it burnt to the ground. Fortunately, those two years were highly successful, and the group built the Salmar Classic Cinema in 1949. The Salmar was a good business, and the goal of subsidizing a memorial arena was realized in 1958. Impressed by the group's achievements, the city gave the group land to operate a drive-in theatre and the Salmar Community Association (SCA) was formed, a registered nonprofit committed to providing affordable entertainment and employing local youth.

When the popularity of drive-in theatres started to wane, the SCA sold the land to the BC Department of Highways and placed windfall profits in a holding account. At this point Roger Ayles, a successful businessman in the video rental and movie industries, convinced the association to expand the Salmar Theatre before Cineplex or Famous Players came to town. Following Ayles's advice, the association secured an initial loan through the bank, later switching to the Salmon Arm Savings and Credit Union for a lower interest rate. In 1997, the dream of a non-profit community-run four screen theatre—unique in North America at the time—was realized. In early 2000, the SCA saw an opportunity to both rekindle its initial goal of supporting local veterans and address the shortage of theatre parking. The aging Legion building adjacent to the theatre was in disrepair and the local Legion branch in danger of folding. The SCA entered into an agreement to build the legion a new building in exchange for their land to use for parking.

Today, the SCA is financially self-sufficient and earmarks 10 percent of its net income for various community initiatives. In 2010, for example, the association had a net income of $125,322 even after giving $18,500 in grants, $12,000 in scholarships to local high school and college students, and $3,500 and numerous free movie passes in sponsorship of various community events and organizations (Joan Sholinder, interview by the author, 28 June 2011).

The old Salmar Classic Theatre remains a fixture in Salmon Arm's historic downtown. In addition to housing the SCA's new 3D projector, it provides a space for community events and the screening of various award-winning movies from around the world by the Shuswap Film Society.

The SCA has served as a model for other communities exploring similar local cinema schemes. Some examples include the now completed cinemas in Dauphin, Manitoba (www.countryfestcommunitycinema.ca), and Burns Lake, BC, (www.bltheatre.com), as well as the proposed cinema in Merritt, BC (http://merrittmovietheatre.com/project-progress/).

Cannon, Kailey. 2011. Interview with Joan Sholinder, Salmar Association Director. 28 June.
Merritt Movie Theatre: Merritt Community Cinema Society. 2015. http://merrittmovietheatre.com/project-progress/.
Salmar Community Association. 2014. http://www.salmartheatre.com/.

Heritage buildings embody the history of places and can evoke an emotional attachment, a caring that translates into engagement, participation, and empowerment: "affective bonds to places can help inspire action because people are motivated to seek, stay in, protect, and improve places that are meaningful to them";

furthermore, "processes of collective action work better when emotional ties to places and their inhabitants are cultivated" (Manzo and Perkins 2006, 347).

Collective memory. People who share experiences and events in a place add something not only to their personal memories but also to the broader, collective history (memory) of the place itself (Boyer 1994). Memory binds people together, "recharging their commonality by reference to the physical spaces and previous instances, often founding a moment, of that collective identity" (Crinson 2005, xiii). This more collective sense of memory is written into the landscape through architecture. As Donovan Rypkema, the founder of PlaceEconomics, a real-estate development consulting firm based in Washington, D.C., observes, "The city tells its own past, transfers its own memory, largely through the fabric of the built environment. Historic buildings are the physical manifestation of memory—and it is memory that makes places significant" (Rypkema 2010, 4). One artifact of this social layering is the "collective memory" that is physically, texturally, and metaphorically embedded in architecture, which affects and is affected by the trends, beliefs, and values of each social era. In *The Architecture of the City*, architect Aldo Rossi claims that "a city remembers through its buildings" (cited in Crinson 2005, xiii). But, as Dolores Hayden (1997) reminds us, memory is not unitary. In the city, she argues, memories are shaped by the diversity of experience of a place's citizens. Advocacy groups and environmental organizations often take on the task of recuperating these diverse memories, while heritage buildings offer a unique opportunity for such agencies to give these memories a concrete presence (Hayden 1997). Our examples of the alliances between social economy actors and those involved in saving heritage buildings show how collaboration not only saves buildings but also brings back a part of what philosopher John McMurtry calls the civil commons. Embodied in many heritage buildings, and shared with previous generations of citizens, is a social democratic ideal. Workers, unions, marginalized classes, and the general public recognize in these buildings, and in the activities that have occurred within them, their own investments, as Canadians, in social justice (Kennah 2008). When buildings like schools, fire halls, or hospitals are repurposed for social economy practices, we align heritage with social democracy.

Consider some of the positive outcomes of non-profits locating in heritage buildings. Authenticity and continuity of the buildings' role in the community seems palpable. In many cases, the structure shelters almost the same services for which the building was originally built. Alex Taylor School, for example, had a long history as a community school and as a place that provided outreach programs to new Canadians and hot lunch programs for children in various schools in the multicultural inner-city neighbourhoods. Today, many of the same food and drop-in programs continue. Alex Taylor is a social economy hub that shelters and co-locates a cluster of progressive organizations working in the inner city. Urban fragments like Alex Taylor or the Flat Iron in Edmonton, or Calgary's Old Y "provide a context in which the more obvious heritage assets are located, but should not be treated as mere context, because it is often the ensemble of objects and their context that create value" (Tweed and Sutherland 2007, 63).

In urban landscapes that are under pressure for renewal and gentrification, social economy actors in heritage buildings become legitimate advocates for heritage preservation. They represent not only a historic and aesthetic asset but also a political asset—the social democratic values that originally shaped these inner-city districts. This is all the more important in this age of globalization, when narrow calculation and financial capital flows dictate much decision making. Calgary's Old Y building is one example of a structure that has been linked with the city's social development since its inauguration. Since 1911, the YWCA provided a safe hostel for single women arriving to the city. "The building became the "Old Y" in 1971 after the YWCA vacated the premises and completed their new building on 5th avenue. . . . Since that time, the Old Y building has housed dozens of diverse community-serving, grass-roots and non-profit agencies" (CWRC 2014b).

When the building was threatened with demolition in 1979, "the groups renting offices united to form a tenants association called the Old Y Action Groups. Together they rescued their beloved building from demolition" (CWRC 2014b). The tenants worked to designate the building with provincial heritage status and the Old Y became a registered historic resource in 1982. The tenants grew closer, changing the name to the "Old Y Centre for Community Organizations." Since 1982, the building "has functioned under the umbrella of the tenant organization as affordable office space for dozens of diverse grassroots and non-profit agencies, in sectors ranging from arts and culture, immigrant community associations, youth agencies, LGBTQ community resources, environmental groups, social justice advocacy and more" (CWRC 2014b). In 2012, the Old Y changed its name to Community Wise as a sign of "the role that the facility plays in linking all these diverse groups together, through Calgary's past, present and future" (CWRC 2014b).

The Old Y and the Alex Taylor School are particularly good examples of authentic expression of heritage values. Both are good, but not outstanding, candidates for architectural heritage. Their heritage strong suit is their social and cultural roles and the alignment of current uses with the activities of people who inhabited these buildings in the past. For both places, contemporary use by social economy actors rehabilitates the building's authentic original function and role in the community. Conservation protects the building and maintains recognition in the public mind of the deep historical continuity of social justice, volunteerism, and social innovation in the inner city. This convergence of authentic representation of place, as remembered and enacted in heritage buildings by social economy practitioners, confers "ontological security"—a sense of continuity and purposeful existence through time—on members of the community (Grenville 2007).

CONCLUSION

Ultimately, the well-being of our communities can be better served by more deliberate attempts to link the practices of social economy and sustainability with heritage conservation. We identified three important dimensions of this intersection. Heritage buildings are saved from demolition and both buildings and neighbourhoods are given a new life. At the same time, social agencies are given new space and visibility, often in socially significant and dynamic or transitioning parts of the city. And finally, embodied energy and building values are conserved. The success stories told in this chapter suggest the potential for future alliances (beyond lodging or co-location solutions) as cities and communities meet the challenges of rising social inequality caused by the disruption of economies and societies. We have been inspired by those working from within the social economy to consider heritage buildings at more than architectural or economic face value and seeking instead their value as embodied social history and their intrinsic sociopolitical worth. Conserving architecture conserves solidarities with the most vulnerable sectors of the Canadian public. It defends and keeps active the memory of Canadian social democracy. It establishes continuities in our commitments to fairness and equality in urban politics and urban design.

REFERENCES

Anielski, Mark, 2009. *The Economics of Happiness*. Gabriola Island, BC: New Society Publishers.
ASMI (Athena Sustainable Materials Institute). 2009. *A Life Cycle Assessment Study of Embodied Effects for Existing Historic Buildings*. Report prepared for Parks Canada. Merrickville, ON: Athena Institute.

Beltline Urban Society. 2014. "Old Y Centre." Beltline.ca. http://2.beltline.ca/3rd-sector/old-y-centre.

Boyer, M. Christine. 1994. *The City of Collective Memory: Its Historical Imagery and Architectural Entertainments*. Cambridge, MA: MIT Press.

Boyle McCauley News, March 1994. "Gibson Block Begins New Life" http://bmcnews.org/pdf/01-MAR-1994.pdf.

Bubelis, Romas. 2009. "Sustainability by Design: Tricks of an Old Trade." H□ritage 12 (1): 5–11.

Calgary Public Library. 1988. "The Y.W.C.A., Calgary, Alta., Canada." Calgary: Calgary Central Library. Canadiana Discovery Portal. http://search.canadiana.ca/view/ac.pc_149.

Canada's Historic Places. Hillhurst Cottage School, Calgary. http://www.historicplaces.ca/en/rep-reg/place-lieu.aspx?id=5181.

Cariou, Darryl, N.d. "Heritage and Citizens: Building Public Will and Engaging Canadians." Calgary: Calgary Heritage Authority, City of Calgary.

City of Calgary. 2007. "ImagineCalgary Plan for Long Range Urban Sustainability." Calgary.

City of Calgary. 1986. "The Connaught-Beltline District: A Heritage Walking Tour." Calgary: The City of Calgary Information Centre, Planning and Building Department.

Cole, Raymond J., and Raul C. Kernan. 1996. "Life-Cycle Energy Use in Office Buildings." *Building and Environment* 31 (4): 307–17.

Crinson, Mark. 2005. *Urban Memory: History and Amnesia in the Modern City*. London and New York: Routledge.

CWRC (Community Wise Resource Centre). 2014a. "CommunityWise." Calgary: Community Wise Resource Centre. http://communitywise.net/communitywise/.

———. 2014b. "Old Y Building." Calgary: Community Wise Resource Centre. http://communitywise.net/old-y-building/.

Dannenberg, Andrew, Howard Frumkin, and Richard J. Jackson, eds. 2011. *Making Healthy Places: Designing and Building for Health, Well-being, and Sustainability*. Washington, D.C.: Island Press.

Fairbairn, Brett. 2009. "A Rose by Any Name: The Thorny Question of Social Economy Discourse in Canada." Canadian Social Economy Research Partnerships / Centre canadien de recherche partenariale en économie sociale, Occasional Paper Series: Canadian Perspectives on the Meaning of the Social Economy, No. 1, October.

Fennell, C. 2009. "Combating Attempts at Elision: African American Accomplishments at New Philadelphia, Illinois." In *Intangible Heritage Embodied*, edited by F. Ruggles and H. Silverman, 147–68. New York: Springer.

Gehl, Jan. 2011. *Life Between Buildings: Using Public Space*. Washington, D.C.: Island Press.

GHPNS (Greening of Historic Properties National Summit). 2006. "Pinpointing Strategies and Tactics for Integrating Green Building Technologies into Historic Structure." White Paper. Green Buildings Alliance and Pittsburgh History and Landmarks Foundation.

Grenville, Jane. 2007. "Conservation as Psychology: Ontological Security and the Built Environment." *International Journal of Heritage Studies* 13 (6): 447–61.

Harrison, Stephan, Steve Pile, and Nigel Thrift, eds. 2004. *Patterned Ground: Entanglements of Nature and Culture.* London: Reaktion Books.

Hayden, Dolores. 1997. *The Power of Place: Urban Landscapes as Public History.* Cambridge, MA: MIT Press.

HERMIS (Heritage Resources Management Information System). 2013. "Gibson Block." Alberta Register of Historic Places. https://hermis.alberta.ca/ARHP/Search. aspx?DeptID=1&st=gibson+block.

Herzog, Lawrence. 2002. "The Rebirth of Alex Taylor School." *Edmonton Real Estate Weekly*, vol. 20, no. 37, 12 September.

———. 2003. "The Gibson Block at 90." *Edmonton Real Estate Weekly*, vol. 21, no. 4, 19 June.

ICOMOS (International Council on Monuments and Sites). 1996. "The Declaration of San Antonio." Charenton-le-Pont, France: ICOMOS. http://www.icomos. org/en/charters-and-texts/179-articles-en-francais/ressources/charters-and-standards/188-the-declaration-of-san-antonio.

Ivany, Kathryn A. 2000. "Bridging Downtown and Inner City: The First Thirty Years of Edmonton City Church Centre Corporation." Edmonton: Edmonton City Church Centre Corporation. http://e4calberta.org/wp-content/uploads/2012/11/ E4C30yearhistorybook.pdf.

Ivany, Kathryn A., and Beckie Garber-Conrad. 1995. *Flatiron Legacy One of Heritage and Help: The Story of a Building with a Provocative Past and an Exciting Future.* Edmonton: Edmonton City Centre Church Corporation.

Kennah, Mel. 2008. "Putting Out Fires–Reclaiming Moncton's Fire Station for Youth at Risk." *Heritage* 11 (3): 22–33.

Lee, Celia. 2009. "Case Study of AWA for the BC-Alberta Social Economy Research Alliance." Available from authors.

Lewis, Mike. 2007. "Constructing a Sustainable Future: Exploring the Strategic Relevance of Social and Solidarity Economy Frameworks." Port Alberni, BC: Centre for Community Enterprise on behalf of BC-Alberta Social Economy Research Alliance.

Lewis, Mike, and Pat Conaty. 2012. *The Resilience Imperative: Cooperative Transitions to a Steady-State Economy.* Gabriola Island, BC: New Society.

Logan, John, and Harvey Molotch. 1987. "Places as Commodities." *Urban Fortunes.* Berkeley and Los Angeles: University of California Press.

Manzo, Lynne, and Douglas Perkins. 2002. "Finding Common Ground: The Importance of Place Attachment to Community Participation and Planning." *Journal of Planning Literature* 20: 335–50.

Mason, Randall. 2008. "Be Interested and Beware: Joining Economic Valuation and Heritage Conservation." *International Journal of Heritage Studies* 14 (4): 303–18.

Massey, Doreen. 1994. "A Global Sense of Place." In *Space, Place, and Gender*, 146–56. Minneapolis: University of Minnesota Press.

Mercier, Guy. 2001. "The Useful Ambiguity of Urban Heritage." *Journal of the Society for the Study of Architecture in Canada* 26 (3–4): 37–44.

Onyschuk, Bohdan, Michael Kovecevic and Peter Nikolakatkos. 2001. *Smart Growth in North America: New Ways to Create Livable Cities*. Toronto: Canadian Urban Institute.

Roberts, Tristan. 2007. "Historic Preservation and Green Building: A Lasting Relationship." BuildingGreen.com. *Environmental Building News*, January. http://www2.buildinggreen.com/article/historic-preservation-and-green-building-lasting-relationship.

Ross, Susan. 2006. "Saving Heritage Is Key to Sustainable Development." *Heritage*, Spring.

Rypkema, Donovan D. 2010. "Preservation: More Than Bricks and Mortar." Presentation at Kansas Main Street Conference. Hutchinson, Kansas. http://www.placeeconomics.com/wp-content/uploads/2011/04/preservation-more-than-bricks-and-mortar.pdf.

Schwartz, Joan. 2010. "Complicating the Picture: Place and Memory Between Representation and Reflection." In *Placing Memory and Remembering Place in Canada*, edited by James Opp and John C. Walsh, 293–312. Vancouver: University of British Columbia Press.

Shipley, Robert. 2007. Guest Editor. "Measuring Progress and Building Heritage." *Alternatives Journal* 32 (2–3).

Shipley, Robert, Steve Utz, and Michael Parsons. 2006. "Does Adaptive Reuse Pay? A Study of the Business of Building Renovation in Ontario, Canada." *International Journal of Heritage Studies* 12 (6): 505–20.

Taylor, Charles. 1991. *The Malaise of Modernity*. Toronto: House of Anansi Press.

Throsby, David. 1995. "Culture, Economics and Sustainability." *Journal of Cultural Economics* 19: 199–206.

Tweed, Christopher, and Margaret Sutherland. 2007. "Built Cultural Heritage and Sustainable Urban Development." *Landscape and Urban Planning* 83 (1): 62–69.

Vinokur-Kaplan, Diane. 2001. "Nonprofit Landlords Leasing to Nonprofit Tenants: Legal and Managerial Strategies Used at Nonprofit Co-location Enterprises in the United States." Paper presented at International Conference on Nonprofit Enterprises: Governing Development and Funding Innovation Faculty of Economics, University of Trento, Italy, July 8–9, 2001.

Wendt, Allyson. 2009. "Building for People: Integrating Social Justice into Green Design." BuildingGreen.com. *Environmental Building News*, October.

Wilson, Alex. 2007. "Driving to Green Buildings: The Transportation Energy Intensity of Buildings." With Rachel Navaro. BuildingGreen.com. *Environmental Building News*, September.

Strong Institutions, Weak Strategies

Credit Unions and the Rural Social Economy

Sean Markey, Freya Kristensen, and Stewart Perry

Over the past few decades, the shift away from the traditional welfare state toward neoliberal policies has had a profound impact on rural communities in Canada. As they grapple with this restructuring, rural communities suffer government withdrawal, weakened linkages with traditional resource industries, and a loss of local services. When those difficulties are combined with the added effects of economic restructuring, labour shedding due to advanced production techniques, and industrial flexibility, it becomes clear that rural communities must find ways to buttress their economies if they are to flourish. Looking beyond traditional private and public sector solutions, we suggest that the social economy may offer viable solutions to address gaps in rural areas affected by political and economic restructuring. Social economy solutions take a place-based approach to building a resilient local economy from within. This involves reorienting a community's focus inwards, finding value and strength in local attributes and resources, and creating local capacity-building and reinvestment opportunities in order to decrease dependency on external resources.

The purpose of this chapter is to explore the role that social economy organizations (SEOs) may play in revitalizing rural communities. Specifically, we are interested in the activities of credit unions, since credit unions, as both SEOs and local financial institutions, have a unique role to play in financing the very sector in which they operate. As part of their mandate, credit unions have a commitment to provide financial and other related services to their members; however, their work serves their members not only directly but also indirectly, insofar as depository funds are reinvested locally. This is in contrast to conventional banks, which often invest at a distance in order to maximize profits. In rural settings, access to financial services is more limited, and thus credit unions have an even greater significance, particularly with respect to the small enterprises and non-profit organizations typical of the rural context. Given their mandate of member and community service and their commitment to a set of co-operative principles (outlined below), we propose that credit unions are a natural source of financial assistance for social enterprises and other organizations operating within the social economy that may provide valuable services to many individuals and communities not adequately served by the for-profit or public sectors. We explore this proposition in the context of several case study rural communities in British Columbia and Alberta. Although the social economy is by no means an understudied concept, to date there is very little research on the social economy in a rural context in general and, more specifically, in rural Canada (Wittman, Beckie, and Hergesheimer 2012; Teitelbaum and Reimer 2002; Reimer 2005; Neamtan and Downing 2005). We hope that this chapter contributes to a more thorough understanding of how the social economy operates in rural areas in Canada and of the particular roles of credit unions within the sector.

THE SOCIAL ECONOMY IN THE RURAL CONTEXT

The earlier chapters of this volume provide a comprehensive overview of the definitions and debates surrounding the social economy. We will not reiterate this material other than to state that for the purposes of our research, we view the social economy as being a limited part of the third sector of the economy. We exclude such non-profits as hospitals, universities, charities, and recreational societies and include only those bodies that seek a different economic process of ownership, work, production, and surplus distribution—a process focused on equity for all stakeholders. It is these companion initiatives and organizations that credit unions might assist through their financial and granting services.

Rural Restructuring and Community Economic Development

Globalization and the changing economy, driven by neoliberal values, have had profound effects on rural communities in Canada (Young and Matthews 2007). With the values and traditional redistributive practices of the welfare state under increasing scrutiny, many governments have repositioned themselves as partners in the provision of community services rather than primary deliverers or funders of those services. As a result, there have been dramatic shifts in the responsibilities of the voluntary sector (Gray, Healy, and Crofts 2003). This societal shift away from the traditional welfare state and toward an emphasis on market-driven mechanisms and business-based approaches for addressing social problems is one reason for the emergence of the social economy (Dart 2004).

Rural restructuring in Canada can be characterized by the growth in the service sector and the subsequent decline in primary industries, upon which many rural communities rely. This restructuring has resulted in high rates of unemployment and emigration of young people (Markey, Halseth, and Manson 2008). Lower populations in rural areas makes providing services in these areas more expensive and a lack of services may discourage businesses or people from moving to the community (Green 2003; Halseth and Ryser 2006). Indeed, the closure of businesses that provided services to the community can have significant social and economic consequences. A seven-year study of the availability of services in rural and small-town places across Canada found a reduction over time of the local availability of all services tracked, including education services, health care, police and fire services, and government services (Halseth and Ryser 2006).

Rural restructuring is also fundamentally linked with the degradation of natural resources and the decline of ecosystem services associated with resource exploitation and, increasingly, with climate change (Wall and Marzall 2006). These issues elevate the importance of sustainable development to rural places— and highlight specific contradictions and tensions associated with the conceptual and practical dimensions of rural sustainability. For example, Katherine Scott and colleagues (2000, 433) summarize the contradictions of defining sustainability in the rural setting by stating that "on the one hand it might imply stasis, but it might also suggest an ability to respond positively to change." This tension is evident in the perceptual barriers to recognizing the relevance of sustainable development to the rural setting. The first barrier concerns the common rural economic practice of attracting large resource-intensive industries. In colloquial terms, this "smoke-stack chasing" is a stubbornly consistent development strategy, despite research that points to its relative impotence in terms of net gain for community economies or long-term gain related to capturing sustainable benefits for the future in rapid-growth settings (Markey et al. 2005; Markey, Halseth, and Manson 2012). Sustainability principles within this context may be seen as a threat to traditional rural economies. At best, sustainability is ignored as irrelevant; at worst, it is targeted as a distinct threat to community viability and a rural "way of life," reflecting the tendency to prioritize economic capital at the expense of the other forms of community capital. This situation is particularly evident in resource boom regions of the country. At a deeper conceptual level, combinations of the rural idyll and frontierism may hinder the connection between rural lifestyle and the need to adopt more sustainable living practices, such as increased density (Markey et al. 2010). While many rural communities are beginning to explore sustainable planning principles, the pressures of finite space and resources that impact their more densely populated urban neighbours do not confront rural people in Canada to the same degree. As a result, rural populations are, for example, less likely to embrace sustainable planning practices like Smartgrowth (Wells 2002). It is also important to note that sustainable community development research has done little to apply a rural lens or to engage seriously with robust case research in the rural setting. Too often, sustainable community planning principles and strategies are urban concepts with little cultural or contextual adaptation to the rural setting.

Faced with these challenges, many rural communities are searching for ways to revitalize their economies in situations of decline or to protect and localize economic activities in situations of resource booms. Community economic development (CED) is an approach being adopted by rural and urban communities alike (Perry 1987). CED emphasizes the need for communities to develop their own local solutions to economic problems and the importance of building long-term community self-reliance and incorporating environmental and social considerations into economic plans and decision-making (Markey et al. 2005). The CED approach recommends that rural communities reorient away from a space-based economy context and toward a place-based economy as a way to become more resilient. A place-based approach encourages communities to look beyond natural resource exploitation and instead to consider the unique attributes of their particular place in order to generate sustainable development opportunities (Markey, Halseth, and Manson 2012).

Credit Unions and the Rural Social Economy

Many researchers see encouraging the growth of the social economy and social economy organizations (SEOs) as a viable strategy for revitalizing local communities (Berkes and Davidson-Hunt 2007; Greffe 2007; Gertler 2004). Because SEOs are not profit oriented, they are able to look at both long-term and short-term prospects and thus to "distil and disseminate values and processes that are intrinsic to local development" (Greffe 2007, 96). Credit unions are important social economy organizations that operate in rural areas, providing crucial financial services. Credit unions, also known as co-operative banks, emerged from the co-operative movement that began in Europe in the nineteenth century, in an era characterized by rapid industrialization and urbanization across Europe and North America. In

British Columbia, the provincial government has been encouraging the development of co-operatives since the 1890s in the agricultural sector, in order to enhance the quality of produce and reduce the price of farm supplies for farmers. In the 1930s, BC farmers, who were well informed about co-operative movements in Europe and other parts of Canada, established the first co-operative marketing organizations in the Okanagan Valley and the Fraser Valley. Consumer co-operatives were also organized in the Kootenays and Vancouver Island, generally as a way to compete with chain stores and reduce the cost of goods. These consumer and marketing co-operatives provided great support for the establishment of the BC credit union movement (MacPherson 1995).

When credit unions finally emerged in British Columbia in the 1940s and 1950s, they were very successful, since there was a real need for banking services for those who were poorly paid or underemployed and who were not being served by existing banking systems. Co-operative banks in British Columbia in the mid-1900s focused on the character and the reputation of each member rather than on individual wealth (MacPherson 1995).

In Alberta, farmers who were frustrated by the terms and conditions under which they were forced to sell their grain formed co-operatives in the early 1900s. First, farmers formed co-operatively owned country elevators and then started to pool their crops for sale through marketing co-operatives. Through this system, farmers received higher prices for their products than if they had sold through the regular grain exchange. Aside from a few short-lived examples, there was no single pioneer that pushed forward the credit union movement in Alberta; rather, the credit union idea "dribbled into the province a little bit at a time, taking root among tiny isolated groups gathered in kitchens, living rooms, and small meeting rooms" in the 1930s (Turner 1984, 40). Alberta passed its Credit Union Act in 1938.

Today, credit unions still have a mandate to lend to members, and they have become heavily involved with community economic development. Since CED "draws on the community's needs and resources, the same way a credit union does" (Fairbairn, Ketilson, and Krebs 1997, 11), credit unions are ideally suited to this role. Credit unions have a unique advantage when it comes to CED: working to build community skills, capacity, and leadership, and even create jobs, they are able to operate beyond the traditional economic development role of financing (Fairbairn, Ketilson, and Krebs 1997; Heenan and McLaughlin 2002).

Credit unions are particularly valuable to rural areas. Since it is part of their mandate to provide loans to those who have less access to credit and because investment decisions are based on the idea of strengthening community, credit unions are able to fill the credit gap experienced in many rural areas (Green 2003). Furthermore, the success of the credit union is dependent upon the vitality of the community in which it is rooted, so economic surpluses are reinvested or redistributed back to the community (Fairbairn, Ketilson, and Krebs 1997). In documenting how four small towns in Australia were affected by the loss of a local bank branch, Deborah Ralston and Diana Beal (1999) found that the number of business and home loans dropped and that the local economy of the town was affected as people stopped shopping locally and instead shopped where they banked. When a credit union opened up in each of these towns, there was a dramatic improvement in community confidence, and the majority of people in these towns felt that the credit union had improved employment opportunities, encouraged new business, and reduced the potential for crime in the community.

Brown (2001) remarks that the size of the community in which the credit union is situated will have a bearing on the kind of impact the credit union will have. In large urban areas, for example, large credit unions are in competition with other banks, so formal community relationships are likely to be more important. Small credit unions in urban areas will be more likely to have an impact on "very particular aspects of community involvement and to mobilize particular segments of the community" (50). Finally, credit unions located in small communities will likely have "high penetration and strong member loyalty" and will therefore be able to address broad-based community concerns (50).

Brett Fairbairn and colleagues (1997), in an extensive article on the roles of credit unions in CED, show that one of their most critical roles is in helping to start up and expand local businesses. Because credit unions redistribute and reinvest surpluses and because they are committed to education and community vitality, they "embody community economic development and can act as powerful bulwarks of their host communities. Co-operatives and credit unions have a greater capacity to influence their community environment than do most businesses" (15). Kimberly Zeuli (2001) finds that co-operatives build human capital through leadership development in rural communities, a prerequisite for local development efforts—for example, through providing skills development like business management, communications, or group problem-solving to those who serve on a co-operative board. These roles for credit unions in smaller communities are also supported by evidence which indicates that credit unions are ranked first in meeting the business needs of small- and medium-sized companies (CFIB 2013).

One area where credit unions can make a positive contribution to strengthening and supporting local economies falls under the broad concept of "community investment." Community investment (CI) refers to "capital used to finance deep-seated needs of local communities that cannot ordinarily be addressed by traditional investment models" (RIA 2007, 16). CI usually supports low-income communities, both in Canada and in developing countries, and is sometimes known as "cause-based, socially directed, social impact, or alternative investing" (Strandberg 2004, 6). The importance of CI is noted by Coro Strandberg (2004, 14), who writes, "Community investing can help turn around communities, create opportunities for the disenfranchised, support environmental regeneration and underwrite affordable housing for the poor." It is this particular role of credit unions that we sought to investigate through our case research.

RESEARCH DESIGN AND CONTEXT

We implemented our research design in three phases. First, we began our exploration with a literature review on the social economy and, specifically, credit unions. Second, we conducted semi-structured interviews with twelve key-informant leaders in the social economy and credit union sectors in order to gain a better understanding of credit union roles and social economy related programs. The perspectives of the informants helped us significantly in moving to our third phase in terms of identifying appropriate case studies. Finally, using the information provided in the interviews and combined with a scan of credit union websites in British Columbia and Alberta (collecting a set of comparative indicators), we completed case studies of eight credit unions. The research emphasized the role of rural credit unions in supporting and promoting the social economy and in facilitating economic development more generally across the rural region. Research with each credit union consisted of a review of annual reports, semi-structured interviews with the CEO and manager(s) of community programs/loans, and an interview with the manager of the Community Futures Network of Canada office in the region in order to gain an external perspective and overview of the rural regional economy.

Our selection of case sites was based upon several criteria, including an assessment of the rural character of each credit union community as indicated by its population and its non-adjacent distance from larger metropolitan centres. Descriptions and rationales for various definitions of *rural* exist elsewhere in the literature (see, for example, Berkes and Davidson-Hunt 2007; Markey et al. 2005). Our approach fits well with the concept of "degrees of rurality," according to which territorial units can be assigned several measures of rurality (Du Plessis, Beshiri, and Bollman 2004). Other selection criteria included the presence of community-oriented programs identified on the host website and an invitation by the credit union's CEO to conduct research on the organization.

Given these factors, the populations of our case communities ranged from 6,000 to 17,000. (See table 10.1 for a breakdown of town population and credit union characteristics.) Overall, the credit union sector in both British Columbia and Alberta is significant. In Alberta, there are approximately forty-six credit unions with over 640,000 members and $17 billion in assets.[1] British Columbia also has about forty-six credit unions, but, with more than 1.6 million members and assets of $48 billion, they are significantly larger (CUCC 2010).

Table 10.1 Characteristics of credit unions studied

	Population*	Branches	Assets	Members
Case 1	13,000	8	$524 M	20,000
Case 2	11,000	3	$169 M	11,000
Case 3	17,000	4	$221 M	10,000
Case 4	7,000	1	$154 M	5,000
Case 5	16,000	3	$458 M	20,000
Case 6	16,000	3	$158 M	12,000
Case 7	7,000	1	$303 M	9,000
Case 8	6,000	7	$163 M	7,000

*Town population refers to main branch location and is based on 2006 Canada Census data.

THE ROLE OF CREDIT UNIONS IN RURAL ECONOMIES

In this study, we use credit unions as representatives of the social economy to investigate how the social economy can contribute to the revitalization of rural communities. As we have outlined above, rural communities commonly employ a CED approach to rebuilding and strengthening their local economies, orienting toward a place-based approach to development that emphasizes social and environmental aspects of development, including the social economy. Credit unions are in a unique position in that they both operate within the social economy and have the

---

1 The number of credit unions will vary because of a continuing process of mergers, on the one hand, and the founding of new credit unions, on the other.

means and the mandate to make meaningful financial contributions to strengthen the sector. In the following sections, we review select opportunities and barriers that exist for rural credit unions as institutional representatives of the social economy. Our research reveals that credit unions possess a number of "competitiveness attributes" that make them invaluable to rural communities, helping to counteract the negative impacts associated with restructuring. These attributes—which include community rootedness, the ability to make locally appropriate decisions, and the ability to provide services tailored to non-profit organizations and marginalized communities—represent operating dynamics that may apply to the rural social economy as a whole. In addition, a significant potential advantage posed by rural social economy actors is their ability to reinvest in the local and regional economy.

Place-Based Economic Competitiveness

As place-based organizations operating within the social economy, credit unions have an obvious and unique advantage in supporting their local communities. Instead of exploiting this competitive advantage, credit unions seem encumbered by the pressure to compete with banks. A common theme among informants in the course of our research was that credit union managers feel compelled to pursue a more traditional business model in order to effectively compete with larger financial institutions. Such a competition is weighted toward the banks because of their sheer size as compared to most credit unions, making it difficult for credit unions to offer competitive financial products and services. One response to this challenge has been for credit unions to merge or simply to work together with other credit unions in a region to offer broader, shared services.

In general, credit union managers are aware of the limitations they face in competing with banks. Indeed, this seemed to be a common sentiment among the informants interviewed in the course of this research: although credit unions find it difficult to compete with banks in offering financial services, informants stressed that they are able to offer to their customers a different type of value, which they can use to compete with banks. This value encompasses strong community roots and an awareness of local issues, which informants report gives them the ability to personalize financial services, stepping outside the typical boundaries to tailor financial products to individual customers and offer services to marginalized groups and non-profit organizations.

Community rootedness. Credit unions differ quite dramatically in structure and mission from banks. Being member-owned, democratic, locally based financial institutions that adhere to a distinct set of regulations in each province in Canada, credit unions operate in a small and well-defined geographic area. Despite notable exceptions to this last point—there are several large credit unions in Canada that have a broad service area, though never extending past provincial boundaries—the majority of credit unions in Canada are set up to serve a particular rural area, town, or city. Some urban credit unions even have branches attuned to particular neighbourhoods. Accordingly, our interviewees identified rootedness in community and a strong community identity as significant not only to the informants themselves but also to credit union customers.

Community rootedness is a product of the structure of the credit union itself. As member-owned co-operatives, credit unions adhere to the seven co-operative principles as set out by the International Co-operative Alliance. Adherence to this set of principles—which includes voluntary and open membership, democratic member control, autonomy and independence, and a concern for the community—is, for the most part, what separates credit unions from traditional financial institutions. Although some credit unions are organized solely for a particular subgroup in a community (such as the employees of a local industry), anyone is welcome to join a credit union, and all members have decision-making power.

In general, the people we interviewed saw their credit unions as being in touch with the needs of their community, a characteristic that they believe sets them apart from the banks. According to one credit union representative, the average person may be unaware of the seven co-op principles but may still perceive credit unions to be community based, an attribute that many informants believe could give the credit union a competitive advantage over banks and other financial institutions. One interviewee emphasized the need for credit unions to engage in more self-promotion:

> When we are out at community events with our credit union shirts on, people can make that connection between the credit union and the community. However, people don't really understand us but we don't say enough about ourselves. We need to beat our own drum more. I think people generally care about the same things as credit unions and if they were more aware of what we stood for there's no way they wouldn't bank with us.

It is clear from our interviewees that "community rootedness" is a characteristic that credit unions can leverage to their advantage in competing with other financial institutions.

Local decision making. Credit unions' community rootedness is manifested in a variety of ways. In terms of community involvement and investment, several informants pointed out that credit unions are able to make their own internal decisions about the kinds of community events, initiatives, charities, and activities they wish to support. In contrast, banks make these kinds of decisions at the head office level, with the result being that sponsorships and donations may not be responding to specific community needs. Although banks also make claims about their community investments, they have a different vision of how to do this and are more inclined to invest in large national charities, events, and festivals. Credit unions are likely to support similar activities but at the local level.

The ability to make decisions that respond to local needs, combined with the community rootedness of credit unions, was seen by interviewees to give credit unions a competitive advantage, particularly in an era of economic uncertainty and at a time when there may be a general wariness about the trustworthiness of traditional financial institutions. This apprehension may result in a surge of interest in more locally based economies. With already established strong roots in their local communities, credit unions are poised to respond to that interest. Like banks, credit unions also strive to make a consistent profit, but this aspect of their operations is tempered by the aforementioned strong commitment to their members and to the communities in which they are situated, an inherent aspect of being a co-operative. According to one informant, credit unions should be able to pursue both an economic and a social mission, provided the two missions are balanced: "Being a co-op is making a good balance between community and profits. For example, even in a time of trouble, you don't lay off people to cut costs." Interviewees clarified that although making profit is important and credit unions must consider the bottom line, an important consideration is how to balance community investment with profit making.

Services for marginalized communities and non-profit organizations. The ability to offer personalized service and tailor financial services to meet individual customers' needs were two competitive attributes also mentioned by a number of interviewees. One informant discussed how staff at his credit union regularly meet with individuals to give financial advice, an example of the kind of service that he believes has earned his credit union a reputation for its integrity and credibility. He noted that while banks require loan applicants to fit into a predefined profile, credit unions are able to be more flexible since credit union staff have the time to get to know customers well and can often find solutions to individual financial needs. In discussing loans, one interviewee reported that although there are standard criteria to be met, staff are often able to step beyond the usual boundaries because of the solid relationships his credit union has been able to build with customers. It was noted that credit unions are not often able to offer better loan terms or a cheaper interest rate, but they do have the ability to offer loans when other financial institutions will not.

Credit unions also have the opportunity to invest in local non-profit organizations, which tend to work in areas not served by the public and private sectors, such as advocating for marginalized communities. In rural and small-town communities, where local non-profit organizations have a smaller population on which to draw for financial support, credit unions have the opportunity to lend financial support to these organizations. Such financial support may go a long way toward strengthening local economies in general, which in turn strengthens the membership base of credit unions. This type of alternative investment has the potential to make real change in communities, especially those that are struggling economically. In addition to giving grants, one credit union involved in our study is supporting non-profits and social enterprises through providing long-term financial advice, organizational development, and general sectoral support. This credit union exemplifies the type of alternative financing and support that credit unions are able to provide, yet our research shows that most credit unions have largely ignored this opportunity.

Select rural credit unions in our study have also established a niche for themselves in offering financial services to traditionally marginalized communities, including loans that banks might consider too risky. One informant pointed out that his small credit union is able to support almost anyone who comes in because unlike banks and other financial institutions that are accountable to policies of a distant head office, credit unions are able to make decisions more independently.

Community (Re)Investment

Social economy policies and programs within credit unions are closely aligned with the institutions' corporate social responsibility (CSR) functions. The definitional obscurity (or emergent qualities) of the social economy presents both opportunities and barriers in terms of linking with the more widely recognized field of CSR. On the positive side, CSR may serve as a gateway—both organizationally and conceptually—to introduce the social economy more broadly within the credit union sector. CSR investments by credit unions are significant: in Canada, credit unions contributed more than $41.4 million to their communities in the form of direct donations, financial services, sponsorships, and scholarships and bursaries (CUCC 2013). On the negative side, however, interviewees expressed concern that CSR may be a barrier to social economy development, as the conventional CSR activities of credit unions—while serving very positive community and marketing roles—are not structurally relevant to elevating the strength and awareness of the social economy or making significant shifts toward environmental sustainability. If the social economy and movement toward sustainability is confused with these "CSR-lite" activities, the broader transformative potential of the social economy and sustainable development is overlooked.

Our research shows that rural credit unions are investing a certain proportion of annual profits into local organizations and events, but they are not engaging in the kinds of investments in the social economy that could potentially bring about structural changes in the economies or environmental sustainability of local communities. Rather, the credit unions examined in our study overwhelmingly tend to focus on charitable donations and sponsorships—for example, funding scholarships for high school students, sponsoring community events like golf tournaments and community breakfasts, and donating to youth sports and local charities. Some credit unions also run financial literacy programs for adults and youth. While supporting these kinds of community initiatives is certainly worthwhile, we characterize them as "traditional investments" since they do not make a meaningful contribution to strengthening the social economy of local communities in long-term, structural ways.

Several interviewees raised the idea that credit unions could play a role in bringing about societal change through, for example, reducing poverty, building community, and supporting youth. Some of the credit union representatives mentioned the importance of CSR in helping credit unions to better engage with communities. However, according to one informant, there is a general lack of understanding of how to affect social change, and engaging in community events is a simple and obvious way for credit unions to invest.

The place-based rootedness of credit unions, combined with their financial resources, makes these organizations strong social economy institutions across the rural landscape. Our study also identifies areas in which credit unions are adopting strong social economy strategies in terms of providing financial services to marginalized communities. Overall, however, the lack of strategic intentionality and structural relevance of credit union programs within our sample indicates that rural credit unions are not translating their strong institutional presence into strong social economy and sustainability investments and practices. CSR-lite will not contribute to the transformation of conventional economic and societal structures.

In the following section, we discuss several barriers that credit unions face in advancing the social economy and sustainability. We explore reasons why many credit union staff and management lack awareness about the social economy and how to contribute to it, and we examine the lack of measurement tools (e.g., social and environmental audits) for gauging the success of community-related investments.

Credit Unions and Green Initiatives
Sean Markey

A number of credit unions in British Columbia and Alberta are using their financial resources to support green initiatives and facilitate sustainable choices for their members. For example, the Vancity enviro Visa has raised $5.7 million in grants since 1990 to help support green initiatives (VCU 2014a). In 2014, the enviroFund provided support toward the development of a sustainable, local food system. Grants were given to two organizations to support the growth of successful farmers' markets, small-scale food processors, and small and medium producers (Vancity 2014a).

In another program, Vancity offers eco-efficiency loans to businesses and non-profit organizations to help finance energy improvements. Loans of up to $250,000 are offered at a preferred rate, with financing for up to 100 percent of capital upgrades and flexible repayment terms to help manage cash flow (Vancity 2014b). Lake View Credit Union, a small BC credit union operating in Tumbler Ridge, Dawson Creek, and Chetwynd, offers members eco-friendly vehicle loans. Members receive a low rate on vehicles that are specifically designed for superior environmental performance and those that emit significantly less CO2 than the average car. The program is pitched as helping to reduce carbon emissions and improving member financial well-being by reducing fuel costs.

One final example, from Alberta, First Calgary Credit Union, launched their Environmental Promise, a commitment to making environmentally responsible decisions as they impact their members, employees, communities, and the organization as a whole, including green purchasing and building LEED certified buildings (First Calgary Financial 2012).

These projects span the continuum of weak to strong sustainability, but they serve as powerful forms of member and community engagement and represent a convergence of the institutional social economy strength of credit unions and sustainable community development.

First Calgary Financial. 2012. "2012 Annual Report." https://www.firstcalgary.com/SharedContent/documents/Corpcomm/FCF_2012_AR.pdf.

LVCU (Lake View Credit Union). 2013. "Eco-friendly Vehicle Loans." http://lakeviewcreditunion.com/your-life-2/go-green/green-car-loans/.

VCU (Vancity Credit Union). 2014a. "The Benefits of Visa." https://www.vancity.com/BusinessBanking/AccountsAndServices/PaymentServices/enviroExpenseGoldVisa/VisaInformation/.

———. 2014b. "Eco-efficiency Loans." Vancity Credit Union. https://www.vancity.com/BusinessBanking/Financing/Loans/EcoEfficiencyLoans/.

Barriers to Structural Influence

Measuring awareness of the social economy within the credit union milieu is obviously a critical starting place for determining the level of engagement of credit unions with the social economy and social enterprise. Some interviewees noted that since the Governor General's Speech from the Throne on 5 October 2004, through which the social economy sector received a jolt of mainstream recognition, broader public and government engagement with the sector has waned (Clarkson 2004). This affects credit union involvement in two ways. First, as responsive agents to the marketplace, and particularly as member-driven organizations, credit unions are heavily influenced by consumer and member interest. Second, as social economy entities themselves (at least in principle), credit unions are, theoretically, central players in representing and showcasing the social economy. The inherent tension between these two roles—responsive agents and proactive institutions—emerged in our interviews.

As institutional entities (i.e., substantial and systemic structures), credit unions are uniquely placed within the social economy, a sector that is more often associated with smaller entities despite the presence of a number of larger cooperatives and non-profit institutions. Even though credit unions, as co-ops, are social economy organizations, linking the co-operative reality with the broader principles of the social economy is not part of the mainstream culture within the credit union sector. Our interviewees offered a number of thoughts that help to explain this apparent contradiction. We will start with factors internal to credit unions and follow with the influence of the social economy sector as a whole.

First, knowledge of the social economy among credit union staff is low. While this is, in part, related to the general public's lack of awareness of the social economy, it is also a function of credit union practices. As one credit union representative put it, "There is high-level comfort around supporting community events, but unless you have people involved who understand the full continuum of roles that CUs could play and how social change is motivated and mobilized, it will not happen."

Interviewees also offered insightful comments on the role of the social economy sector itself in promoting or inhibiting its own development. As they were aware, the language of the social economy can at times be alienating to the mainstream (including credit union personnel) and, in particular, to mainstream business practices. "There is a business capacity issue in the co-operative sector," one respondent noted. "The people involved carry a hippie persona and have not brought business ethos. There is also a general lack of understanding about co-ops among the public. They seem to have a negative image and are not viewed as mainstream." Echoing this comment, another pointed to the lack of fit between the social economy and the criteria by which business operations are typically judged: "We don't know how to evaluate this animal. We set a basic module for evaluating business models and the social economy is not included in this. We don't know what to look for and don't understand the social economy business model and organization. There is a need for more training." Social economy leaders generally either assume a higher level of awareness than exists in reality or situate the social economy in opposition to, or as serving a higher purpose than, traditional business. Thus, to the extent that credit union personnel are oriented to general business practices (as they indeed must be to operate a financial institution), they may be turned off.

Second, interviewees noted that the social economy sector could be doing a better job of communications. There are clear challenges here in terms of resources available to spread the word; however, respondents wanted more examples of successful performance and commented specifically on how the co-op sector, for example, needs to do a better job of sharing and communicating the co-op model. Awareness of the co-op sector (even within co-operatives and members who may belong to a co-op) was seen as being very low. The social economy sector needs to be doing a better job at communicating its benefits: it needs to highlight its ability to make a value-added contribution to organizations and to the economy, thus countering the misunderstanding of the social economy as a sector that drains valuable and limited resources. One interviewee attributed this misperception to the unrealistic expectations that are placed on emergent social economy actors and enterprises. The pressure to achieve short-term benefits and realize short-term financial viability may crush potentially viable organizations.

In offering their comments and critiques, interviewees were aware of the many good works and programs offered and supported by the credit union sector overall. However, the interviews provided a clear sense that organizational and structural barriers are preventing the social economy from reaching a critical tipping-point of awareness and action that could lead to a more inclusive economy.

Several informants suggested that the reluctance on the part of credit union management to move away from traditional investment may be due in part to a lack of knowledge about what the social economy is and how investing in it may benefit the larger community and the credit union itself. Although there is some evidence for the value of a strong social economy, data on how the social economy contributes to a stronger economy overall are scarce. Because of a lack of specific data on what aspects of the social economy are successful, credit unions may, understandably, perceive investment in the social economy as involving too many risks—risks that, according to some informants, credit unions are unfamiliar with and do not know how to handle.

Finally, despite the efforts of select credit unions, performance metrics (where they are being used) generally do not incorporate social economy or sustainability criteria. If social economy and sustainable development variables are not part of the information feedback system within credit unions, then those sectors will continue to be programmatically marginalized. In no instances were case study credit unions tracking or measuring the impacts of their community investments, donations, scholarships, or programs, except to measure membership growth.

Performing a social and environmental audit is one technique used to measure the impact of CSR-related activities. Generally, auditing serves three purposes. First, it allows organizations to evaluate their performance in relation to their social, environmental, and economic commitments and goals. Second, auditing helps organizations to respond to changing expectations in the business environment: for example, it allows them to demonstrate their commitment to social or environmental responsibility. Third, given increasing consumer concern about social and environmental risk, triple bottom-line accounting can position an organization favourably in the marketplace (Brown 2001).

Although auditing may not capture the drawbacks associated with engaging in various investments or initiatives, it may help credit unions to define what kinds of risk they can assume and to identify the limitations of traditional forms of community investments. One informant proposed that in the absence of measurement tools, credit unions might become mired in more traditional investments.

Although there is nothing wrong with traditional investments, they are unlikely to lead to the societal changes to which credit unions are ostensibly capable of contributing by virtue of their co-operative principles and their scale. Despite the strong argument for using social and environmental audits, however, one credit union employee suggested that auditing may not be as critical for smaller communities because the effects of investments are more clearly visible. Measurement may still be necessary in rural and small towns, but perhaps it should be done using a tool that is less complex than comprehensive auditing. "'Community' is a real phenomenon here," the credit union employee noted. "You see results faster in the community here in a small town. The impact of investments is easier to see, so measurement of these investments is less formal."

THE POTENTIAL FOR CONVERGENCE

Although credit unions have a distinct history from banks and are founded on different values and principles, the qualities that distinguish credit unions are generally not being expressed fully in terms of offering tangible and measurable facilitation of the social economy and sustainable communities. Credit unions certainly have the capacity, based on their mandate and resources, to finance the social economy and the transition to more sustainable communities: they are rooted in community, are democratic institutions, and are themselves part of the social economy. But can credit unions overcome the strong compulsion to compete with banks on traditional grounds, a compulsion that may very well detract from the overall mission and structural potential of credit unions?

Informants from all case study credit unions discussed their firm rootedness in the communities they serve and their familiarity with local issues and struggles. Yet most credit unions have not taken advantage of these qualities in order to make strategic investments that would build the foundations of a social economy and more directly align with credit union principles. The credit unions in our study are making meaningful investments in traditional areas such as sponsorships of local festivals or sports teams, but there is a widespread lack of broader strategic, structural visions or plans associated with building the social economy and sustainable communities. Our research indicates that an underlying cause for this lack of structural vision is the failure of many credit unions to recognize the importance of the social economy and their role within it. In particular, the lack of staff education about the social economy and its contribution to local economic development is a significant finding. More awareness of the importance of the social economy is critical for the strengthening of the sector and the organizations within it. In addition, further research about the social economy's role in economic development will be a critical contribution.

Our interviewees suggested that most credit unions are struggling to find a niche for themselves. Credit union managers and staff recognize that their institutions are unable to compete with banks solely on financial services but they are constrained by members who may not recognize the value of supporting environmental initiatives or less mainstream traditional investments that could lead to a strengthening of both the local economy and the credit union itself. Many informants reported that despite the distinctive attributes that set them apart from banks, credit unions have strayed from their mission and are more strictly focused on profit making. Those credit unions that have tried to position themselves to compete with banks are now trapped in the market and do not see that they could have an altogether different position in the economy. Recent findings from the Global Alliance for Banking on Values (GABV) may provide some support for adopting more sustainable operating principles. Its 2013 study shows that leading sustainable banks and credit unions outperformed the world's largest banks in all key measures for the years 2003 to 2012 (GABV 2013, 5, 8):

- They lend almost twice as much of their assets on their balance sheet (75.9% compared to 40.1% for the big banks).
- They rely on customer deposits to a greater degree to fund their balance sheet (73.1% versus 42.9%).
- They maintain stronger capital positions, especially when measured by equity/total assets (7.2% versus 5.5%, relative to their larger contemporaries).
- They deliver a higher return on assets (0.53% versus 0.37%) with lower levels of volatility.

The study concludes that overall, sustainable banks are resilient, support the real economy, and provide stable returns.

In facing the challenge posed by restructuring in rural communities, credit unions have the potential to play a critical role in helping to strengthen rural community economies by building on existing strengths and local capacity. In order to be successful and meaningful in their communities, credit unions must compete on the basis of financial products while also looking for ways to support people, local organizations, and their communities as a whole. Interviewees stressed that the social economy may provide a balanced way (i.e., appealing to both enterprise and social and ecological dimensions) to pursue competitive advantages that are still rooted in the principles and practices of the credit union ideal. It is here where we find the seeds of a convergence within the credit union sector. At a strategic level, rural credit unions in our study are implementing weak social economy and sustainability strategies; however, their connectedness to community and their place-based development orientation could provide a foundation for making local investments that achieve the principles of integrated development, balancing economic needs with a commitment to social equity and environmental sustainability to ensure a long-term and prosperous future for the community.

REFERENCES

Berkes, Fikret, and Iain J. Davidson-Hunt. 2007. "Communities and Social Enterprises in the Age of Globalization." *Journal of Enterprising Communities* 1 (3): 209–21.

Brown, Leslie. 2001. *Social Auditing and Community Cohesion: The Co-operative Way*. Final report submitted to the Co-operatives Secretariat and Department of Canadian Heritage.

CFIB (Canadian Federation of Independent Business). 2013. "Battle of the Banks: How SMEs Rate Their Banks." Toronto: CFIB.

Clarkson, Adrienne. 2004. "Speech from the Throne to Open the First Session of the Thirty-eighth Parliament of Canada." Government of Canada, Privy Council Office, 5 October. http://www.pco-bcp.gc.ca/index.asp?lang=eng&page=information&su b=publications&doc=aarchives/sft-ddt/2004_2-eng.htm.

CUCC (Credit Union Central of Canada). 2007. *Social Responsibility and Canada's Credit Unions: Fresh Approaches, Stronger Communities, the Spirit of Co-operation*. http://www.cucentral.ca/Annual-Reports/10141_CUCC_2013_Social%20 Responsibility%20Brochure%20Final.pdf.

——. 2010. *System Results, Fourth Quarter 2009*. March. http://www.cucentral.ca/ FactsFigures/4Q09SystemResults.pdf.

——. 2013. *Fast Facts on Canada's Credit Unions*. Pamphlet. Toronto: Credit Union Central of Canada. http://www.cucentral.ca/Documents/Fast%20Facts%20 Leaflet%20Q2%202013%20Update_Final(secured).pdf.

Dart, Raymond. 2004. "The Legitimacy of Social Enterprise." *Nonprofit Management and Leadership* 14 (4): 411–24.

Defourny, Jacques, and Patrick Develtere. 2000. "Social Economy: The Worldwide Making of a Third Sector." In *Social Economy: North and South*, edited by Jacques Defourny, Patrick Develtere, and Bénédicte Fontenau, 17–47. Translated by Stuart Anthony Stilitz. Leuven: Hoger instituut voor de arbeid, Katholieke Universiteit Leuven; Liège: Centre d'économie sociale, Université de Liège.

du Plessis, V., R. Beshiri, and R. Bollman. 2004. "Definitions of Rural." In *Building for Success: Explorations of Rural Community and Rural Development*, edited by G. Halseth and R. Halseth, 51–80. Brandon: Rural Development Institute.

Fairbairn, Brett, Lou Hammond Ketilson, and Peter Krebs. 1997. *Credit Unions and Community Economic Development*. Saskatoon: Centre for the Study of Co-operatives, University of Saskatchewan.

GABV (Global Alliance for Banking on Values). 2013. *Real Banking for the Real Economy: Comparing Sustainable Bank Performance with the Largest Banks in the World*. Zeist, Netherlands: GAVB.

Gertler, Michael. 2004. "Synergy and Strategic Advantage: Co-operatives and Sustainable Development." *Journal of Cooperatives* 18: 32–46.

Gray, M., K. Healy, and P. Crofts. 2003. "Social Enterprise: Is It the Business of Social Work?" *Australian Social Work* 56 (2): 141–54.

Green, R. 2003. "Social Work in Rural Areas: A Personal and Professional Challenge." *Australian Social Work* 56 (3): 209–19.

Greffe, Xavier. 2007. "The Role of the Social Economy in Local Development." In *The Social Economy: Building Inclusive Economies*, edited by Antonella Noya and Emma Clarence, 91–117. Paris: OECD.

Halseth, Greg, and Laura Ryser. 2006. "Trends in Service Delivery: Examples from Rural and Small Town Canada, 1998 to 2005." *Journal of Rural and Community Development* 1: 69–90.

Heenan, D., and R. McLaughlin. 2002. "Re-assessing the Role of Credit Unions in Community Development: A Case Study of Derry Credit Union, Northern Ireland." *Community Development Journal* 37 (3): 249–59.

MacPherson, I. 1995. *Cooperation, Conflict and Consensus: B.C. Central and the Credit Union Movement to 1994*. Vancouver: B.C. Central Credit Union.

Markey, Sean, Greg Halseth, and Don Manson. 2008. "Challenging the Inevitability of Rural Decline: Advancing the Policy of Place in Northern British Columbia." *Journal of Rural Studies* 24: 409–21.

Markey, Sean, Sean Connelly, and Mark Roseland. 2010. "'Back of the Envelope': Pragmatic Planning for Sustainable Rural Community Development." *Planning Practice and Research*, 25 (1): 1–23.

———. 2012. *Investing in Place: Economic Renewal in Northern British Columbia*. Vancouver: University of British Columbia Press.

Markey, Sean, John T. Pierce, Kelly Vodden, and Mark Roseland. 2005. *Second Growth: Community Economic Development in Rural British Columbia*. Vancouver: University of British Columbia Press.

Neamtan, Nancy, and Rupert Downing. 2005. "Social Economy and Community Economic Development in Canada: Next Steps for Public Policy." Issues paper. Montréal, PQ: Chantier de l'économie sociale. http://ccednet-rcdec.ca/sites/ccednet-rcdec.ca/files/Issues%20Paper_Sept_2005.pdf.

Perry, S. 1987. *Communities on the Way: Rebuilding Local Economies in the United States and Canada*. Albany: State University of New York Press.

Ralston, Deborah, and Diana J. Beal. 1999. "Credit Unions: Filling Finance Gaps in Rural Communities." *Economic Analysis and Policy* 29 (2): 173–86.

Reimer, Bill. 2005. "A Rural Perspective on Linkages Among Communities." Prepared for Building, Connecting and Sharing Knowledge: A Dialogue on Linkages Between Communities forum (Infrastructure Canada), 3 March, Ottawa. http://nre. concordia.ca/__ftp2004/reports/Linkages_Reimer%20-%20EN.pdf.

RIA (Responsible Investment Association). 2007. *Canadian Socially Responsible Investment Review 2006: A Comprehensive Survey of Socially Responsible Investment in Canada*. Toronto: RIA.

Roseland, Mark. 2005. *Toward Sustainable Community Development*. Gabriola Island, BC: New Society.

Scott, Katherine, Julie Park, and Chris Cocklin. 2000. "From 'Sustainable Rural Communities' to 'Social Sustainability': Giving Voice to Diversity in Mangakahia Valley, New Zealand." *Journal of Rural Studies* 16: 433–46.

Strandberg, Coro. 2004. "The Emergence of Community Investment as a Strategy for Investing in Your Community." With assistance from Susannah Cameron. Presentation at the Investing in Your Community Conference, Saskatoon, March. http://corostrandberg.com/wp-content/uploads/files/CommunityInvestment_E. pdf.

Teitelbaum, Sara, and Bill Reimer. 2002. *The Social Economy in Rural Canada: Exploring Research Options*. A report to the Concordia Section of Centre de recherche sur les innovations sociales dans l'économie sociale, les entreprises et les syndicats, October. http://nre.concordia.ca/__ftp2004/reports/ SocialEconomyReport3wb.pdf.

Turner, A. E. 1984. *Forging the Alternative: A History of the Alberta Credit Union Idea*. Calgary: Credit Union Central of Alberta.

Wall, L., and L. Marzall. 2006. "Adaptive Capacity for Climate Change in Canadian Rural Communities." *Local Environment* 11 (4): 373–97.

Wells, Barbara. 2002. *Smart Growth at the Frontier: Strategies and Resources for Rural Communities*. Washington: Northeast-Midwest Institute.

Wittman, Hannah, Mary Beckie, and Chris Hergesheimer. 2012. "Linking Local Food Systems and the Social Economy? Future Roles for Farmers' Markets in Alberta and British Columbia." *Rural Sociology* 77 (1): 36–61.

Young, N., and R. Matthews. 2007. "Resource Economies and Neoliberal Experimentation: The Reform of Industry and Community in Rural British Columbia." *Area* 39 (2): 176–85.

Zeuli, Kimberly A. 2001. "Business Attraction as a Rural Community Development Tool: Arguments for More Comprehensive Evaluations." In *Rising Tide: Community Development Tools*, Models, and Processes, edited by David Bruce and Gwen Lister, 47–56. Sackville, NB: Mount Allison University.

Conclusion

"Social Economizing" Sustainability

Mike Gismondi, Sean Connelly, and Sean Markey

In this book, we explore the convergence of the social economy and sustainability. Our analysis is grounded in a commitment to sustainable community development and is guided by a conceptual framework that allows us to place organizations, projects, and perspectives on a weak-strong continuum. As stated in our introduction, we are drawn to convergence as a means of addressing inherent limitations in the social economy and sustainability sectors. We propose that meaningful structural change can be achieved by "social economizing" sustainability—that is, by combining the social economy with sustainable development in order to create a whole greater than the sum of its parts. The many case examples explored throughout the book illustrate how the two sectors are converging through strong social economy/strong sustainability practices that emphasize building capacity, making decisions democratically, seeking structural change, creating market demand for green social economy services, building networks, and challenging existing regulations and policies. We found innovative organizations that have begun to intertwine the best of both fields and are developing into strong, viable alternatives to unjust and unsustainable practices. Using this empirical evidence, we have identified patterns, revealed mechanisms, and proposed models of structural change that embrace strong-strong practices in numerous settings: food, social care, energy, resource economies, ecotourism, housing, transportation, heritage conservation, land tenure, and banking and finance. In this diverse array of examples, we discovered a conjunction of organizational and institutional strategies, community building, social innovation, and new knowledge. This convergence, we believe, can be scaled up and out to accelerate a fair transition to sustainability.

True, the examples we have described in this volume are modest in scale relative to counterparts in the mainstream economy. Nevertheless, they are by no means marginal: their individual and collective significance is substantial. Many arose out of the need to address critical elements that are lacking or underdeveloped in our economy and society and have begun to move from the fringes to the centre. Within the framework upon which our analysis is based, it is significant that they represent more than just incremental change: individually and collectively, they suggest alternatives to current systems and plant the seeds of real transformative change— change that has structural implications for the whole economy and society. If we are to realize sustainability, it will be crucial to scale out and scale up these innovations—to multiply their impact through diffusion into new sectoral and geographic contexts (scaling out) and through moving each innovation from the fringe to the centre of its sector (scaling up).

ANALYSIS: OPPORTUNITIES AND BARRIERS

At the end of this chapter is a series of charts that recount how organizations described in this book carry out a convergence of social economy and sustainability in each of seven sectors. The first three columns in each table identify the name, organizational structure, and socio-ecological mission of the organization. The last two columns list actions and outcomes related to scaling up the activity and policy changes that would support scaling out each initiative. In these two columns, we specify key political actions and policy directions that support convergence.

In table 11.1 we summarize findings in the food sector. In their discussion of food provision in chapter 3, Mary Beckie and Sean Connelly recognize that scaling out the local food system will require much more extensive storage, processing, and distribution infrastructure. In addition, informed consumers and knowledgeable, skilled producers are needed to build sustainable local food systems. In fact, only by strengthening and expanding the social infrastructure can these initiatives challenge current systems of food provision. Partnerships, coalitions, and networks of actors along the entire supply chain are essential to attract and maintain investment in a strong physical infrastructure. Without strong social infrastructure, we run the risk of re-creating the mistakes of the conventional food system, albeit on a more local basis.

Beckie and Connelly advocate for various types of coalitions that cluster small producers to increase their market opportunities and scale up volume and access for consumers but do not require investment in physical infrastructure. Strong social networks have real potential for changing systems of food provision. By strengthening the moral imperative to make fresh local food accessible to all, not just to those who can afford it, such coalitions help to overcome the current elitist trend in the local food market. And when investment in physical infrastructure is required, strategic partnering also spreads the financial risk. Beckie and Connelly identify a strong need for intermediaries and activists to co-ordinate a widespread group of food consumers, producers, and go-betweens. Collective building of social infrastructure will lead to increased capacity, shared knowledge, and stronger leadership skills, all of which are critical to increasing overall food security. As some of their examples show, partnering with the municipal government or the public sector to build social and physical infrastructure can lead to strategic collaboration and policy support. Such tactics help to address the challenges of scale, scope, accessibility, and organizational capacity that niche or grassroots local food initiatives often face. Policy support, in particular, is crucial to regionalizing food systems (Sonnino and Griggs-Trevarthen 2013).

In chapter 4, John Restakis tackles the topic of social care (see table 11.2). He notes that in an age of neoliberalism, applying market language and working with market forces in the provision of social care is risky, since conservative forces have co-opted market entrepreneurialism and seek a stripped-down, privatized model of public sector service delivery. Social economy actors who advocate operating in the market like a business must be wary. Restakis proposes instead the social use of market forces. Reciprocity is the basis for the type of social care that he champions. The aim of social care, he argues, should be to create local involvement in care delivery so as to ensure an equitable provision of care to all social classes and an increase in local employment. Even if money changes hands, both caregiver and recipient share in the generation of care as a human relation, not as a purchased commodity or a charitable offering. Restakis also anticipates that social care runs contrary to the traditional thinking of labour unions and left-wing political parties. His own research uncovers in the Canadian public a persistent wariness of co-operatives. He also notes the reluctance of co-operatives in other sectors to enter the arena of social service provision.

While the current politics of social care is challenging, it is encouraging to see in Canada the rise of new kinds of co-operatives and social enterprises that focus on relational goods. Over the last few years, The Cleaning Solution, Free Geek, and various bicycle cooperatives have all been integrating human care and the reduction of social inequality with specific green services (see chapter 4). The

Cleaning Solution is a good strong-strong example. It is a green social enterprise that promotes ecologically sound practices while collaborating with government mental health departments and private firms to provide employment to the marginalized. Many readers might know of similar stand-alone or networked social enterprises in their own locales that create a blended return on investment.[1] In its role as a social economy intermediary, Enterprising Non-Profits (2009) has found other ways to add value. ENP's political and lobbying work focuses on increasing social procurement (using one's purchasing power to create social change) and creating "intentional demand" for social economy services. The organization has proposed an enabling policy framework of social purchasing that would have the potential to scale up the activities of social enterprises (LePage 2014). Social purchasing policy would require that an annual proportion of budgeted purchases come from the social economy. Thus, public institutions, government, and even private corporations working on public projects would have to secure a percentage of their labour, products, and services from social enterprises and non-profits. In a remarkable move, ENP and others have lobbied for "event-based" social purchasing targets at the 2015 Commonwealth Games in Toronto, as they did at the recent Vancouver and London Olympics (Hamilton 2014). Social purchasing is another key to transition politics.

In her discussion of energy and sustainability in chapter 5, Julie MacArthur identifies key barriers to scaling up and out alternative energy sources: global market pressure (capitalist imperatives); insufficiency of local production; uneven free markets that make it hard for a small energy co-operative (or any small social innovator) to break in and compete for clients; a scarcity of capital investment for high-cost infrastructure; and the threat of private buyouts of successful community projects, even in good times (see table 11.3). Collective ownership is not a guaranteed defence against market pressures and lucrative buyout offers. Recently, members of a large regional rural electrical co-operative in Alberta (Peace Country REA, founded in the 1960s) voted to sell their electrical distribution lines and systems to ATCO Electric, a large private firm. MacArthur introduces two additional threats: the shallow understanding of the term *community*, in which a few community members make money on a "good" energy project at the expense of the most vulnerable groups in the community, and the greenwashing of social economy projects that provide local jobs or achieve energy autonomy but cause

---

1 For many more examples and for information about community work oriented toward social change and innovation, see the tools, resources, and research of the Demonstrating Value Resource Society, http://www.demonstratingvalue.org.

long-term environmental damage. She believes that local ownership and control and the adoption of appropriate technology can counter these equity and ethical threats. Strong local involvement in the NaiKun wind energy project, for example, ensures that the Haida Nation benefits in terms of employment opportunities and financial gain: half of all future revenue will flow to the community. Moreover, connection of the wind turbines to the local grid will reduce the nation's dependence on diesel generators for electricity. In Ontario, a government feed-in tariff started off strong in 2009 but has met countervailing forces of late. The feed-in-tariff (FIT) policy guaranteed both the price for clean energy and the amount of electricity that could be supplied to the power grid by microproducers from alternative energy sources such as wind, solar, microhydro, and biogas. The FIT policy also encouraged up to 10 percent community-owned energy production. Considerable investment was attracted and long-term contracts signed, some of them by renewable energy co-operatives (Lipp, Lapierre-Fortin, and McMurtry 2012). In recent years, however, political opponents have questioned the high prices paid by government to FIT producers and have raised concerns about the effects of wind farming on communities, a range of land-use impacts, and government rules for local procurement (Stokes 2013). Prices for electricity fed into the grid from alternative sources have since been reduced. To improve scaling out, Stokes argues, the state and the renewables sector must collaborate to support the FIT beyond the policy stage and start-up and must be willing to adapt and modify the program in order to scale it out. Stokes concludes that a greater percentage of community-owned renewables would help to spread the innovation and reduce resistance (Stokes 2013). That said, FIT policies in general have heavily influenced the growth in investment in alternative energy technologies worldwide, whether by individual householders or by co-operative and community-owned energy producers (Lipp, Lapierre-Fortin, and McMurtry 2012).

For communities in regions responding to a decline in primary resource extraction—by transitioning from mining, fisheries, or logging to tourism and services, for example—Kelly Vodden, Lillian Hunt, and Randy Bell, in chapter 6, suggest a balanced mix of resource use and conservation, all underpinned by strong ecological principles (see table 11.4). They are cautiously optimistic about this approach, which they call "eco-cultural tourism." They remind us that community control of local resources and ecotourism are vulnerable to cycles and events at macroeconomic levels and that the role of local governments is particularly critical to this approach. They are also wary of the dangers of traditional tourism, which tends to exploit both non-human nature and First Nation cultures. Their three examples emphasize the critical importance of cultural capital and its links to ecosystems and resources for planning both the conservation and the use of nature. The multistakeholder, multiple-use, community-coalition principles proposed by the authors are sound not just for First Nations communities but for any community that faces boom-bust resource cycles and depends on global market demands for primary goods.

Table 11.5 lists organizations and issues related to housing, transport, and community land trusts. In their discussion of affordable housing in chapter 7, George Penfold, Lauren Rethoret, and Terri MacDonald identify opportunities for collaboration among social housing organizations, green housing advocates, and social co-ops delivering care to seniors and to the poor. Once again, local-government tools and cross-sector collaboration are crucial to advancing sustainability and equity goals in housing. Marena Brinkhurst and Mark Roseland, in chapter 8, confirm that the community land trust model has great potential because it makes entry-level housing more attainable through common ownership of the land base: rents are lower, and the potential for equity ownership of social housing emerges. The affordable housing complexes associated with Station Pointe Greens (Edmonton), the Irvine Community Land Trust (California), and the Boyle Renaissance project (Edmonton), are strong-strong examples of sustainable housing projects that have made social and ecological sustainability integral to design, ownership, and operations. Other examples in this volume demonstrate links between transportation and affordable housing, particularly in car-centric cities and regions. Transitioning from private vehicles to more sustainable modes of transportation such as walking, cycling, and public transit will have health and social benefits. Most importantly, it will reduce household transportation budgets by thousands of dollars a year, freeing up cash for rent, mortgage payments, and other costs related to family well-being. Poorer people may then be able to afford to rent or purchase housing in a greater number of city neighbourhoods. This in turn will diversify those neighbourhoods and increase social equality.

In Canadian municipalities, links between bicycle culture and the use of public transit have strengthened. The bike lobby, which has long been active, has benefitted from the synergies it has developed with a series of federal and provincial funding programs now available for municipal sustainability planning and infrastructure: Canada's Federal Gas Tax rebate, the Alberta Municipal Infrastructure Fund, and the BC Climate Change Plan are three examples. Programs such as these have emerged over the last decade and have required local governments to adopt municipal sustainability plans and, in some cases, climate change plans.

The "traditional" strategies of bike riders, like mass actions to close roadways and bridges, now align with opportunities to open up the discussion of urban transport and to influence urban planning. The discussions go well beyond such practical solutions as bike and commuter lanes. Across all levels of governments, critics raise larger questions of mobility and transport disadvantage. They challenge the automobile culture that is embedded in state and municipal infrastructure planning. They prod City Hall planners to rethink transport and lifestyle, parking, noise, zoning, and development plans. In short, public transit, walking, biking, and carsharing are elevated into public discussions of urbanism, climate change, mobility justice, and social equity (Grieco and Urry 2012).

In chapter 9, Noel Keough, Mike Gismondi, and Erin Swift-Leppäkumpu discuss heritage-building conservation as a political act that reminds the broader public of a time when progressive governments assumed responsibility for investing in Canada's public services and buildings (see table 11.6). The preservation of place, social memory, and authenticity in the built environment affirms that place is more than just a physical environment; place is a social construct. Again, examples of collaborations between heritage and social activists and municipal staff are many. In Edmonton, a derelict building was transformed into a women's shelter and an inner city school converted to a multicultural community centre. In Moncton, New Brunswick, a century-old fire hall now shelters a non-profit that provides services across the province for homeless and at-risk youth. Most important of all, these collaborations reassert in bricks and mortar a long-standing Canadian cultural and political allegiance to the ethos of social democracy.

Table 11.7 addresses organizations and issues that concern financing sustainability. In the final chapter of this book, Sean Markey, Freya Kristensen, and Stewart Perry report their finding that many credit unions remain weak in the provision of financial support for the social economy, in part because credit union directors have a poor understanding of the social economy. There are some bright lights, nevertheless, and although more urban-centric, the ideas could translate to rural credit unions. Vancity Credit Union is a good example of a large credit union (Canada's largest, in fact) that, through engagement in a wide range of initiatives, promotes both social innovation and sustainability. Two internal dynamics drive the structural potential of Vancity's efforts. First, the credit union's governance and risk management are guided by a policy of "no contradictions." As the 2011 annual report states, "By 2013, we'll implement a process to enable us to identify and correct systemic contradictions between what we say and what we do" (Vancity 2012, 71). This decision elevates social well-being and environmental sustainability from the portfolio of a sub-department or grant program to a corporate mandate. The entire capacity of the credit union has been mobilized to do things differently. Second, Vancity now defines and measures its community investment activities in terms of "demonstrable positive community impact" (43). Investment must be "impact investment": it must improve people's lives and/ or sustain the natural environment. Among the strategic impact categories are affordable housing; social-purpose real estate; local, natural organic food; energy and the environment; and social enterprise and social venture. In 2011, Vancity exceeded its target and invested $361 million in impact investments. Vancity's "no contradictions" policy and impact investing (in addition to the scale of the investments themselves) speak to the potential of credit unions to apply their considerable resources to effecting structural change. Vancity's example also affirms the feasibility of the convergence of the social and the environmental, as outlined in this book. These efforts—and the fact that Vancity had its best net earnings ever in 2011—illustrate how initiatives and investments that combine strong sustainability and strong social economy do not have to diminish returns or make members nervous. These were two of the concerns that the researchers discovered could impede strong social economy/strong sustainability actions in the credit union sector.

As noted by Mike Gismondi, Lynda Ross, and Juanita Marois in chapter 2, the search for local capital in Alberta has taken a slightly different turn. Faced with capital withdrawal by large private rail companies, two communities in rural Alberta made creative use of the new-generation co-operative model and generated millions of dollars of investment from residents. In Westlock, the capital was used to secure local ownership of a large grain terminal. In Battle River, it was needed to purchase a rail line in the agricultural heartland. Both businesses are thriving. Other examples of local capital retention co-operatives in Alberta are those in Sangudo and Crowsnest Pass.[2] In late 2013, the Alberta Community and Co-operative Association facilitated the spread of opportunity development co-operatives, co-ops that attract capital from local sources and invest it in local businesses, to six communities: Athabasca, Didsbury, Smoky River/Fahler, Three Hills, Drumheller, and Vulcan (Gismondi, Marois, and Strait, forthcoming; ACCA, n.d.). Local or micro-options such as these are essential to the development of models of money creation and credit that support local economies.

---

2 See "Sangudo Opportunity Development Co-operative," Agriculture and Rural Development, http://www1.agric.gov.ab.ca/$department/deptdocs.nsf/all/info13989, and Crowsnest Opportunity Development Cooperative, http://www.codcoop.org.

Taken together, the examples described in this volume suggest that with a more supportive government and policy context, the convergence of social economy and sustainability, together with the scaling up and scaling out of local innovations, could accelerate changes in the current system. Still, the questions remain: Can green social economy innovations shift the capitalist growth paradigm? Can they gain wide acceptance and become emulated across Canada? It depends.

Noam Bergman and colleagues (2010) describe a fixed bias among policymakers toward technological rather than social innovation. Policymakers presume bottom-up social innovations to be limited, localized, and context dependent (Gismondi and Cannon 2012). The evident success of local or small-scale green and social economy innovations notwithstanding, specialists are wary of the relevance of innovation from "bottom-up" sources (i.e., small-scale innovation generated by individuals, community groups, and so on) to major policy development. Dan van der Horst (2008) found that policymakers tend to believe that larger firms are more likely sources of sustainability innovation. They assume that large-scale change requires a "top-down" process, led by large private firms, and that the role of social economy or grassroots sustainability actors is to "fill in the gaps" and to ameliorate the shortcomings of the capitalist marketplace or state services. The social economy is considered incapable of transforming larger structures like markets; government programs, standards, and codes; the practices of financial institutions; or the habits of regional socio-economic planners. Community or co-operative energy sources, shared municipal/community forestry operations, socially infused organizations like bike and carshare co-operatives, and community land trusts all fall under the same rubric: they are deemed unlikely to spark widespread behavioural changes, let alone transformations in overarching structures of provision, business procedures, codes, practices, law, planning, and policy (Bergman et al. 2010; Brock and Bulpitt 2007). Van der Horst (2008) argues that successful privately owned local or small businesses receive a similar reception: they are downplayed as a source of social learning relevant to widescale change.

Given the evidence we have presented here, why does this remain the case? One reason for policy specialists' tendency to privilege technological innovation is because it is difficult to measure the benefits of social innovation (Bergman et al. 2010). Policymakers prefer clear-cut statistical approaches. They struggle to calculate the value of such benefits as employment for marginal groups, community cohesion, resilience, carbon reduction, increased social capital, and reciprocity.

Recently, the City of Vancouver demanded that the New City Market local food hub demonstrate a business case based on the same parameters as the large-scale food industry. Although city officials recognized the social and environmental benefits of local food, these factors held less weight than a business plan that answered the question: How will this make money? Bergman et al. argue that "it is hard to quantify the effects of a phenomenon that is not standardized or traded and which might include potentially nebulous outcomes" (7). A further complication arises when attempting to measure low-carbon contributions (like those of bicycle co-ops, carshares, or local food initiatives). The multiple ways in which the green social economy benefits the health of an urban living environment appear even harder to measure. They are less visible and "emerging in localized niches like communities and workplaces" distant from government power. These benefits take a form "which fits less well with mainstream, market-oriented ways of diffusing novelty across society" (2).

To address the perceived need to measure such benefits, grassroots sectors and their supporters have taken political steps and developed alternative measurement tools. Advanced social accounting and sustainability indicators include ways to measure different kinds of capital (social, cultural, ecological, heritage, and economic), their impacts, and progress (Mook and Sumner 2010; Sustainable Calgary 2011). Recently, the Vancity Community Foundation sponsored the Demonstrating Value project (demonstratingvalue.org). Its Web tools and Internet presence can help groups show their value to the community and in the long run "use data as a management and learning tool." Other innovative indicators are now implemented municipally and even nationally, including measures for carbon emissions. For instance, Sustainable Calgary groups indicators into six indices: community, economy, education, natural environment, resource use, and wellness (Sustainable Calgary, n.d.). Each index contains five or six measures, ranging from safety of streets, adult literacy, and daycare worker turnover, to domestic waste, energy use, locally produced food, and the use of transit for trips to work. City councillors and staff use these sustainability indicators to measure their annual performance against goals. They can adjust municipal practices and policies accordingly. The public can use indicator trends to pressure elected officials and the administration for improvements.

Sometimes social innovations and sustainable alternatives meet resistance because of the beliefs embedded in the approaches, processes, and culture of the policy community. One such belief is that it is individual behaviour that needs to change rather than the social and economic practices that shape behaviour. What is required is a shift away from focusing on the individual in the explanation of behaviour (Shove 2010, 203; Gismondi and Cannon 2012). A number of social scientists and activists now focus instead on "systems of provision" and policies that "play a crucial role in establishing, stabilizing and transforming practices," most often in unsustainable ways (Shove 2010, 203). Practice theorists argue that over time, the ways in which a society deals with energy and water provision, waste disposal, communication, and transport can lead to "lock-in," a dependency on a particular practice not because it is optimal in terms of cost or performance but because it is part of a complex system that has been established over time and is difficult to escape. To alter a locked-in practice "may require significant changes to large scale technical networks, which are themselves maintained and reinforced by aspects of social structure (be it government policy, social norms, etc.)" (Büchs, Smith, and Edwards 2011, 7).

In each of our chapters, we have tried to demonstrate how social economy and sustainability actors seek changes in social structures, organizations, and systems of provision. These actors challenge conventional ways of providing a service, focusing their efforts on disrupting group-think and group-behaviour in order to alter norms, codes, and conventions. They question the attitudes and practices of professions and trades and the mainstream practices in sectors like finance, policy, law, planning, and taxes.

A good example of this is Light House, a non-profit company in Vancouver (see chapter 7). Light House is working to convince government, the real estate and construction industries, and consumers of the importance of sustainability in building design and performance. Company staff work to alter the policy landscape through advocacy and social marketing, a green technology trade show, and consulting services. They also directly work with construction unions and real estate developers in order to promote more equitable work practices. At the policy level, Light House staff network with different levels of government to support planning and programming change and with the construction industry to change rules, codes and construction training. They lobby construction manufacturers to meet demand for green building supplies, products, and competent trades and labour. They also collaborate with financial institutions like Vancity Credit Union to alter lending policy and to create new green mortgage products. They work with other sectors to improve, for example, insurance and lending policy for smart homes. Similarly, Light House uses strategic collaboration with the real estate and construction industry, financial institutions, and municipal government to promote sustainable housing construction education and awareness. Their networking and educational work allows them to influence practices at every stage of building construction: design, finance, planning, governance, construction practices, consumer education, labour force availability, sales and marketing, and aftercare. They create demand for the services they offer at every level and scale.

On the human services side, there is the example of Free Geek, a social enterprise that approaches the question of social inclusion and sustainability from a different angle (see chapter 4). Free Geek targets the negative side of rapid technological development and the digital divide between those who have access to computers and training (a prerequisite for many jobs and schooling today) and those who do not. The company does not simply give computers to marginal groups, however. Because the digital divide is social, Free Geek focuses on building capacity within marginal groups, including job skills training in the use and repair of computers. The organization addresses the global dimension of the divide as well. Computer technology is consumed en masse in the global North, and a corresponding amount of often toxic e-waste is shipped to the global South to be sorted by the working poor in e-waste dumps. Free Geek changes how we see the problem by reusing or by ethically recycling e-waste in accordance with the Basel Convention (www.basel.int). Since the founding of Free Geek Portland in 2000, eleven additional autonomous Free Geek organizations have sprung up in the United States, Vancouver, and Toronto.

Many of the organizations introduced in this book demonstrate significant social reach. They are part of national or international networks or federations that influence government policy at the municipal, provincial, and federal levels. They also work "horizontally" to alter their immediate policy contexts: they have influenced local bylaws, private business, finance, and other non-profit actors. They are creating change, not simply reacting. We are optimistic that the new ideas and exciting organizational practices of green social economy organizations are indeed "opening windows" of change (Schmidt 2011, 108) and catalyzing the scaling up and out of sustainable practices (Parrish 2008; Parrish and Foxon 2009, Smith 2006, 2007).

Yet, as some critics argue, biases against bottom-up policymaking can still effectively trump social innovation. How do we overcome that? Adrian Smith, Andy Stirling, and Frans Berkhout (2005, 1496) urge niche actors who wish to alter "the dominance of an incumbent [policy] regime" to exert "selection pressure" and simultaneously offer "the resources to respond to this pressure." In a number of our examples, effective organizations increase pressure for sustainability by means of education, social marketing, and the building of alliances and networks.

Their activities prepare the landscape for policy change and create demand for innovative change. They then meet this demand with services and products. In other words, many of these innovative organizations and initiatives are simply bypassing the policy actors and processes that are stuck in an increasingly outdated institutional past.

Many of the organizations reviewed in our research combine social and ecological issues in ways that disrupt current social practices and policy environments. They pose new questions and create public discussion about new problems. In so doing, they increase the ethical clarity of the issues at stake and alter public thinking. Their actions in the marketplace also generate new alliances among different actors and at different levels and scales. They connect once-isolated and intransigent policy silos and policy actors. And they exert strategic pressure for change and for scaling out innovation in theory and practice.

Can this array of small and modest scale changes result in transformative change? Can we move these innovations from the fringe to the centre and change structures of provision and service? Can the learnings from these innovations help us transition from capitalist growth to a new alternative economy that will contract resource use and redistribute income and wealth?

Scaling Up discloses example after example of green social economy actors who have been leading the development of alternative practices and policies that integrate sustainability and socio-economic justice. While obstacles and barriers remain, we are inspired by this bundle of successes, and even some failures. It is our hope that the examples collected in this book will change the direction of research, stimulate more intensive study into factors that enable or thwart change, and generate new hypotheses about how policy can be created or changed to support transition. We hope that the mixture of mission, practice, and theory in this book brings new ideas to your community, stimulates public discussion, and inspires new sustainable and just practices. In this convergence of social economy and sustainable community development lies the beginning, if not the core, of a new ethos and a fair and structurally relevant transition to sustainability.

Table 11.1 Food: Summary of findings

Convergence	Organizational structure	Socio-ecological mission
Rimbey Farmers' Market	Community non-profit	Increase consumer access to fresh, local food
		Increase market venues for local producers
		Strengthen community
Good Food Box, Edmonton	Social enterprise	Increase consumer access to fresh, local food
		Increase market venues for local producers
		Strengthen community
Westlock Grain Terminals	New-generation co-operative	Purchase and operate grain terminal destined for closure
		Increase capacity to move grain to market
New City Market Food Hub, Vancouver	Community non-profit	Strengthen local food system
		Provide infrastructure for distribution of local food

Actions Toward Scaling Up	Actions Toward Scaling Out
Increase the family and community orientation	Collaborate across sectors: farmers, municipalities, consumers
Provide bus for seniors	Create local as social space, seek zoning changes
Use local labour	
Collaborate with local organizations, government, businesses, and other farmers' markets in the region	Strengthen social infrastructure
Initiate affordable access to local food	Build relationships of trust and reciprocity between producers and consumers
	Spread buy local practices
Invest capital locally	Promote local capital investment in agriculture
Blend investment from members and the community	Work with community based financial intermediaries like Alberta Futures and Alberta Treasury Branch
Keep the control with producers-owners	
Upgrade rail lines and add new terminals	Combine independent terminals into a federation to purchase and operate large rail and storage terminals
Community renewal	
	Develop new markets
Collaborate across sectors	Collaborate with social enterprises across sectors
Raise public awareness	
Create local as a social space	Develop a year-round space for small businesses and family-owned producers
	Coordinate marketing and sales across the local food sector
	Build links between social and physical infrastructure

Table 11.2 Social care: Summary of findings

Convergence	Organizational structure	Socio-ecological mission
Social care co-operative	Membership-based co-operative	Provide social services (e.g., health, disabilities, funeral care) through democratic decision making
The Cleaning Solution	Social enterprise	Provide environmentally friendly cleaning services Provide meaningful employment for local residents who have experienced mental illness
Free Geek	Social enterprise	Reduce environmental impact of e-waste by reusing and recycling donated technology Provide education, job skills training, Internet access, and free or low-cost computers to the public

Table 11.3 Energy and natural resources: Summary of findings

Convergence	Organizational structure	Socio-ecological mission
Dawson Creek Peace Energy Co-op (Generation)	Co-operative social enterprise	Generate renewable energy Maintain local control of energy production Employ local individuals and contractors
SPARK Energy Co-op (Retail)	Co-operative	Provide residents with opportunity to purchase green energy Provide investment capital to renewable projects Demand management initiatives

Actions and outcomes (scaling-up)	Policy change (scaling-out)
Extend services from members to the wider community, including the marginalized Employ disadvantaged individuals Strengthen bonds of trust and mutuality between caregivers and users (reciprocal relational services)	Increase variety and quality of social care Improve working conditions, wages, and professional competence of staff Focus on front lines of care Encourage social procurement policies Develop social public partnerships
Workers assigned to one workplace instead of gang cleaning multiple sites in order to create sense of family, and create positive attitudes toward hiring those with a mental illness Collaborate with Canadian Mental Health Association and Western Economic diversification	Create a link to a social procurement strategy Link mental health supports and funding to federal green jobs training and employment support Influence granting and funding formulas
Train marginal groups in computer use and repair Link organization's financial self-sustainability to green initiatives and recycling jobs Increase awareness of global e-waste	Link to social procurement strategy Address global digital divide and global pollution issues associated with computer age

Actions and outcomes (scaling-up)	Policy change (scaling-out)
Shift toward renewable energy Promote development and adoption of renewable energy Build capacity in community wind energy	Raise awareness of broad energy issues Partnerships with local organizations Establish a long-term purchase agreement
Promote development and adoption of renewable energy Build capacity in wind energy	Lobby government to make space for small retailers in field dominated by major electric corporations Seek public and government support for feed-in-tariffs from household and community energy generation

Table 11.4 Eco-cultural tourism: Summary of findings

Convergence	Organizational structure	Socio-ecological mission
U'mista Cultural Society	Community owned	Protect resource base upon which cultural traditions are based
		Repatriate cultural property confiscated by government
		Promote culture and language
'Namgis Nation's eco-tourism	Community owned	Recognize and protect ecologically significant sites
'Namgis Nation's Closed Containment project	Community owned	Practice bio-secure aquaculture that eliminates interaction with marine environment
Revelstoke Community Forestry	Community owned with involvement of municipal government	Transfer value of forestry from harvesting to adding value in place

Actions and outcomes (scaling-up)	Policy change (scaling-out)
Ensure that community benefits directly from cultural activities	Recognize the critical importance of cultural capital
Provide distribution network for local artists	Create cedar strategy to protect red cedar from harvesting
	Set aside natural resources for explicit cultural use
Train guides and outfitters	Arrange co-management with provincial government for forestry and parks
Create local employment	
Re-open ancient trade routes	
Manage protected areas jointly	
Develop resort and land-based whale watching	
Improve rate of fish growth with less feed, controlled use of antibiotics and pesticides	Demonstrate feasibility of salmon farming in land-based pens
Protect resource-based jobs in community	Create sense of place, local control, and self-sufficiency
	Collaborate with municipal government and private sector
	Manage logging for aesthetic values to protect tourism

Table 11.5 Housing, transport, and community land trusts: Summary of findings

Convergence	Organizational structure	Socio-ecological mission
Station Pointe Greens, Edmonton	Mix of co-operative models	Provide passive solar high-rise apartment housing. Create advanced envelope design Lower use and costs of all utilities Provide affordable green housing
Light House Sustainable Building Centre	Non-profit	Encourage green ratings and construction audits Change institutional, commercial, and residential building practices Relate cost of design to efficiencies Shift focus of professionals from designing buildings to designing smart neighbourhoods and regions
Car Share	Co-operative social enterprise	Lower pollution Reduce consumerism
Community Bike Shops	Co-operative	Reduce bikes taken to the landfill Repair and reuse Create car retirement program Increase biking accessibility
Irving California Community Land Trust	CLT non-profit with municipal collaboration	Develop affordable housing by separating the two cost elements: the market price of the land and the price of house

Actions and outcomes (scaling-up)	Policy change (scaling-out)
Create main floor commercial rental space for revenue generation	Address fuel poverty and utility costs
	Extend passive solar to northern climates
Provide mix of regular co-operative housing and equity-based ownership in co-operative	Extend green housing to low-income and middle-income social sectors
Involve construction trades and labour	Create national and provincial building codes
Encourage community energy planning and business engagement	Create national, provincial, and municipal green building incentives
Create home renovation guides	Link into municipal sustainability plans and provincial and national codes and standards
Advise, manage, and facilitate projects	
Provide life cycle analysis of efficiency	
Source carbon footprint materials	Create banking and finance policy as well as real estate and construction policy
Reuse and reduce waste	
Alter automobile culture	Create location-efficient mortgages
Increase disposable cash	Reduce parking requirements
	Prioritize walkable neighbourhoods
Make bikes, parts, and repairs available to all regardless of social status	Encourage biking as a means of transport and not just recreation
Empower people to do their own repairs	Create healthy communities
Create queer-only shops and women-only shops	Promote accessible mobility as a principle to be supported by local, provincial, and national governments
Provide access to housing for people earning 30 to 60 percent of average income of community	Encourage collaboration among municipalities, developers, non-profits, and community land trust
	Increase civic commitment and involvement of poor and low-income families in decisions

Table 11.6 Heritage-building conservation: Summary of findings

Convergence	Organizational structure	Socio-ecological mission
Gibson Block and WEAC	Foundation	Preserve and reuse heritage building
Alexander Taylor School/E4C	Social service agency	Preserve and reuse heritage building Preserve community place
Old YWCA	Non-profit	Preserve heritage building
AWA Hillhurst Cottage School	Non-profit	Raise awareness of wilderness Create more Ideologically diverse neighbourhood

Actions and outcomes (scaling-up)	Policy change (scaling-out)
Provide women's shelter Add to renewal of neighbourhood Educate public about heritage building and how it plays a social purpose and has "value" beyond real estate appraisal	Create alliance between heritage and community development actors and women's movement Preserve architecture and collective memories of social democracy
Provide space for social economy cluster Create a community asset Use land base for local food productions	Conserve social memory of school as multicultural haven Promote value of multiculturalism
Provide affordable office space for non-profits/service agencies Encourage co-location synergies	Conserve social memory of space and its functions in a social democratic polity
Play role heritage preservation Provide free office and meeting space for organizations	Provide model of municipal ownership and affordable lease with non-profit for social purposes

Table 11.7 Financing and sustainability: Summary of findings

Convergence	Organizational structure	Socio-ecological mission
Nelson and District Credit Union	Credit union	Provide financing and banking services
		Finance green Innovations
Battle River Railway Co-operative	New generation co-operative—includes producer-owners and community investors	Prevent closure of 100 km rural rail-line
		Invest local capital to establish collective ownership of transport option for farmers
		Provide means of transport that has less ecological impact than trucking
Sangudo Opportunity Development Co-op	Co-operative—local development investment	Retain rural capital
		Develop rural business (abattoir and café and affordable housing)

Actions and outcomes (scaling-up)	Policy change (scaling-out)
Extend services from members to wider community	Partner in SmartGrowth initiatives
Make commitment to place	
Encourage youth entrepreneurialism	
Provide in-kind and financial contributions to range of community programs and organizations (health, sports, arts, economic development)	
Retain rail line and railway culture	Provide new model of co-operative that allows various classes of non-owner investors (with proportional representation) but retains ownership in hands of core agricultural producer-owners
Invest local capital for profit making	
Expand rural agricultural services	
Include other communities	
Create diversification of goods hauled	
Develop learning modules explaining steps in founding a local investment co-operative	Partner with Unleashing Local Capital Project to develop affordable legal, accounting, securities
Assemble leadership team and develop an offering document	Offer templates for local capital investment co-operatives at provincial level

ACCA. N.d. "Unleashing Local Capital!" Alberta Community and Co-operative Association. http://acca.coop/unleashing/.

Bergman, Noam, Nils Markusson, P. Connor, Lucie Middlemiss, and Miriam Ricci. 2010. "Bottom-Up, Social Innovation for Addressing Climate Change." Symposium conducted at the conference Energy Transitions in an Interdependent World: What and Where Are the Future Social Science Research Agendas, Sussex, UK, 25–26 February.

Brock, K. L., and C. Bulpitt. 2007. "Encouraging the Social Economy Through Public Policy: The Relationship Between the Ontario Government and Social Economy Organizations." Paper presented at the annual meeting of the Canadian Political Science Association, 30 May–1 June, Saskatoon.

Büchs, Milena, Graham Smith, and Rebecca Edwards. 2011. *Low-Carbon Practices: A Third Sector Research Agenda*. Third Sector Research Centre: Informing Civil Society, Working Paper 59, May. http://www.birmingham.ac.uk/generic/tsrc/documents/tsrc/working-papers/working-paper-59.pdf.

ENP. 2009. *The Social Enterprise Purchasing Toolkit*. Vancouver: Enterprising Non-Profits. http://www.socialenterprisecanada.ca/en/toolkits/purchasingtoolkit/.

Gismondi, Mike, and K. Cannon. 2012. "Beyond Policy 'Lock-In'? The Social Economy and Bottom-Up Sustainability." *Canadian Review of Social Policy* / Revue canadienne de politique sociale (67). http://pi.library.yorku.ca/ojs/index.php/crsp/article/view/35371.

Gismondi, Mike., Juanita Marois, and Danica Straith. Forthcoming. "Unleashing Local Capital: The Practice of Local Investing." In *Consumers, Activists, and Environmental Governance: Advances and Applications in Social Practice Theories*, edited by Emily Huddart Kennedy, Maurie J. Cohen, and Naomi Krogman. UK: Edward Elgar.

Grieco, Margaret, and John Urry. 2012. "Introduction: Introducing the Mobilities Turn." In *Mobilities: New Perspectives on Transport and Society*, edited by Margaret Grieco and John Urry, 1–3. Farnham, UK: Ashgate.

Hamilton, Sandra. 2014. *Social Procurement: The Olympic, Commonwealth & Pan Am Games, and the Growing Case for Social Procurement Policy in Canada*. EMBA: Social Enterprise Leadership. University of Fredericton July 2014. http://www.sandrahamilton.ca/assets/uploads/sandra_hamilton__social_procurement_july_2014_web_59814.pdf.

LePage, David. 2014. *Exploring Social Procurement*. Vancouver: Accelerating Social Impact CCC, Ltd. http://buysocialcanada.ca/files/2014/05/Exploring-Social-Procurement_ASI-CCC-Report.pdf.

Lipp, Judith, Émanuèle Lapierre-Fortin, and J. J. McMurtry. 2012. "Renewable Energy Co-op Review: Scan of Models and Regulatory Issues, Preliminary Research Findings, January 2012." Measuring the Co-operative Difference Research Network. http://www.cooperativedifference.coop/assets/files/National/RE_Co-op_Review_RegulatoryScan_Jan2012.pdf.

Mook, Laurie, and Jennifer Sumner. 2010. "Social Accounting for Sustainability in the Social Economy." In *Living Economics: Canadian Perspectives on the Social Economy, Co-operatives and Community Economic Development*, edited by J. J. McMurtry, 155–178. Toronto: Emond Montgomery.

Parrish, Bradley D. 2008. "Sustainability-Driven Entrepreneurship: A Literature Review." Working paper. Leeds, UK: Sustainability Research Institute, School of Earth and Environment, University of Leeds.

Parrish, Bradley D., and Timothy J. Foxon. 2009. "Sustainability Entrepreneurship and Equitable Transitions to a Low-Carbon Economy." *Greener Management International* 55: 47–62.

Ponto, Jason. "Edmonton Bicycle Commuters Society." BALTA Case Study.

Restakis, John. 2011. "The Co-operative City: Social and Economic Tools for Sustainability." Working paper, British Columbia Co-operative Society, June. http://p2pfoundation.net/City_of_Vancouver_as_Cooperative_City.

Schmidt, Vivien. 2011. "Speaking of Change: Why Discourse is Key to the Dynamics of Policy Transformation." *Critical Policy Studies*, 5(2): 106–126.

Shove, Elizabeth. 2003. *Comfort, Cleanliness, and Convenience: The Social Organization of Normality*. Oxford: Berg.

———. 2010. "Beyond the ABC: Climate Change Policy and Theories of Social Change." *Environment and Planning* 42 (6): 1273–85.

Shove, Elizabeth, Mika Pantzar, and Matt Watson. 2012. *The Dynamics of Social Practice: Everyday Life and How It Changes*. London: SAGE.

Smith, Adrian. 2006. "Bringing Sustainable Technologies into the Mainstream." Innovation Brief. https://grassrootsinnovations.files.wordpress.com/2012/03/at-innovation-brief-final-dec-06.pdf.

———. 2007. "Translating Sustainabilities Between Green Niches and Socio-Technical Regimes." *Technology Analysis and Strategic Management* 19 (4): 427–50.

Smith, Adrian, Andy Stirling, and Frans Berkhout. 2005. "The Governance of Sustainable Socio-Technical Transition." *Research Policy* 34: 1491–1510.

Sonnino, Roberta, and Christopher Griggs-Trevarthen. 2013. "A Resilient Social Economy? Insights from the Community Food Sector in the UK." *Entrepreneurship and Regional Development: An International Journal* 25 (3–4): 272–92.

Stokes, L. C. 2013. "The Politics of Renewable Energy Policies: The Case of Feed-in-Tariffs in Ontario, Canada." *Energy Policy* 56: 490–500.

Sustainable Calgary. N.d. "Sustainability Indicator Research." Sustainable Calgary. http://sustainablecalgary.org/home/sustainability-indicator-research/.

Sustainable Calgary. 2011. *State of Our City Report*. Calgary: Sustainable Calgary. http://sustainablecalgary.org/wp-content/uploads/2012/03/2011-SOOC-Report.pdf.

Vancity. 2012. *2011 Annual Report*. Vancouver: Vancity Credit Union.

Van der Horst, Dan. 2008. "Social Enterprise and Renewable Energy: Emerging Initiatives and Communities of Practice." *Social Enterprise Journal* 4 (3): 171–85.

Contributors

Mary Beckie is an associate professor at the University of Alberta in the Faculty of Extension, where she conducts teaching and research in sustainable community development, municipal sustainability planning, local and regional food systems, the social economy, and community-university engagement.

Randy Bell works with the 'Na̱mgis First Nation and lives in Alert Bay.

Marena Brinkhurst holds an MA from the School of Resource and Environmental Management, Simon Fraser University.

Kailey Cannon is a graduate of the School of Political Studies at the University of Ottawa. She was formerly a research assistant with the BALTA project.

Sean Connelly is a lecturer in geography at the University of Otago in Dunedin, New Zealand, and a research associate with the Centre for Sustainable Community Development at Simon Fraser University. His teaching and research interests include human-environment relations, urban geography, planning, and sustainable community development. His post-doctoral research with BALTA focused on local food movements as a bridge between sustainability and the social economy. He is a provisional member of the Canadian Institute of Planners. His doctoral dissertation explored the role of community mobilization in the implementation of sustainability initiatives in urban, rural, and aboriginal communities in Canada. In 2002, he worked for ICLEI–Local Governments for Sustainability, preparing for and participating in the World Summit on Sustainable Development in Johannesburg. He holds an MA in international studies from the University of Northern BC and a PhD in geography from Simon Fraser University.

Mike Gismondi is a professor of sociology and global studies at Athabasca University in the Centre for Social Sciences. He has been a member of the BALTA steering committee since 2006. His research interests include environmental sociology, grassroots sustainability, socio-ecological transition, the political ecology of natural resource extraction, and global development. Gismondi is co-lead for Scaling Innovation in Sustainability, a SSHRC-funded research partnership exploring the transition to sustainability (www.balta-sis.ca).

Lillian Hunt is a member of the 'Namgis and Ma'amtagila First Nations. She has been directly involved in protecting the cultural heritage of her people since the first cultural tourism training program was initiated by U'mista Cultural Centre in 1999. The recognition that tour operators from around the world were making substantial money based on the culture and territories of the Kwakwaka'wakw peoples prompted the U'mista Cultural Society to direct staff to develop and market their product. With the society's support, Hunt connected with regional tourism associations, and she now serves on the boards of Tourism Vancouver Island, the Aboriginal Tourism Association of British Columbia, and Go2 British Columbia. She is also on the Vancouver Island North Tourism Advisory Committee, which works with the Regional District of Mount Waddington (RDMW) to develop a regional marketing plan for Northern Vancouver Island. Hunt held the tourism portfolio while serving two terms on the Alert Bay Municipal Council. Her tenure as director with the RDMW provided valuable insight on working with community leaders in office.

Noel Keough is a co-founder of Sustainable Calgary Society and CivicCamp Calgary. He is also an assistant professor of sustainable design in the Faculty of Environmental Design at the University of Calgary.

Freya Kristensen is a PhD candidate in the Department of Geography at Simon Fraser University and a researcher with the SFU Centre for Sustainable Community Development. Her work examines how international municipal sustainability networks influence policy learning around sustainability, focusing particularly on the social dimension of sustainability. Prior to starting her PhD, she spent almost two years with the Columbia Institute's Centre for Civic Governance, a non-profit organization that works to engage locally elected officials around social and environmental issues.

Celia Lee holds a Master of Environmental Design from the University of Calgary and is currently research and community liaison at Vibrant Communities *Calgary*. She won the Outstanding Master's Thesis Award from the Association for Nonprofit and Social Economy Research in 2011 for her thesis, "Growing a Social Economy: A Case Study of Hillhurst-Sunnyside," which was based on research she did for BALTA on mapping social enterprise in the area.

Mike Lewis is executive director of the Canadian Centre for Community Renewal, lead investigator with BALTA, and co-author, with Pat Conaty, of *The Resilience Imperative: Cooperative Transitions to a Steady-State Economy* (New Society Publishers, 2012).

Julie L. MacArthur teaches political science at Simon Fraser University and Kwantlen Polytechnic University and is a lecturer in political studies and public policy at the University of Auckland. Her political economy research on human security, sustainability, and community energy ownership has appeared in a number of publications, including *Monthly Review*, *International Journal*, and *i4*.

Terri MacDonald, Selkirk College's BC Regional Innovation Chair in Rural Economic Development, holds a PhD in Educational Studies from the University of British Columbia and an MA in Policy and Administration from the University of Calgary. Dr. MacDonald has worked for over 10 years in economic development across British Columbia, primarily in the Kootenay region.

Sean Markey is an associate professor with the Simon Fraser University School of Resource and Environmental Management and an associate with the SFU Centre for Sustainable Community Development. His research focuses on issues of local and regional economic development, rural and small-town development, community sustainability, and sustainable infrastructure. Markey works with municipalities, non-profit organizations, Aboriginal communities, and the business community to promote and develop sustainable forms of community economic development. He serves as co-chair on the Board of Directors with the Vancity Community Foundation.

Juanita Marois is a research assistant at Athabasca University and is working on the Unleashing Local Capital project and the BALTA mapping project. She is the former executive director of the Métis Crossing Cultural Interpretive Centre near Smokey Lake, Alberta, and holds an MA in recreation and leisure studies with a focus on sustainable tourism from University of Alberta.

George Penfold is former Regional Innovation Chair at Selkirk College, British Columbia. He has retired from academic life and is practicing community development.

Stewart Perry is a staff associate with the Canadian Centre for Community Renewal and has long been active in community economic development (CED) in the United States and Canada as both a policy adviser and a designer and manager of CED institutions. As head of the (US) Center for Community Economic Development, Perry helped create the first finance institution for CED, the Massachusetts Community Development Finance Authority. He also helped start Canada's first community development corporation, New Dawn Enterprises, and from 1988 to 1993, he headed the Community Economic Development Centre in Cape Breton, Nova Scotia. A consultant, researcher, and author, Perry currently specializes in community and development finance.

John Restakis, a co-lead of BALTA, has been executive director of the British Columbia Co-operative Association in Vancouver since 1998. The BCCA is the umbrella association for the co-op and credit union movement in British Columbia. He is the author of *Humanizing the Economy: Co-operatives in the Age of Capital* (New Society Publishers, 2010).

Lauren Rethoret is a full-time researcher with the Columbia Basin Rural Development Institute at Selkirk College, working primarily in the environmental and economic pillars. She holds a Master's degree in Resource and Environmental Management (with a specialization in land use planning) from Simon Fraser University and a Bachelor's degree in Geography (with a specialization in globalization, society and the environment) from Carleton University.

Mark Roseland is professor of planning in the Simon Fraser University School of Resource and Environmental Management and director of the SFU Centre for Sustainable Community Development. Roseland lectures internationally and advises communities and governments on sustainable development policy and planning. The fourth edition of his book, *Toward Sustainable Communities*, was published in June 2012 (New Society Publishers). Roseland is leading the development of Pando | Sustainable Communities, a new network for sustainable communities researchers and practitioners. He is a founding member of the SFU Community Trust's Board of Directors, responsible for the award-winning UniverCity sustainable community development project.

Lynda Ross is an associate professor of women's and gender studies in the Centre for Interdisciplinary Studies at Athabasca University, where she also coordinates the University Certificate in Counselling Women program. She holds a PhD in psychology from the University of New Brunswick. Her research interests focus on the social construction of psychological "disorders," attachment theory, and motherhood. She also has an extensive background and interest in quantitative and qualitative research methodologies, as well as in statistics.

Erin Swift-Leppäkumpu is a Canadian intern architect and designer and holds a Master of Architecture from the University of Calgary. She has been working in architecture offices in the Helsinki metropolitan area since September 2010.

Kelly Vodden is an associate professor (research) in environmental studies and geography at Memorial University. She also serves as a research associate with Municipalities Newfoundland and Labrador. Vodden's research focuses on collaborative governance and sustainable community and regional development, particularly in Canadian rural and small-town communities and coastal regions. Her publications include the co-authored book *Second Growth: Community Economic Development in Rural and Small Town British Columbia* (UBC Press, 2004), along with numerous book chapters, journal articles, and reports. Vodden is a former research coordinator and instructor with the Centre for Sustainable Community Development at Simon Fraser University and has acted as a consultant to all levels of government, non-government, and private sector organizations.